D0893793

.

THE CONQUEST OF NEW GRANADA

BEING THE LIFE OF
GONZALO JIMENEZ DE QUESADA

FROM HERRERA'S "HISTORIA DE LAS INDIAS."

THE CONQUEST OF NEW GRANADA

BEING THE LIFE OF
GONZALO JIMENEZ DE QUESADA

BY

R. B. CUNNINGHAME GRAHAM

93611

COOPER SQUARE PUBLISHERS, INC.
NEW YORK
1967

Published 1967 by Cooper Square Publishers, Inc.
59 Fourth Avenue, New York, N. Y. 10003
Library of Congress Catalog Card No. 66-30734

Printed in the United States of America

A

DON GUILLERMO VALENCIA

EXCELSO POETA

ORADOR ARMONIOSO É IRRESISTIBLE

HONRA DE LAS LETRAS ESPAÑOLAS

EN AMÉRICA

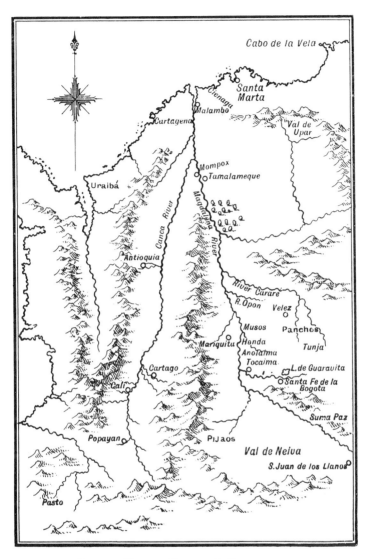

SKETCH MAP OF QUESADA'S EXPEDITION.

PREFACE

THE names both of Pizarro and Cortés are household words. The conquests of Peru and Mexico are known to everyone.

The Aztec and the Inca empires are generally assumed to have been the only two states in the Indies the conquerors found, that were well organized, and had evolved, or were evolving, a civilized society. The story of their conquest reads like a fairy-tale, and Pizarro and Cortés are taken as the archetypes of the conquerors. The history of the conquest of New Granada—that is, Colombia—has passed almost unnoticed as far as English letters are concerned. Quesada's name is fallen into oblivion, even in Spain itself.

Gonzalo Jimenez de Quesada was as great as were Pizarro or Cortés, confronted equal perils and endured far greater hardships, conquering an empire just as interesting as was Peru or Mexico, far more remote and inaccessible. Pizarro and Cortés knew more or less where they were going to; Quesada fell upon his conquest by accident, just as a chance stroke with a pick sometimes reveals a rich lode in a mine.

There has been but one real conquest worthy of the name—that of the New World. The human race in all its annals holds no record like it. Uncharted seas, unnavigated gulfs; new constellations, the unfathomable black pit of the Magellan clouds; the Cross hung in the sky; the very needle varying from the pole; islands innumerable and an unknown world rising from out the sea; all unsuspected races living in a flora never seen by Europeans, made it an achievement unique in all the history of mankind.

vii

This was a conquest worthy of a race of heroes, nor were the men who undertook it, vanquishing difficulties rendered more arduous by the element of the unknown, in the main unworthy of their task. Cruel, no doubt, they were; but yet not all of them—witness the names of Alvar Nuñez, Balboa, and of him I am to write about. Cruel, perhaps; but who are we to cast a stone at them? Steadfast, enduring, patient in hardships to an incredible degree, resourceful, valiant, loyal to their King and country to a fault, they had the virtues and the vices of "conquistadores." Money they loved; but they loved glory more. Through all their actions ran a vein of true nobility.

It was no craven spirit that impelled Cortés to burn his ships.

When, in the Isle of Tumbez, Pizarro and his thirteen companions waited alone for reinforcements from Panama, preferring death to giving up their enterprise, knowing there was a populous empire to confront, even when the scanty help they could expect arrived, fear was a word beyond their comprehension.

So of all of them. In the dank everglades upon the Magdalena, when racked with fever, starving, and exposed to ceaseless and unseen attacks; with poisoned arrows rained upon them from the thickets killing the soldiers and the precious horses—for after God, as say the chroniclers, they owed the victory to the horses—Quesada never faltered for an hour.

The conquerors plundered, and they slew, all in God's name, holding, just as we do ourselves, that they were chosen to bring light into the darkest places of the world.

In all the chronicles of this great adventure, no name stands higher than Quesada's for prudence, valour, and, on the whole, for his good treatment of the Indians.

Pizarro and Cortés had wider theatres and a better press in Spain, for they brought gold, and were received as only those who bring gold with them ever are received.

Quesada only brought renown, a history of marvellous adventures, an account of perhaps the strangest meeting in the Colombian uplands on the wind-swept plains of Bogota, of three brave captains, fate-led and brought together by the invisible loadstone of chance, that the world ever saw.

He brought the tidings of an unknown empire, rich both in interest and antiquity, having its calendar, its own theology, traditions of the creation of mankind almost as reasonable as our own, and, lastly, a system of society adequate to its needs, almost Arcadian in its simplicity. It may be that the years I have spent with the descendants of the conquerors have fitted me in some degree to write the life of one of them, to whom scant justice has been done.

The music of the wind in the dried grasses of the Southern Pampa, the icy nights upon the frosty sierras, dank trails in Paraguay and in Colombia through the impenetrable forests, where lianas whip you as sharply when you pass as does a sheet torn from your hands at sea, and humming-birds flit jewelled in topaz and in amethyst across the clearings—all these, and the long days behind the cattle, on a tired horse with heels a-jogging ceaselessly against his sides, the ache between the shoulders growing intolerable as the slow hours move on, may serve as links between me and the man of whom I write.

Those weary hours were the true sauce to the hospitality of the straw rancho, camp-fire beside the stream, or of the white hacienda, buried in its grove of peach-trees, when the day was done, for hunger is as old as is the world.

For all his perils, his adventures, for the great empire that he conquered with such scant resources, Quesada had the usual guerdon of the conqueror from the Court of Spain, ingratitude and base neglect of his past services. That it was usual, witness the chains Columbus ever carried with him—for remembrance; the lonely deathplace of Cortés in Castillejos de la Cuesta and the adobe building near the sulphur springs hard by Tocaima where Quesada, himself a leper, by his last testament left a jar of water always to be kept for travellers on the road. Yet, if the conquistadores were men of blood and iron, careless of life and suffering, and mostly dying either by violence or broken-hearted by the ingratitude of those they served, the Indians owed them little, either in valour or in the fortitude with which they met their fate.

Their chieftains, treated as gods, borne on the shoulders of their subjects, refined, intelligent, and far more reasonable in controversy than were their conquerors—boldly met the onslaught of a race of men who fell upon them, as it were, from the skies—a race of beings sheathed in steel, riding on animals that seemed a part of them, who breathed out fire, as the Indians thought, taking the harquebus as in some way connected with the horse. With their poor arms and quilted cotton doublets, their poisoned arrows and their fire-hardened spears, they faced those " children of the sun," dying in heaps, just as Leonidas and his three hundred Spartans died for their fatherland.

No chronicler has preserved the fame of their heroic deeds; yet still the conquerors, here and there, when they were soldiers who had taken up the pen after the sword had grown too heavy for their hands, now and then have done them scanty justice, calling them " valiant Indians," just as a man may pat his bull-dog on the head when it has battled valiantly.

Wrapping themselves in the stoicism of their race, no men have died more bravely than did their chieftains and their kings. Guatimozin upon the bed of coals, in Mexico, when he reproached his followers' groans, saying, " Am I upon a bed of roses?" the Inca Atalhualpa, strangled and betrayed, and the last King of Bogota, tortured inhumanly, the blot upon Quesada's name that he paid for so bitterly in after-years, in money and in pangs of conscience, died like the martyrs that they were, showing themselves the conquerors' equals, both in high feeling and in contempt of death.

A wondrous adventure it was most certainly, calling forth all that was best and worst, both in the victors and the vanquished. No man that is a man can read the history of the Spanish conquest of the New World unmoved. Of all the stirring episodes of the strange epic, there is none stranger than Quesada's life. He and the conquest are so bound up together, that to write either of them is to write the other. He was the conquest, and the conquest both made and marred him; but still left his name one of the first in all its chronicles. As a conquistador he is the equal of Pizarro and Cortés, and far less bloodthirsty than was either of them. His one lapse was remembered and is recorded to his shame, for he brought little treasure with him on his return to Spain. Theirs were washed out in gold.

If there is justice anywhere on earth, in heaven, or in the waters underneath the earth (those of oblivion), surely the errors of his youth must be wiped out by the achievements and the sufferings of his eighty years of conquest and of strife.

R. B. CUNNINGHAME GRAHAM.

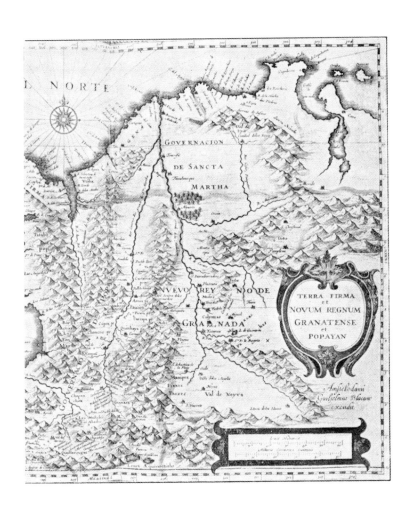

Gonzalo Jimenez de Quesada

CHAPTER I

GONZALO JIMENEZ DE QUESADA was born either in Cordoba or in Granada, in or about the year 1506.

Fray Pedro Simon,[1] the most complete authority upon the conquest of New Granada, says: "Gonzalo Jimenez de Quesada was a native of the city of Cordoba. He was no degenerate descendant of his country in letters and in valour, for it appears that, in him, Mars and Minerva were joined in a close friendship, a juncture that is seldom found.[2] His father was El Licenciado Jimenez, a lawyer, and his mother Isabel de Quesada, both of noble blood, and natives of the same city. He was brought up in the district (Coleccion) de Nuestra Señora de la Fuen Santa, until his parents removed to the illustrious city of Granada."

There he remained ten or twelve years. His father practised as an advocate, and this inclined Gonzalo to the same career. He lived there till the year 1535, and had become " consummate in grammar and in the law, in which he graduated, and began to practise in the same court[3] as his father," for several years.[4]

---

[1] " Noticias Historiales de las Conquistas de Tierra Firme en las Indias Occidentales," por Fray Pedro Simon, del Orden de San Francisco, del Nuevo Reino de Granada. Bogotá, 1882. The original edition was printed in Spain at Cuenca, in the year 1627. Only the first volume was issued, and thus the first complete edition is that of Bogotá.

[2] " Gonzalo Jimenez de Quesada, natural de la ciudad de Cordoba, que no degeneraba de los demas hijos de su patria en letras y valentia, pues parece que se juntaron en el con amistad estrecha, Marte y Minerva, junta que raras veces se halla." Cap. IX., Segunda Parte, p. 32.

[3] La Cancilleria Real.

[4] Fray Simon, " Noticias Historiales."

I

Other authorities, as Oviedo,[1] Piedrahita, and Castellanos, state that he was born in Granada, whilst Ocariz,[2] again, sides with Fray Simon and gives Cordoba as his birthplace.

The matter is of slight importance. The two old Moorish towns are not far distant from each other, and whether Quesada first saw the light in Cordoba or no, it is certain that his youth was spent in the city of the pomegranate, set on its tawny hills. As he was born in 1506, or at the earliest in 1505, he must have grown up amongst the Moriscos, and probably spoke a little Arabic, for the Moriscos formed at least three-quarters of the population of the town. One thing is certain, that, though a lawyer himself, he must have passed muoh of his youth with men accustomed to the use of arms. Many of the old soldiers of the Catholic kings had settled in Granada, revolts were frequent amongst the conquered race, and there Quesada, although an accomplished grammarian,[3] must have learned the horsemanship and the dexterity in arms that, in his future life of action, stood him in good stead.

No better cradle for an adventurous youth could have been found than the Granada of those days. The Alhambra still retained its Moorish impress; the clinging scent of atar and of spices that strikes all those who enter any house in Northern Africa, could scarcely have evaporated. The palm-trees that the Moors had planted could not all have been cut down. The baths, of course, had gone, for they were anathema to all good Churchmen, unable to divorce hygiene from immorality and sloth. A rough trail paved with cobbles, La Calle de los Gomeles, led up to the great horseshoe archway of the Pomegranates and to the Gate of Justice. Great rocks most probably stuck up through the surface of the track, just as they do to-day in paths that lead to mountain Kasbahs in North Africa. The palace of the Emperor Charles was slowly rising, a monument of artistic vandalism,

[1] "Historia Natural de las Indias," por el Capitan Gonzalo Fernandez de Oviedo.

[2] "Genealogias del Nuevo Reino de Granada," por Juan Flores de Ocariz. (Madrid, 1674.)

[3] Consumado en la gramatica.

It seems an architectural palimpsest, superimposed on a foundation even finer than its own. The Moorish town lay out below the walls, its houses small and flat-roofed (as Navagiero, the Venetian envoy, tells us), buried in fig-trees; each house a microcosm of Islam, shut to the outside by walls with little slits for windows, and inside rich with coloured carpets; hung with brass lamps if the owner were a wealthy man, or bare, clean, and austere if he were poor; but, in both cases, hermetically sealed against the world. In such surroundings Gonzalo must have felt himself always in presence of the enemy: an enemy that did not attack, but still was there, hostile and unappeasable, keeping the Christian ever on the watch.

As he strayed up and down the stony and steep paths that led from the Alhambra to the banks of the Genil and Darro, in whose sands probably people searched for the minutest particles of gold as they still do to-day, he must have had a sense of always being spied upon by eyes, invisible, but subtly felt by those they spied upon.

No cactus thickets[1] could have crowned the rocks above the Moorish suburb of the Albaicin, that refuge of the people of Baeza,[2] after it was lost. Amongst its narrow streets and tortuous lanes, he probably would never have been allowed to penetrate alone, for danger lurked in them to any unprotected Spaniard in those early days. Still he must have looked down upon the little stronghold of the enemy of race and faith, from the mirador that rises above Lindaraja's garden, or, seated on the walls, felt that there was something there to conquer and subdue. The palaces both of the Generalife and the Alizares must have been intact. Nothing was wanting to stir his imagination as he looked out across the Vega, towards La Zubia with its

[1] Strange as it may appear, the cactus, that has an air in Spain, in Sicily, and in Morocco of being indigenous, is really an American plant and could hardly have been naturalized at the time of which I write.

[2] El Baezi, a man from Baeza. This became the name of the suburb, and has been but little corrupted in its transition from Arabic to Spanish.

gigantic laurel, under whose shade the Catholic Queen and the ladies of the Court were glad to hide, when a sudden razzia of the Moors nearly surprised them. He knew the white-coned, solitary Mulahacen with the red sunset falling on the snow; and in the tawny glow, when yellow walls, red castles, green plain, and distant sierras blend into a vast, but always changing scheme of colour, such as no earthly palette could ever have devised, he may have dreamed of conquering another Mexico. Throughout his studies, till the time that he emerged a full-fledged advocate, practising in the Real Cancilleria, he must have often joined in those mock battles known to the Spaniards as " El Juego de Cañas," when, mounted on the Moorish saddle,[1] they threw canes at one another, in imitation of the javelins thrown by the Arabs and the Moors. He must have gone on many a hunting expedition into the Alpujarras, and thus acquired his skill in horsemanship and arms, by practice, at first hand.

Whether he was born in Cordoba or in Granada, Quesada formed no exception to the general rule that all the conquerors came from the south of Spain.

Pizarro and Cortés, Hernando de Soto, and Alvar Nuñez came from Estremadura; Don Pedro de Mendoza, the discoverer of the River Plate, from Guadix, in Almeria; Sebastian de Belalcazar, from the village of that name, also in Estremadura; Balboa, from the same province; and so

---

[1] The Moorish saddle with the short stirrups and high cantle, so often to be seen represented on Talavera plates and bowls, long maintained its hold in Spain. Even so late as 1820-23 Blanco White, in his " Letters from Spain," speaks of the herdsmen of his native Andalucia appearing almost " to kneel upon their horses' backs." To ride in the Moorish saddle implied using the lance overhand, and not under the arm, as in the demipique saddle first used by the knights. The Inca, Garcilasso de la Vega, in his celebrated " Comentarios," says, " mi tierra [*i.e.*, Peru] se ganó á la gieta." Cervantes uses the phrase, when Don Quixote meets the Discreet Gentleman of La Mancha on his handsome grey mare, for he says, " el aderezo de la yegua era de campo y de la gineta." To ride well in both saddles (" ser ginete en ambas sillas ") was such a feather in a man's cap that it was often mentioned in his epitaph.

on of the rest. The long, slow conquest of the Moors had eventually pushed the more adventurous spirits into the south, as the Moors sullenly retreated into Africa.

Thus, after the discovery of the New World, the south became the breeding-place of the conquerors. Nothing more natural than that men who had heard their fathers recount their prowess in the wars against the infidel, should wish to follow in their steps.

Robertson, Prescott, and other Protestant and English-speaking writers on the Spanish conquest of the New World have pandered both to religious and to racial pride and prejudice. For them, all Spaniards were cruel, blood-thirsty, and treacherous. This came in some degree from ignorance and more from the atavism of the time when Spain and England were rivals for the dominion of the seas.

Some conquerers were cruel, as Pizarro, Almagro, Valdivia, and, to a less degree, Cortés. Others, as Quesada, were, at times, overborne by their followers, in whose power they were, without support from Spain. Balboa and Alvar Nuñez were tolerant and liberal; but all were men deeply imbued with a stern faith in God and in their creed. This creed, to them, was half religious and half racial; the Cross, not a mere emblem of salvation, but a labarum that each man saw hung in the skies above his head. Spain was God's chosen country; the Spaniards His chosen people; the town from which the individual Spaniard came the centre of the country; and himself the central figure in it—for Spaniards then, as now, were the most individualistic people on the earth. Thus fortified, both by religious and by racial pride, holding their faith with fierce intensity, they felt they had a mission to fulfil, laid on them from on high. Gold was not always their chief aim, as Protestant historians aver, although they loved it, wading ankle-deep in blood in its pursuit. When all is said and done, they were much like ourselves, not knowing, and not caring much to know, where their greed ended and their faith began.

Quesada probably throughout his youth heard constant

stories of the deeds of the chief conquerors. All through his early years, the world's map was receiving the " augmentation of the Indies," and countries which a year or two ago were being conquered, settled, and still more empires were appearing on the horizon of the conquerors.

It must have seemed to the Spaniards of those days as if the earth was daily growing larger, and as each conqueror came back, with his wealth gained by the sword, in a few years, all Spain must have shaken to the core; a very fever of adventure boiled in each Spaniard's blood. One of the writers of that time says, " Even the tailors wanted to go a-conquering, and looking out for mines."

The conquests of Peru and Mexico had stimulated everybody's hopes. The oft-repeated tales of Eldorado were in all men's mouths. Raleigh had sailed to find it, and Orellana and the Pizarros never ceased seeking for it. It was the ultimate goal of nearly every enterprise in these times, luring on everyone who sought it, to ruin and defeat. No doubt Quesada, even at that early date, had dreams about it, dreams that in after life were so disastrous to him

His opportunity came to him, not specially by any effort of his own. In the year 1535 or 1536—for once again the various authorities are all at variance—Don Pedro Fernandez de Lugo, Perpetual Governor[1] of the Canary Islands, was named the Governor of Santa Marta, a city founded in 1525, that lacked advancement, and was in fact " one of the cities most combated by evil fortune that was to be found in all the Indies."[2]

The town was founded in 1525 by Rodrigo de Bastidas. From the first, ill-luck attended it, and Bastidas soon was murdered by his lieutenant, Juan de Villafuerte.

Situated nearly in latitude 6° north, it stands at the head of an almost landlocked horseshoe bay. The islands called El Morro Grande and El Morro Chico lie across

---

[1] " Gobernador perpetuo ": " Noticias Historiales," Fray Pedro Simon, cap. xv.

[2] " Una de las ciudades mas combatidas de las que se halló en las Indias ": Fray Simon.

the harbour's mouth and form a natural breakwater. Steep cliffs come down close to the water's edge on all sides of the bay. The town, flat-roofed and Oriental-looking, with its domed churches rising from the sandy, ill-kept streets, mere watercourses in the rainy season, has an air of Magazán, of Azimur, or of Arzila, or any of the towns on the Moroccan coast. The difference is that, whereas in Morocco, only a few date-palms stand up to defy the sun, in Santa Marta, coco-palms, looking like vegetable ostrich feathers, fringe all the beach, and the fierce-growing vegetation almost invades the town. The older houses cluster round the cathedral, and some of them have coats of arms above the heavy, iron-studded doors. The iron grating in front of every window, and the raised footpaths, paved with brick, all speak of Spain, and possibly some of the older mansions date from the early times of the first conquest. Gradually the town trails off into a negro village, with its bright hedges round the shanties, of red and yellow crotons, until at last, a sandy road, broken here and there by clumps of cactus and hedged with aloes, runs into the forest. Beyond the forest, passing the ancient Spanish country house, with its trim boxwood hedges, fountains, and secular trees that tower above the roof, where died Bolivar, the Washington of South America,[1] the road gradually rises to three or four thousand feet, and reaches a zone of coffee plantations, a zone in which the flora both of the tropics and of Southern Europe flourish side by side. Twenty miles off the snow-clad sierra runs to a height of seventeen thousand feet, and beyond the mountains lies the wild country of the Valle de Upar, upon whose rivers still dwell tribes of Indians, never subdued, whose arms are poisoned arrows, and who are reported to be cannibals.

This range of snowy mountains, cutting off the coast from the interior, was the reason of the ill-success of the

[1] The house is called La Quinta de San Pedro de Alejandria, and is a resort of patriotic pilgrimage, and deservedly so, for Simon Bolivar was the greatest genius ever born either in North or South America.

colony of Santa Marta, for, as there was no gold upon the coast, the Indians all were hostile and most warlike, and the Spaniards of those days were not concerned with agriculture, having left Spain to follow arms and seek adventures rather than the plough. The newly founded settlement was in the last stage of decay, when Don Pedro Fernandez de Lugo was appointed Governor.[1] Don Pedro must have been either a patriot or a born adventurer, to leave his comfortable home in the Canaries and his quiet hereditary office of Perpetual Governor to take command in such a miserable place as was the Santa Marta of those days.

Perhaps the fact that his governorship had been acquired by marriage with the heiress of the last Governor impelled him to show what mettle he was made of, or perhaps the fury of adventure that possessed all Spain drove him forth, as it had driven out a thousand others, to put his fortune to the touch.

Fray Simon, Castellanos, Piedrahita, and the rest of the historians of the time speak well of him, dwelling upon his honour, his capacity, and his fitness for command. A man of his position in those days never lacked followers, and soon he had a well-appointed fleet, assembled in the port of Santa Cruz de Tenerife. Captains, destined to be famous in the conquest of New Granada, flocked to him, as Cespedes and San Martin, Manjarrés, Lazaro Fonte, and a score of others, bringing their followers, their horses, and the best weapons that they could procure. Don Pedro offered the post of chief magistrate of Santa Marta to a young man, unknown in arms, and who had passed his life in study and the practice of the law. His name was Gonzalo Jimenez de Quesada, destined to be the foremost person in the expedition, and take a front place in the annals of the conquerors.

[1] His Spanish title was that of Adelantado, a distinction often bestowed in those days on governors in South America.

It seems to have carried more dignity with it than that of Gobernador (governor,) and perhaps may correspond to the more modern Spanish office of Capitan General.

There is no record of how or where Don Pedro de Lugo met Quesada; but the young lawyer must have stood high in his profession to have been offered such an important post.

The expedition sailed from Santa Cruz de Tenerife, according to Fray Simon, in 1535, and thus Quesada was about thirty-six years of age.

The fleet arrived off Santa Marta, without novelty,[1] as goes the Spanish phrase, after a passage of about forty days—not so very slow considering all things at the time.

The Adelantado found a miserable state of things in his new capital. The so-called city was a wretched hamlet built of mud hovels thatched with reeds. Only one stone-built house existed, and a most miserable church. The expedition had to live in tents. Dysentery scourged the newcomers, unaccustomed to the tropics, and fevers played great havoc in their ranks.

Provisions were so scarce that the Adelantado tried every means he could to force the inhabitants to leave the town and settle on the land. Those who attempted it were attacked at once by hostile Indians, and many lost their lives. Inside the city, civil strife was raging dangerously, and the sailors in the fleet were clamouring for pay.

The colonists who had accompanied the fleet were horror-struck at the poverty and wretchedness of the miserable village, that no doubt they had been told was a fine thriving town.

Especially the women, so says Colonel Acosta[2] in his "Descubrimiento de la Nueva Granada," were disgusted, and could scarce believe that, after having been founded for ten years, the settlement presented such a famine-stricken air.

The colonists lived in their miserable huts, without a

[1] "Sin novedad." Novelty may take many forms. In those days it included the risk of pirates, being becalmed, dying of thirst, and other acts of God, as such matters are referred to in bills of lading.

[2] Colonel Joaquin Acosta, "Compendio Historico del Descubrimiento de la Nueva Granada." (Paris, 1848.)

garden, nor was any land ploughed up for crops. Their clothes and food they forced out of the Indians, for they did nothing for themselves. Thus they were like a band of gipsies dressed in skins and roughly woven cotton cloths, made by the Indians. In fact, they had fallen as low in the social scale as were the natives whom they had come to educate and civilize.

When the brilliant cavaliers, all dressed in silks with velvet cloaks and shining arms, gilt morrions and waving plumes, disembarked upon the beach, they were met by the interim general Don Antonio Bezos and the members of the town council, all dressed like muleteers.[1] One of the captains of the newcomers asked them if their clothes were cut after the fashion-plates in the celebrated book on "Indumentaria," by Lazaro Buonamico. They did not know that amongst the men they derided were to be found the celebrated baquianos, who were to be so useful in the conquest.[2]

Castellanos,[3] in his rhymed chronicle, has a vivid picture of the settlers.

Few governors of colonies in the New World have found themselves in a more miserable plight than did Don Pedro in his new government.

[1] En traje de arrieros.

[2] Son los baquianos los que aconsejan á propósito, rastrean, caminan y no se cansan, cargan lo que se ofrece, sudan, sufren el hambre, la sed, el sol, agua y sereno . . . ni les pesan las armas ni huyen del trabajo; buscan y conocen las comidas silvestres. . . .

The word "baquiano" originally meant a pioneer. It is now commonly used all over Spanish America for a guide.

[3] Juan de Castellanos, "Historia del Nuevo Reino de Granada." (Madrid, 1886.) His MS. lay unpublished in the Archivo de Indias for three hundred years. "Los antiguos con sus camisetillas, tan delgados de zancas y pescuezos que pudieran contarlles las costillas. Contemplaban aquellas maravillas de trajes y costosos aderezos." The newcomers asked them,

> Como podian vivir desta manera
> En chozuelas cubiertas con helecho.
> Una pobre hamaca vuestro lecho
> Una India bestial por compañera.
> Curtido cada cual, seco y amarillo
> Como los que castiga Peralvillo.

His entire future was at stake, his reputation in the balance. Something had to be done, and done at once, to avoid a mutiny and the loss of the new colony.

There was no time to plant or sow or to build houses: the immediate need was both for food to give his troops and gold to pay the clamorous sailors of the fleet.

He did the only thing he could have done in the circumstances, and, taking with him a thousand of his best soldiers under the Captains Cespedes, Cardoso, Villalobo, Manjarrés, and San Martin, he set out resolutely for the interior.

Up to that time, the Sierra Nevada had barred the way to the interior. From the beginning the Adelantado, who had the instinct of a conqueror, seems to have seen that he had either to cross the mountains or to find a way round them, for he could not remain cramped up against the coast and at the same time save the colony.

With his thousand chosen men and his best captains, Don Pedro set out to attack the town of Bonda, whose inhabitants had from the first been hostile to the new settlement.

Colonel Acosta[1] talks about a punitive expedition just

---

[1] Acosta, " Descubrimiento de la Nueva Granada," p. 151. In one of these expeditions in the wild country behind Santa Marta occurred the following adventure, told in the curious and homely style of many of the chroniclers. It is preserved by Fray Pedro de Aguado in his " Historia de Santa Marta y Nuevo Reino de Granada." One Captain Palomino, having been sent out to explore, came on a river that was unfordable: " Pidio Palomino su caballo Matamoros, para pasar el rio que iva muy crecido, y aunque los que con el estavan, le decian que no lo pasase, propusó y determinó de pasallo, no embargante que el caballo lo rehusaba, y se bolvia á subirdel agua, pero como Palomino estubiere tan obstinado en seguir aquel su propósito, contra toda fortuna, herió recimente de las espuelas al caballo Matamoros, y haziendole que se metiese en el mas hondo y caudaloso del rio, fué sumido debajo del agua, sin que pareciese mas. Su caballo salió por la mar á la otra vanda, y el capitan Juan de Cespedes y el capitan Juan de Escobar tomaran el caballo Matamoros y lo llevaran encubertado de luto, adonde el gobernador estaba." Palomino evidently thought that he knew more than his horse, a common error amongst horsemen; but it cost him his life.

as men to-day, writing about some tribal warfare above the Khyber Pass or in South Africa, would write of " punishing the natives " for their hostility.

In either case it is a little difficult to see how the word " punishment " applies to such an expedition conducted against men in their own country, whose only crime is that they prefer their liberty to any foreign rule. Don Pedro hoped to find gold in Bonda wherewith to pay his men. However, as it happened, the inhabitants made such a stout defence that many of his men were killed and wounded, and, when at last he took the place, he found nothing of any value in it. The inhabitants, having left the town, still shot their arrows and rolled down boulders on his men from all the mountain peaks. This so much irritated Don Pedro that he burned the town and seven other villages in the adjoining valleys of Coto and Valhermoso, and, with his wounded followers, fell back upon the coast.

He left his son Don Luis Alonso de Lugo to continue the " chastisement of the inhabitants."[1]

Don Luis divided his forces into two divisions, being determined not to return to Santa Marta without some booty.[2]

The division that he sent under the command of Captain Suarez was driven back, and then the two commanders advanced to a town upon the coast called San Juan de Guia, from which they determined to penetrate into the mountains of Tairona, where two chiefs, called Marobaré and Arobaré, had taken refuge with their followers. Advancing cautiously up mountain paths so steep they had to hold each other by the hand to avoid falling over precipices, they surprised and took the town. In it they found gold to the value of fifteen thousand " castellanos "[3] in images and ornaments.

So far, so good: gold is the only real salve to national honour, and these gold-producing Indians had all been hostile to the new settlement.

[1] Continuar el castigo de aquellos habitantes.
[2] Sin algun botin.
[3] The " castellano " was worth about eleven dollars.

Had there been nothing more than that to chronicle, the history of the expedition would have been little different from the account of half a hundred other raids of the same kind, but for a curious episode that befell them on their march. As they struggled up the mountains towards Tairona, to set their ambush, ragged, half-starved, and shivering in the light clothes that they had brought from Santa Marta, by paths so steep and rugged that they had to go in Indian file, just at the top of a high pass they heard a donkey bray. All knew that asses were not indigenous to the New World, so each of them began to comment on the astounding sound. Some said that, unless the beast had wings, he could not possibly have got to such a place. Others, that the Indians, having heard the animal in Santa Marta, were imitating him, to mock at them. A foreign soldier,[1] one Edmundo Malatesta, who had a touch of the humanities[2]—one wonders what he was doing in such a galley—said he must be the ass Silenus rode on in the classics, and that the gods had taken him up to Olympus with the other deities, and, having got him there, he must have fallen from his high estate. As his companions wondered at his learning, little enough of the humanities ever having come their way, the Italian said he hoped, when they had won the town, to eat the author of the voice. This fate was not reserved for the poor donkey, who had, in after years, what may be called the benefit of clergy at his death.

After the battle, when the town was duly burned, the Indians punished for defending it, and all the gold collected, the Spaniards solved the mystery of the ass. It then appeared that he had swum ashore from a Spanish vessel wrecked upon the coast. The Indians never having seen or heard so strange an animal, thought he was something, supernatural. They slung him to a pole and, in relays, carried him up the mountains to the village of Tairona, where he had lived for several months, treated with the respect due to his quality.

[1] Un soldado extrangero.
[2] Algo entendido en humanidades.

The Spaniards made them take him down again in the same way, and Fray Simon, with one of his rare flights of humour, says, as the ass was the first of all his species to tread the soil of the New World, he may be justly called a conqueror. This conquering animal went with the Sargento Mayor, Salinas upon a lengthy expedition, and did good service on it. He struggled up to Bogotá in Quesada's expedition, and lost his life under Hernando de Quesada, the Conqueror's brother, upon the Llanos of the Rio Meta. His end was worthy or unworthy of his fame, according to the reader's point of view. The valiant quadruped[1] on his last expedition was ridden by a friar. Provisions failed, starvation stared the expedition in the face, and, as a last resource, they killed the ass, "pushed by the extremity of hunger," so Fray Aguado says, in extenuation of the crime.

Thus were his services, in life and death, considerable. The soldiers called him Marobaré after the cacique of the town where he was captured. His rider's name was Padre Fray Vicente Requesada. Both friar and ass were conquerors, as it were.

The friar, faithful to his vows, we may suppose, has left no progeny. His tried companion and his saviour of the past was the progenitor of thousands of his race, who to-day wake the echoes of the Andean trails as did their ancestor on the hillside above Tairona, when he first stood revealed a conqueror.

After some futile raids upon the neighbouring villages, in which nothing was found, except in one case several large figures made of wood,[2] that the Spaniards took to be the images of departed chiefs, Don Luis de Lugo gave orders to return towards the ships. He had been strictly enjoined by his father to devote the gold they had collected to pay the sailors of the fleet. Instead of doing so, he seized a vessel and secretly embarked for Spain, leaving his father to face the situation as he could.

---

[1] Valiente quadrupedo.
[2] Figuras humanas de madera, toscamente labradas.

A ship was sent out to pursue him, but he eluded it, and arrived in Spain a month before his father's messenger. When they produced the documents to prove his treachery, he was arrested and sent to prison, under an order from the king.

Somehow or other he contrived to get his liberty, either by bribery or by some other means.

Then, with the money he had stolen, he went to Court, and married a lady of position, one Doña Beatriz Neroña de Mendoza, related to the powerful family of the Mendozas, and through her influence became a favourite, and a thorn, both in his father's and Quesada's side, by his intrigues and wiles.

Don Pedro, when he heard his son's defection, was broken down with grief. Still, he could not remain inactive, for something had to be achieved at any cost, as, cooped in their tents upon the beach in Santa Marta, his men died daily, and mutiny was rife.

Summoning his officers, he laid the situation plainly before them, as a wise commander should have done in such a desperate strait.   All joined in the advice that the first thing they had to do was to find out a way to the interior.

To pass the snow-clad mountains was impossible, for no one knew the way, and to push on through the primeval forests still more impossible.   So they determined to explore the River Magdalena, ascend it, and, from its sources, try to reach some country fit for a settlement.   At once they set themselves to build several decked boats, of the kind known to the Spaniards of those days as " bergantines,"[1] destined to carry their provisions and their arms, and ferry across the soldiers and the horses who marched along the river banks when they came to impenetrable swamps and streams they could not ford.   No expedition, in all the history of the conquest, ever set out upon so desperate a march.   The oldest settler in Santa Marta had never penetrated more than a hundred miles inland.   The interior was so shut off from the coast, by the primeval forest, by

---

[1] " Bergantin " means brigantine, but the Spanish chroniclers seem to have used it for any kind of decked sailing boat.

marshes, hostile tribes, high mountain ranges, and the enormous distance that lay between the seaboard and the plains of Bogotá, that not a whisper had ever reached the Spaniards of the existence of the Chibcha[1] kingdom, nine hundred miles away. Yet, so great was the spirit that animated the conquistadores, no man hesitated, and all were keen to plunge into the wilderness.

The first point was to choose a leader, for upon him the failure or the success of the adventure would ultimately lie. Tried captains were not wanting, for camped upon the beach of Santa Marta were men who had made their name in the Italian wars. Others had fought in Venezuela, in Mexico, and in Peru.

Don Pedro's choice fell upon none of his tried captains, for, without hesitation, he named Quesada general of the expedition, having found out that he was born to be a leader, although not bred to arms. His choice was justified, as the young general proved himself valiant in action, patient in hardships to an incredible degree, tactful in council, and, in the difficulties that at once beset his path, staunch, and as true as steel.

[1] The Chibchas were the original inhabitants of Bogotá, as the Aztecs and Toltecs were of Mexico.

CHAPTER II

THOUGH at the time the Adelantado, Don Pedro, was hard pressed for money,[1] and the defection of his son had made things still more difficult for him, he yet pushed on the preparations for the expedition, pledging his credit to the last doubloon.

In a short time[2] he had six brigantines prepared and ready for the voyage.

Remembering the medieval saying, " Let death come to me from Spain,"[3] the " breve tiempo " might seem doubtful to those who know the Spains. However, the conquistadores were capable of boundless energy, as is shown on this occasion, and at the time when Cortés constructed another fleet of brigantines, during the siege of Mexico. Wood certainly abounded in the jungle, and all must have known that the position, hemmed in on the coast, was quite untenable. No doubt the heavy work was done by the forced labour of the Indians, and, in a fleet in those days, men abounded who could construct a wooden sailing vessel, just as they abound to-day on the Ligurian coast.

When all was ready and the ships victualled and duly blessed, Don Pedro solemnly delivered his commission[4] to Quesada as General-in-Chief, before the assembled host:

" I, Don Pedro Fernandez de Lugo, Adelantado of the Canary Islands and Perpetual Governor of Santa Marta and all its provinces, for His Majesty at present, name as my lieutenant-general the Licentiate Quesada. I name him

---

[1] " Sin reparar en lo poco que tenia trató luego de que se dispusiese lo necesario al viage y empresa " (Padre Simon).

[2] En breve tiempo.

[3] Que la muerte me venga de España.

[4] Titulo=commission: in this case Quesada was, of course, lieutenant-general under the Adelantado Don Pedro.

general both of the infantry and of the cavalry of the army that is ready to set out on the discovery of the sources of the great River Magdalena."

The commission was dated " Santa Marta, April the first, 1537," and signed " El Adelantado."[1]

The date of the commission seems to be wrongly stated in the document,[2] as there is no doubt the expedition sailed on April 6, 1536. At that time there were in Santa Marta, according to contemporary accounts, about one thousand men capable of bearing arms.

From these the Adelantado selected eight hundred, and formed six hundred of them into six companies, appointing Captain Juan de Junco to replace Quesada, if he should happen to be killed.

In case both should be killed, he named Captain Gonzalo Suarez Rondon, to take command.

As captains of infantry of the six hundred men who were to march by land, followed up by the fleet, went Juan de Cespedes, Juan San Martin, Pedro Fernandez de Valenzuela, Lazaro Fonte, Juan de Madrid, Lebrija, and several others. As ensigns he named Gonzalo Garcia Zorro[3] and Anton de Olalla.

[1] Herrera in his " Decadas " (5 and 6) makes the date 1536, but Fray Simon expressly says Herrera is mistaken ("se engaña Herrera"), and affirms that he himself had seen the date on the original document in Bogotá. Juan Rodriguez Fresle, a native of Bogotá, the author of the famous " Carnero Bogotano," who wrote in 1639, agrees with Fray Simon as to the date. So also does Juan Florez de Ocariz, who wrote his " Genealogias del Nuevo Reino de Granada " in 1764. Moreover, two of Quesada's captains, Juan de San Martin and Antonio Lebrija, who sailed from Santa Marta with Quesada and fought beside him during the entire conquest, in a joint letter that they wrote to the King, copied by Nuñez the historian from the Archives of the Indies at Seville, give the date 1536. Padre Juan Castellanos, the author of the rhyming chronicle, and Piedrahita, the Bishop of Santa Marta, also agree as to the date 1536.

[2] Quesada himself in the " Relacion" that he wrote, dated July 5th, 1576, fixes the date, for in the first paragraph he says, " thirty years ago " (" treinte años á esta fecha ") in speaking of his companions who set out with him from Santa Marta.

[3] Alferez.

Two hundred men were put aboard the brigantines under the command of Captains Antonio Diaz Cardoso, Luis de Manjarrés, and Juan Cespedes. Diego de Urbina, a Biscayan,[1] was appointed " Cabo."[2] Ortun Velazquez de Velasco was appointed general overseer.[3]

The fleet was well provisioned and equipped with everything required for such an expedition. Not the least important was the care for spiritual matters, in taking two religious with them, Padre Fray Domingo de las Casas and Padre Anton Lescano, with requisites with which to celebrate Mass, when opportunity occurred.[4]

As even conquerors do not live by bread alone, this care for matters spiritual does great credit to the Adelantado's orthodoxy, and, as it proved, both the two friars were men of learning and of liberal views.

After a solemn Mass, the expedition started, as full of spirit as of hope.[5]

The fleet put out to sea with all the population of the almost illusory settlement standing on the beach to gaze at them. The lions and the castles of Castile, no doubt, made a brave show, fluttering from the jackstaffs of the ships, and such artillery as they possessed thundering out a salvo to speed them on their way. The Adelantado had done his duty like a man, and, without doubt, Quesada took up his first command with that self-confidence that never once deserted him through all the perils of his life. He himself, mounted on a fine charger, led the six hundred men that the Adelantado had chosen and equipped with his last funds.

His cavalry numbered only eighty, but as we are so often told that, after God, the conquerors owed their victory to

[1] Diego de Urbina, Vizcano.

[2] " Cabo " literally means " corporal."

[3] " Veedor " also means " caterer," and there is nothing to show which office is meant.

[4] No era lo menos el llevar prevencion en las cosas espirituales, sino lo mas para lo que tocaba á ellas con buen recaudo para poder decir misa donde se ofreciere oportunidad.

[5] Tan llenos de brios como de esperanzas.

the horses, they counted for far more than their mere number would suggest. With them went the celebrated Marobaré,[1] the valiant quadruped that they had acquired, as it were, fallen from the skies. Unluckily, Fray Simon was not a horseman, as was Bernal Diaz del Castillo, so no one has preserved for us, as he did, in his history of the conquest of New Spain, the names, the colours, and the qualities of any of the horses who marched from Santa Marta on that eventful day. All we know is that they were good and fit for war. Now and again, during the history of the conquest, we get a glimpse of one of them, as, for instance, of the dappled grey[2] of Captain Cespedes, who scaled the mountain paths, with such discretion and agility[3] note that he owed nothing to the best footman[4] in the host.

All now was in Quesada's hands, and upon him depended the fate and lives of all the expedition. He found himself in a unique position for a man, only thirty-seven years of age, and not brought up to arms. The Adelantado must have seen great qualities in him, and certainly he had that magnetism that onables every great commander to win the confidence of those he has to lead, for, from the first day, all his men followed Quesada implicitly, and none rebelled against him, even when he committed certain harsh actions that would most certainly have brought on a mutiny with other generals.

The expedition was not too well found, as money was scarce in Santa Marta, and arms and powder had to come from Spain. Although in the West Indian Islands horses were being bred, they yet were dear and far from plentiful.

The chiefest want was powder, and, from the first, the expedition had to economize its use.

When once the fleet had put to sea, the army set out on its march, crossing the province of Chimila, a country hot and desolate, sandy and waterless. The Indians all were hostile, having already suffered from the incursions of the settlers, so that from the first day the expedition marched,

---

[1] See Chapter I.   [2] Rucio rodado.
[3] Discrecion y agilidad.   [4] El peon mas suelto.

they had to fight their way. The Indians harassed them
from thickets and from rocks raining their poisoned arrows
on their ranks; but, as they wore the quilted cotton armour
that the Spaniards had found more efficacious against
arrows than the best armour, either of Milan or of Toledo,
their losses were but small. Nothing could well have looked
more curious and awe-inspiring to the Indians than a Spanish
horse-soldier and his horse draped in their cotton quilts.

As a horse was worth at least five men in battle and
almost irreplaceable[1] in those days, and cost, moreover, a
king's ransom to procure, the first thing naturally was to
defend him against poisoned arrows, that killed both men
and horses in an hour or two.

Aguado, in his most curious " History of Venezuela,"[2]
says: " Out of sacking or light linen cloths they make a
kind of surcoat that they call a coat of arms. These fall
below the knee, and sometimes to the calf. They are all
stuffed with cotton, to the thickness of three fingers. The
layers of cotton are quilted between folds of linen and
sewed with rough thread made in the country, and every
thread is strongly knotted. . . . The sleeves are made in
the same fashion. . . . Of the same cotton they also make
a breastplate and a helmet, though some make these of
tapir's or ox hide, formed like a skull cap. Those soldiers
who have a steel helmet often prefer it. . . . In the same
manner and of the same cotton and linen they make armour
for the horse that guards his face and chest, and covers him
in front. Fixed to the saddle is another covering over his
croup that falls down over his legs. A mounted man
armed in this way, upon his horse caparisoned in the same
fashion, looks the most hideous and monstrous thing that
it is possible to see.[3]

" . . . In countries where the Indians place sharp stakes

---

[1] Francisco de Jerez in his " Conquista del Peru " (p. 238) says:
" El precio comun de ellos (caballos) era de 2,300 pesos, y no se
hallaban este en precio."

[2] " Historia de Venezuela," Fray Pedro de Aguado, tomo 1°.

[3] Parece cosa mas disforme y monstruosa de lo que aqui se puede
figurarse.

in holes, they [the Spaniards] make foot covering for the horse of the šame nature as the armour. These stakes the Indians used to sow about the roads to lame the horses of those who were conquistadores."[1]

A monstrous sight indeed a horse and man must have appeared so armed; but all the same the precaution was quite necessary, for Aguado goes on to say the Spaniards often came out of battle with so many arrows sticking in their armour and that of the horses, that Captain Juan de Ribera, in the battle of Labugá, had full two hundred hanging from him and from his horse.

Thus did Quesada's cavalry advance. The infantry were dressed in the accoutrement of Spanish men-at-arms of those days, the settlers from Santa Marta in the linen clothes and cotton armour that the colonists of those days wore when their Spanish clothes and arms had been worn out in the hot and humid climate of the coast. Quesada, mounted on his horse, rode at the head of his strange-looking cavalry. After him came the harquebusiers with their long match and flint lock guns. The infantry composed the vanguard. Then followed a long train of Indians carrying stores and baggage, and the crossbowmen brought up the rear.

None of the chroniclers of the conquest of New Granada mentions any of those troops of Cuban bloodhounds that did such execution under Cortés in Mexico.

It is not difficult to imagine with what feelings Quesada rode amongst his captains. Gone was the dreary poring over deeds in crabbed hands. The long hours in the stifling courts must have seemed like a bad dream to him. At last he had his chance, and was resolved to make the most of it. The line of march was almost due westerly. Some of the colonists of Santa Marta had penetrated about a hundred miles up the great river.[2]

It is uncertain to what point the settlers actually had

---

[1] " Para que se hinquen los que fuesen conquistadores": Aguado, " Historia de Venezuela."

[2] Fray Simon always refers to the Magdalena as " El Rio Grande."

penetrated, but certainly[1] the town of Tamalameque, about
a hundred miles up the river, was known to them by name.
At that point Quesada ordered the commander of the fleet,
El Licenciado Juan de Gallegos, to join him, as he marched
by land along the river's bank.

The province of Chimila, through which Quesada marched,
formed part of what is now the department of Atlantico.
For the first, and perhaps the only, time in the whole conquest, they suffered from a want of water, for the land is
hot and dry, and water-holes are few and far between.   To
the south-west the snow-capped peaks of the Sierra Nevada
towered to the sky.   In front of them rose the thick wall of
vegetation on the Magdalena's bank.   Indian attacks were
frequent, and the skirmishers were ever on the watch.   In
the front of the expedition the " baquianos " acted as
scouts, their experience of the New World rendering them
priceless for such work.   On one occasion, they took several
Indians prisoners, and bought them to the camp.   In a
few minutes an Indian woman rushed into their lines, her
hair loose, weeping bitterly and like one possessed.[2]   The
Spanish soldiers stood aside to let her pass, and she, running
up to a young man whom they had taken prisoner, threw
herself on his neck, shedding " most tender tears,"[3] and
saying, as her son was captive, she would remain with him.
Her tears and desperation so much moved Quesada, that
he at once released the boy and all the prisoners, keeping
one only for a guide.

A moving scene it must have been, with its wild setting
and strange accessories, and one that showed Quesada was
a man who, had not circumstances later on proved stronger
than his will, might have ranked almost alone amongst the
conquerors for his humanity.

The march through the hot, barren country of Chimila
only took Quesada about a week, and then his real diffi-

---

[1] Tamalameque is said to have meant " The City of the Palms "
in the Indian tongue of the district.

[2] Haciendo mil extremos.

[3] Con tiernísimas lagrimas.

culties began. No roads existed on the Magdalena's banks, and none exist to-day. In those times, as in these, the river was the only highway to the interior. Even to reach it was a work of difficulty. On every side there towered a giant vegetation, matted together with lianas so as to be almost impenetrable. To the soldiers' eyes, only accustomed to the tamed-looking European vegetation, that seems to grow just as man wishes it should grow, in the main thornless and with due intervals between the trees, the virgin forest, that had never felt the pressure of a European foot, appeared to threaten and to challenge their advance.

The gigantic trees; the unknown heavy-scented flowers; the ferns as big as European bushes; the palms with their smooth stems and feathery heads; the gaily-coloured birds and butterflies; the hum of insect life that filled the air as with the strains of a great organ; the reptiles hanging from the boughs, or lying with their fangs bared and heads erect to strike, beneath the masses of the heavy vegetation; the thorns like lancets that even pierced their leather jerkins; and now and then the half-seen form of a tiger[1] stealing through the bushes, impressed men used to Europe, with dread and horror, as if they had come into another planet hostile and terrible.

Quesada was not the kind of man to be discouraged by initial difficulties, though they were formidable. At once he formed a force of " macheteros,"[2] who, with their cane-knives and their axes, were set to cut a path through the dense jungle, to the river bank.

Sometimes Quesada, dismounting from his horse, worked for a spell amongst the " macheteros," to show a good

[1] The jaguar is always referred to as " El Tigre " in the accounts of the conquest, whether of Mexico, Colombia, or Paraguay.

[2] " El machete " is the cutlass, that is called in the West Indies and Southern States of North America a cane-knife. It is a most useful weapon, and is used all over Spanish America except in the Argentine Pampas, where it would have no application, as there is no brushwood to cut down.

example, and incidentally to show the kind of stuff that he was made of, and without doubt his men marched the more willingly, seeing their general walk. The first few days gave them a taste of what was in store for them. The enervating heat prostrated men accustomed to the moderate heat of Europe. The perpetual damp rotted their clothes away. Water, though plentiful—too plentiful, in fact—was deadly, for all along the belts of forests, by the Magdalena's banks, stretched vast and feverish swamps, and from the swamps they were compelled to drink. Soon men were falling out, stricken with malarial fevers, against which in those days no remedies existed, and, even if they had, Quesada had no doctors and no hospitals.

The deadly climate, the lack of roads, and the impenetrable swamps he had to wade through, were the first difficulties Quesada met upon his way.

Cortés in Mexico, and Pizarro in Peru, marched through relatively open country, and every day brought them towards climates more suitable for Europeans. Moreover, they both knew that great and powerful Indian empires were in front of them. All this contributed to make the soldiers more contented, and it speaks volumes for Quesada's talents as a leader that his men, plunged in the recesses of the virgin forests, going they knew not where, never rebelled against him, or even murmured, until their sufferings grew intolerable. Those who have wandered in the Colombian wilds to-day, with all the resources of modern times at their command, can form some slight idea of what the conquistadores had to bear, marching waist-deep in stagnant water, almost dependent on the game they killed for their support, for stores from Spain were not to be expected, and those they had they were obliged to use with the utmost parsimony; without quinine or any febrifuge; devoured alive by the mosquitoes and by the innumerable insect plagues that make life miserable. Besides all these, as they toiled painfully along, at any moment from the recesses of the woods a flight of poisoned arrows might be poured upon them, against whose poison no antidote, except the actual cautery, was known to them.[1]

No expedition in the annals of the conquest had to bear greater hardships, and few commanders faced them more stoutly than did Quesada and his captains.

One of the greatest difficulties he had to meet was how to cross the many and considerable streams that fell into the Magdalena.

Struggling through marshes and through swamps, they reached a river after a fortnight's toil, marching at times but a short league[2] a day. The river proved too deep to ford, and there were no canoes or boats at hand, until they joined the fleet that had set out to join them, in the district known to the Indians as Sampollon.

Alligators swarmed upon its banks, just as they swarm in any creek in the hot country of Colombia to-day. The difficulty seemed insuperable, for to adventure into the turbid, swiftly flowing flood, haunted by saurians and the ravenous, bloodthirsty fish known as caribes[3] in some parts of America, without support of any kind, would have been to invite disaster and a certain loss of men.

Quesada, with the eye of the born leader, ordered his men to cut lianas from the trees, and twist them into ropes. Then, a brave soldier having volunteered to swim across holding the end of the extemporized cable in his teeth, a rough and dangerous, but adequate bridge was improvised. All crossed in safety, the horses swimming, whilst men with poles beat on the water to scare the alligators.

Nothing was lost except some stores,[4] and then the expedition, having come out upon the Magdalena's bank, halted to rest, and seek for tidings of the fleet.

---

[1] Later on we read of " La contrayerva," probably the Waco plant so well known to the Indians in both Americas. " Yerva " (probably " hierba ") was the name that the Spaniards always gave to the poison the Indians used for their arrows.

[2] The Spanish league may be taken at three miles.

[3] " Caribes "—*i.e.*, caribs.

[4] Matalotage.

CHAPTER III

On leaving Santa Marta, Quesada had fixed his meeting with the fleet at Tamalameque in the province of Sampollon. He had expected that they would easily precede him there; but, when he reached the Indian village of Chiriguana, considerably farther down the stream than Tamalameque, he found no trace of them.

Although he did not know it at the time, the voyage, from the first, had been disastrous. All had gone well as far as the Magdalena's mouth. On entering it, the fleet found it in flood. An enormous yellow mass of water, upon whose surface floated trunks of trees and rafts of brushwood, met the tide and caused a fearful sea upon the bar. These floods, caused by the melting of the snows upon the mountains of the interior, descend so suddenly, that the powerful boats, that to-day ply upon the Magdalena, are often hardly able to make headway, and, now and then, are twisted round and driven on the banks, as if they were mere cockle-shells or Indian canoes. The brigantines, built hastily in Santa Marta, most probably of unseasoned wood, for it is most unlikely that the Adelantado could have risked dismantling any of his ships from Spain, could make but a poor fight in heavy weather such as prevailed just off the river's mouth.

A southerly gale drove them right past the entrance to the river, a place not always easy to negotiate even to-day, and that, in those days, uncharted and without lights or any fairway beacons, must have been a perfect death-trap, in the fierce gales that spring up from the south.

The tempest drove them towards Cartagena, past the long island of Salamanca, which extends for almost five leagues in front of the river's entrance to the sea, so that there are two passes, as it were, into the Magdalena, one at each end of this natural breakwater. Three of the five ships were sunk, and the greater portion of the crews were lost.

The few that got ashore were killed and eaten by the Indians, except some stragglers, who escaped by hiding in the woods, and arrived eventually at Cartagena, after great sufferings.

Captain Cardoso's ship was driven ashore at Punta de los Icacos,[1] near Cartagena, but got afloat again after much labour, and the same fate happened to the vessel of Captain Manjarrés.

Thus only two ships out of the five that sailed from Santa Marta escaped the storm, and even they were badly damaged and scarcely fit for sea.

The Adelantado, with that contempt of difficulty that always characterized him, although in want of money, and in bad health,[2] instantly issued orders to build three more brigantines. As soon as they were built he sent them off to join Quesada at the trysting-place. By this time Captains Cardoso and Manjarrés had got their damaged ships refitted, and, entering the river, had got as far as an Indian town known as Malambo,[3] after the cacique's name.

Several of the captains sent to the assistance of Quesada by the Adelantado had become so much discouraged by their first want of success, that they deserted with their ships, and, crossing to Panama, went to Peru[4] to seek their fortune. One of them, Captain Urbina, joined the Licen-

---

[1] The icaco is the *Chrysobalanus icaco*. It is known in Cartagena as " Uvas de Playa " (Grapes of the Shore), and bears a fruit that has much the appearance of a bunch of grapes.

[2] De bien poca salud.

[3] Many of the towns in Colombia still bear the names of their caciques at the time of the conquest. Cacique, though originally a Carib word, from the Island of Hispaniola, is now used all over Spanish America in the sense of chieftain, or chief. Maiz, hamaca, and many other words now in common use in Spain and her quondam colonies, were originally Carib.

[4] Many of the early chroniclers write " Piru " for " Peru." It would appear that " l'un et l'autre se disait " in those times.

ciate La Gasca, and did good service in the rebellion of the Pizarros.

Quesada all the time was in a miserable plight hemmed up against the river bank, which was perpetually in flood, as the rainy season had begun, with swamps on every side of him, and his men falling sick of fevers from their exposure to the sun. Provisions almost were exhausted, and game existed in such small quantities that they could not rely upon it, even if they had not been forced to economize their powder, as if each grain of it were gold.

The Indians attacked him, coming down in their canoes concealed in floating vegetation, and every wound their poisoned arrows caused was almost certain death.

In this extremity he sent a message to Santa Marta to ask for fresh provisions and reinforcements, for, owing to the deadly climate and the perpetual fighting, he had already lost two hundred of his men. Passing Malambo in his canoe, the messenger encountered Captains Cardoso and Manjarrés with three more vessels, that the indefatigable Adelantado had got ready and dispatched. They were commanded by the Licentiate Juan Gallegos, a man " of great satisfaction, valour, and confidence "[1]—that is to say, the Adelantado had great confidence in him. The evil fortune that had hitherto accompanied all the seagoing ventures of the Adelantado still dogged him, for a caravel that he dispatched to overtake and join Gallegos ran ashore on a shoal at the mouth of the Magdalena, and only fifteen of her men were saved.

The other three vessels had set sail with great precaution, as they well knew the dangers amongst those ever-shifting shoals. However, having got through without mishap, probably by sounding carefully, as not a chart existed, and the few sailing directions that they had, dated from El Bachiller Encisco's[2] voyage in the year 1515, they safely

---

[1] " Persona de gran satisfaccion, valor y confianza." Gallegos eventually died in Peru, fighting under the Licentiate La Gasca against the Pizarros.

[2] The Bachiller Encisco (another lawyer) was dispatched by Pedrarias Davila, the Governor of Panama, to survey the coast.

passed the shoals, and found themselves floating on the great river that hitherto had proved so fatal to the fleet. At once the Indians attacked them. From creeks and swamps, out of the recesses of the dark forest, and from their shelters behind islands, poured such flotillas of canoes that the whole river seemed covered with them. You might have walked across stepping from one canoe to another, as an old writer says. He farther on avers there were one thousand of them; but perhaps his illustration is to the full as apt as his arithmetic. From the canoes the arrows fell like hail, or, rather, like a flight of feathers falling from a flock of cranes, for arrows shot from the loose-strung bows of the river Indian make hardly any sound.[1] The brigantines, taking advantage of their sails, plunged right into the midst of the canoes, their crews sheltered behind a covering of stout canvas, and ran down several of them. Not being able to go about with any speed on account of their build and the swift current of the Magdalena, the ships got separated, and then the Indians' canoes swarmed round each individual vessel, launching their arrows and endeavouring to run aboard. The brigantines made a stout fight with some small cannons they carried that discharged " reasonable-sized bullets,"[2] and did considerable execution on the infidels.

At last the brigantines broke the resistance of the Indians, who turned and fled, leaving the river covered with broken canoes and with innumerable dead bodies floating on it.

The Licenciate Gallegos was now free to prosecute his voyage, and made all speed to join Quesada, who, he was

---

His soundings, distances, and latitudes are strikingly accurate. His most interesting narrative, entitled " La Suma de Geografia del Bachiller Martin Fernandez de Enciso, Alguazil Mayor [a legal dignity] de Castilla del Oro," was published in Seville in 1519, a long time before the foundation of Cartagena and Santa Marta.

[1] Albert Milligan in his " Adventures of an Orchid-Hunter " (London, 1891) says (p. 165), in speaking of an Indian attack on the Opôn River, by which Quesada penetrated to the mountains, " In the direction from which the arrows came we heard nothing— not even a rustling of the foliage."

[2] Razonables pelotas.

well aware, was in great difficulties. The flooded river, with its swift stream and surface full of trees and boughs, proved almost as great a danger as had the Indians' canoes.

Knowing nothing of the seasons at that time they (the Spaniards) went along, making discoveries of everything, including, as we may suppose, the seasons, and slowly gained a few miles every day.

How anxiously Quesada looked for his arrival may well be imagined, situated in such a desperate condition as he was. The Adelantado strained every nerve to help him, knowing well that on the exit of Quesada's expedition was hung the fate of his new government. All his hopes were centred on Quesada's finding gold, for, at that time, they had no men to enter into agriculture, even had the Spaniards been inclined to follow it, as a means of livelihood. Nothing was farther from their thoughts. They came to seek for gold, to court adventure, and, incidentally, to spread their faith amongst the Indians. The gold in the Indian tombs of the Zinu[1] had been collected, and, at that time, the mines in Antioquia had never been explored. In Venezuela all the country about Maracaibo and El Cabo de la Vela had been searched thoroughly, and no gold had been found. All Santa Marta was well known, and it was thought the province was of little value as it contained no mines. The Spaniards of those days had never dreamed either of planting coffee or bananas, industries that to-day have made the country prosperous and rich.

Thus all depended on Quesada finding gold in the interior, and on his expedition the Adelantado put out all his strength.

As ships were his chief want, he sent off Captain Manjarrés to Santa Domingo to build three brigantines and a good caravel.[2]

This Manjarrés, who, not unlikely, was an Andaluz from Seville or from Malaga, was known to everyone in Santa Marta as a sayer of sharp things. His grace consisted in

---

[1] See "Cartagena and the Banks of the Sinú," Cunninghame Graham. London, 1920.

[2] Tres bergantines y una buena carabela.

a faculty to put apt nicknames to almost everyone.[1]   His
wit seems to have led to his undoing, for, on arriving in
Hispaniola, he was thrown into prison for a debt.   A lady
also preferred a suit against him for breach of promise, and
the witty captain found himself obliged to spend a good
deal of the money which should have gone upon the ships
to satisfy the debt.   As to the lady, none of the chroniclers
have set down how Captain Manjarrés settled his plea with
her.   Manjarrés assuredly could not have been an object
likely to capture the affections of an ordinary woman, for
he is described as having " a sun-dried face, a hollow belly,
and thin legs ";[2] in fact, the very picture of the baquiano[3]
that he was, dressed in his linen clothes, with sandals on
his feet, and perhaps a rusty Spanish helmet on his head.
Once free from prison and his affair settled with the offended
lady, he set to work in earnest, and in a short time had a
brigantine and a good caravel built.

News in those days took long to filter from one place to
another, and so Captain Manjarrés never knew of the death
of the Adelantado, though it had happened shortly after
he sailed from Santa Marta, until a year had passed.   Death
took Don Pedro in the midst of preparations to send more
reinforcements to Quesada, worn out with toil and by the
deadly climate, and sick at heart at the defection of his son.

He was indeed the father of the republic.[4]   All mourned
his loss with heartfelt tears, and held themselves for orphans,[5]
for the Adelantado always had specially befriended widows,
old soldiers, and the poor.

We have no portrait of him from the pen of any chronicler;
but it seems clear he was of a noble character, upright and
just; a man not to be dismayed by difficulties, and a tenacious
friend.

His lot was cast in a place that had been the grave of

---

[1] Era muy chistoso y tenia una gracia especial en poner
apodos.

[2] Cara tostada del sol y enjutas piernas y barriga flaca.

[3] " Baquiano " may here be taken as meaning " old hand.'

[4] Habia sido padre de aquella republica.

[5] Se tenian por huerfanos.

many reputations; blow after blow of evil fortune descended on his head, and yet he faced them manfully and died in harness, still striving, ever contriving to make Quesada's expedition a success, like a Castilian gentleman of those days, steadfast in faith and with his face toward the foe. Shortly before his death Don Juan Fernandez de Angulo had arrived from Spain as the first bishop of the unlucky colony. This prelate was with Don Pedro at his death, gave him the last rites of the Church, and buried him.[1] He also composed his epitaph in what Fray Simon describes as elegant distichs in which he wrote down " some of the much that he could have said about his person."[2] The Latin seems a thought canine, although it has a pawky ring about it in the last hemistich, that redeems it from banality.

Quesada, who was all afire to start, as both his spirit and his courage spurred him on,[3] as soon as he was joined by Manjarrés with his brigantine and caravel, set his course again upstream. When he left Chiriguana, where he had been so long delayed, he was guided by some Spaniards whom he found living with the Indians. It is supposed they were deserters from the expedition, made about a year before, by the German General Ambrosio Alfinger,[4] who set out from Venezuela, and, after suffering great hardships, had to return with the loss of great part of his men.

[1] Don Juan Fernandez de Angulo, the first Bishop of Santa Marta, subsequently became Bishop of Bogotá.

[2] Cifro algo, de lo mucho de su persona, que se podia decir. The distich runs as follows:

> Hac Dominus Petrus Fernandez conditur urna
> Excelsus maritis, prosperitate minor
> Expensis multis, quæsivit barbara regna
> Indicat ipse viam
> Sustulit alter opes.

[3] Porque el brio y valor le ponian espuelas.

[4] Alfinger, a German in the Spanish service, started from Maracaibo in 1530, to make an expedition to the interior. He went due west, and entering El Valle de Upar, in what is now Colombian territory, traversed it for the first time, committing hideous cruelties upon the unfortunate Indians. No Spaniard in any of the conquests equalled him in barbarity, and, though an able and a dauntless

The guides soon lost their way and led the expedition into a country entirely uninhabited, in which they wandered for twelve days. Luckily game, especially deer, was plentiful. Their horses, having rested at Chiriguana, were in good condition, and so the mounted men were able to kill many of the deer, by coursing them with spears. The deer were fat and tame, never having seen horses, and very seldom men, except the Indians who occasionally ventured into the uninhabited tract of country in pursuit of game. Had this not been the case, it seems impossible that the Spaniards could have killed them with their spears. Those who have lassoed horses in the open can judge how much more difficult it would be to approach near enough to lance a deer, even when mounted on an active horse. At last the expedition came on an Indian town, and, " taking tongue "[1] with them, found that they were still in the province of Tamalameque. All the land in it is intersected by lakes and swamps that generally have outlets to the Magdalena, and, as they had no guides, nor anyone to interpret with the Indians, it was impossible to march.

The Cacique Tamalameque had withdrawn himself to an island in the Lake of Parabuy, as he had suffered from Alfinger's expedition, who had attacked the place.

In Alfinger's time, having no boats to cross to the island, the Spaniards mounted their horses,[2] and, swimming over,

---

leader, his memory is held in execration for his bloodthirstiness. After enduring many hardships, and committing countless cruelties, Alfinger was killed in battle in the valley of Chinacota, as he was returning to Maracaibo with a considerable amount of spoil.

[1] Tomando lengua.

[2] This feat was repeated by the Llaneros of General Paez, in Venezuela, during the War of Independence. Seeing some Spanish gunboats anchored in the Orinoco, he sent a regiment of cavalry to take possession of them. These men, Llaneros from the great plains upon the Orinoco, half centaurs and half canoemen, as much at home in the water as on land, stripping themselves naked, leaped on their barebacked horses, with their lances in their hands, and, swimming out, attacked the gunboats with such ferocity that they were forced to yield. A wondrous combat, with something classical about it, that needs a painter to commemorate it properly.

put the place to sack. The chief escaped, and this had made him wary, so his canoes had all been taken over and secured. On this occasion, Quesada did not have to swim his men across, for Captain Manjarrés, with his brigantine and caravel, covered the Spaniards' advance along a neck of land from which they all could wade across.

Quesada, having found plenty of provisions in Tamalameque, decided to rest a while after his twelve days' wandering in the wilds. Moreover, Tamalameque was the farthest point to which any of the colonists from Santa Marta had attained.

In front of him all was more absolutely wrapped in mystery than is the remotest portion of the world to-day. The enormous yellow river, a mile or more in breadth, flowed through high walls of vegetation. Flora and fauna, climate, the inhabitants, even the seasons were unknown to any European. As, after Tamalameque, the river takes a southern turn, the latitude was quickly lowering, and thus the very heavens took on an unfamiliar air. The Great Bear now had sunk into the northern hemisphere; above their heads the Southern Cross, inferior to the Bear perhaps in brightness, but far more mellow in its effulgence, was the one friendly thing they saw, and that only on account of its supposed resemblance to the emblem of their faith. The birds and smallest insects differed entirely from those that they had ever seen or heard about: the vampire bats, the gigantic boas, and the alligators were terrible and awe-inspiring. For all they knew, the recesses of the woods might still hold stranger monsters, as huge and terrifying as the great beasts that walked the earth before the waters of the Flood.

In spite of the uncertainty, and notwithstanding all his difficulties, a sort of exaltation seemed to possess Quesada, as is the case with all men born to command, His confidence inspired his followers with hope. For the time being they had lost touch with the Magdalena, having been led into the swamps that fringe its banks in many places. Quesada therefore sent Captain San Martin to get back to the river, and find a way by which the army could advance. This Captain San Martin was one of the best officers Quesada had, and was a man of education, as the curious, but, unfortunately too brief, account of the expedition that he and Captain Lebrija prepared for Charles V. most amply testifies.[1]

Captain San Martin pushed on, with " Spanish courage, to which everything possible seems easy."[2] In the first place, he had to cross the Rio Cesar,[3] though how he managed it is difficult to understand. The river is a full half-mile in breadth, runs swiftly, and is full of alligators. Having crossed over, San Martin encamped, having placed an outpost to protect Quesada when he resumed his march.

Quesada still was waiting for his fleet, encamped near Tamalameque, in a pestilential swamp, losing men every day by fever, snake-bite, and in perpetual skirmishes.

After twenty days of waiting, with nothing but conflicting rumours of the fleet brought to him by the Indians, and, as often contradicted, he set out to join Captain San Martin at his camp on the Rio Cesar. By this time San Martin had got together a fleet of canoes, so that Quesada's army passed the river in safety, though with considerable risk, as it was a perilous passage for raw soldiers.[4]

This is not to be wondered at, considering how ticklish

[1] " Relacion de los Capitanes Sanmartin y Lebrija," translated into French in Ternaux Compans, " Essai sur l'ancien Cundinamarca " (Paris, 1842). Cundinamarca comprehended the provinces of Bogotá, Velez, Pamplona, La Grita, Merida, Muso, Ebaté, Panches, Neiba, Muequetares, Sutagaos, Ubaque, Funza, Lengupa, Sogamoso, and Chita. All these territories now form part of Colombia. They were all conquered by Quesada.

[2] Con animo español, á quien todo lo posible le parece facil.

[3] This river was named after Captain Cesar, the best of Heredia's captains. His career was adventurous, even beyond most of the captains of those days. In one respect he excelled nearly all of them, for he was renowned for his good treatment of the Indians. His chivalrous conduct to Don Pedro de Heredia, when the latter was imprisoned by his enemies, marks him out as a man of real nobility. For an account of his adventures see " Cartagena and the Banks of the Sinú," Cunninghame Graham. London, 1920.

[4] Era pasage bien peligroso para chapetones.

an embarkation is a dug-out canoe. The slightest move-
ment (of a chapeton) upsets it, and to hold horses' halters
as they swim beside adds to the difficulty and risk. Yet
all the horses had to be passed that way, for to have let
them loose to swim across would have been to expose them
to getting lost amongst the woods after they landed on the
farther side. As they swam by the frail canoes, the paddlers
must have had to keep a careful eye upon them, to adjust
the pace to the worst swimmer, for horses differ greatly in
the water, some swimming with their backs exposed and
heads held high, leaving a wake like an electric launch, and
others are almost entirely submerged, except their faces,
and look like tired fish ready to be taken in a landing-net.

Having crossed the Rio Cesar, the expedition once more
came out upon the banks of the Magdalena.

It must have been a dreadful march they had to execute.
No one who does not know by personal experience the
banks of rivers such as the Magdalena, the Orinoco, or the
Amazon, can form the least idea of the difficulties troops
would encounter on the march, even to-day, if they were
forced to hug the rivers' banks.

Quesada had no option, for he was sent to discover the
sources of the Magdalena, and, as no maps existed, and he
had not the least idea of his itinerary, the river was the
only guide he could rely upon. Few rivers in the world can
have a denser vegetation growing on their banks; few streams
can be more absolutely shut in between high walls of vegetation even to-day, when there are settlements at intervals,
with clearings here and there, and wood stations for the
steamboats, that naturally cut deep into the primeval growth.

Swamps often extend at a short distance from the banks,
and these are intersected here and there with deep and
sluggish streams, known locally as " caños," usually unfordable. Floods often sweep the river, almost without
warning, and in Quesada's time, when there was no possi-
bility of receiving any information from the upper waters
of the stream as to their coming, they must have constituted a peril difficult to meet.

Quesada all the while was striving to reach the province of Sampollon, for it was known by Indian report to be both fertile and well cultivated.

Still between him and it lay many leagues of what turned out a veritable *via crucis* to him and to his men.

Simon and Piedrahita, as well as Castellanos,[1] tell us of the difficulties they had to meet. Rivers and marshes, illness, great tracts of flooded ground, mountains, and deluges by night and day, they had to resist upon an empty stomach, for if the proverb, " Every evil is bearable with bread," says sooth, the reverse must be the case that " Every evil, wanting bread, is greater."

Nothing in any work of the imagination can exceed the perils that Quesada had to face: neither Pizarro nor Cortés experienced a tithe of the material hardships that he underwent. They fought with hordes of savage men; but still they had superior arms and discipline to those they fought with, and the great advantage of their cavalry.

Quesada fought in the first instance against a hostile nature, vastly more powerful and challenging than any that mankind had known before his time. He had to break his way into the fastnesses of a world that put out all its strength in heat and rain, in floods, in pestilences, in monstrous and invading vegetation that overflowed the paths his " macheteros " cut through it, and obliterated them almost as fast as they were made. Hunger and thirst —those enemies against which the modern soldier, with all his discipline and courage, hardly resists two days—were with him constantly, the handmaidens of death.

No wonder that in the deadly march to Sampollon, Quesada lost a hundred of his men. They died like bugs,[2] as goes the homely Spanish saying, and many of the rest were ill; especially privations took their toll of the poor

---

[1] A cada paso . . . venian rios, cienegas, enfermedades, añegadizos, espesísimas montañas . . . aguaceros terribles de dia y de noche . . . estomagos vacios mal se resisten aquellas inclemencias, pues si el refran dice, " todos los duelos con pan son buenos," tambien valdria lo contrario, " todos los duelos sin pan son mayores."

[2] Morian como chinches.

chapetones, the soldiers, with their red cheeks and sturdy legs, who a few months ago had disembarked from Spain. Only the " baquianos," with their sun-tanned faces, small bellies, and thin legs like flutes, were proof against the climate, for to them hunger, thirst, and the sun shining through a white miasmic vapour were everyday occurrences.

Quesada, either on foot leading his horse, his armour piled upon its back, possibly covered against the sun with the same helmet that to-day is hung up bruised and rusty as a monument in Bogotá, or, with a machete in his hand, marching beside the pioneers, appeared invulnerable.

His spirits never fell, and so far he had had no fever, and his iron will maintained the spirit of his men. Provisions had run short, and the small store of powder that he had was growing mouldy with the constant rain.

The expedition's fate seemed sealed, and it appeared that all of them would leave their bones to rot in the Magdalenian wilds, for antiquaries to find some day and found their theories on.

As a last resort he halted, and once more sent out Captain San Martin, with his good caravel, to seek for tidings of the fleet.

CHAPTER IV

THIS time Captain San Martin was more successful in his quest. After a day or two of sailing downstream he came upon the vessels slowly struggling against the current, and obliged to anchor every night for fear of Indian attacks.

They only sailed when they encountered a fair wind. Often it blew dead ahead; and then, hugging the shore, they progressed painfully by rowing, punting, and by towing from the bank. Thus do the curious Colombian craft, called "bongos," ascend the Magdalena, their high and ornamented bows giving them an air of caravels. Their low waists, with but a foot or so of freeboard, have a palm-leaf awning over them, and the high stern completes the likeness to a vessel of Quesada's time.

As a general rule, a gang of punters, standing on a platform, urge them along, working like galley-slaves, to the cadence of a chanty, the perspiration falling off their half-naked bodies like dew falls from a corrugated-iron roof, and with blood oozing from their right armpit, for against it they throw their weight upon the pole.

When, after several days' delay, the fleet reached Sampollon, the joy was general through Quesada's camp at Chingalé.[1]

[1] There has always been some doubt as to where the actual town of Tamalameque was situated in those days, for it is certain that the modern town does not occupy its site. Recent investigations have shown that the Cacique Tamalameque's chief residence was in the island or peninsula in the lake, over which General Alfinger's soldiers swam their horses. It is described as " de aspecto gracioso," and was composed of three streets terminating in a square, with the cacique's palace in the centre. The Spaniards first founded the town on the bank of the river opposite to the town of Mompox. They then removed it a little higher up, on a small plain. This place is now

Quesada had almost given up all hope, but the arrival of the fleet renewed the spirits of his men. For almost three months they had been without news from their base, and though the most important news of all, the death of the Adelantado, did not reach them, as the fleet had sailed before he died, it yet brought letters from the soldiers' families.

For the first time since they had sailed from Santa Marta, the expedition had a little bread and a few barrels of Castilian wine. They also got some linen, with which they bound up their wounds, anointing them with oil.

Spirits rose high again, and the army clamoured to advance. Quesada, who was above all things a most cautious leader, as well as valiant in the field, would not consent to it until the fleet had rested for a week. Scouts were sent out, and everything as far as possible arranged for their departure into the unknown.

Before they started Quesada gathered his forces all together and addressed them. His speech is reported or written by his chief chronicler.[1]

" The natural grief I feel, gentlemen, at the loss and death of so many friends, does not drive me to despair. Grief is a part of our nature, in spite of what the Stoics preach. . . . Those who set out for wars or conquests put themselves into close touch with death, and this is the first

---

known as Old Tamalameque. In 1608 it was moved to the plains of Chingalé, where it still stands. The reason of these changes of site is most curious. It appears the priest of the parish, El Licenciado Bartolomé Balzera, was frequently at loggerheads with the civil authorities. When he could not get his own way, he packed the sacred images and the chapel bell upon his Indians' shoulders, and, shaking off the dust (or mud) from his sandals, used to put up a temporary altar in another place. The civil authorities, unwilling to be left without the consolations of religion, used to follow him, and found it more convenient to build new houses round the chapel of their " mustang " priest than to attend Mass from afar. This curious bit of information Colonel Acosta ("Descubrimiento de la Nueva Granada") unearthed in "La Floresta de Santa Marta," by Nicolas de la Rosa.

[1] Fray Simon.

rule of every war. . . . That two of our companions have deserted us—I mean Don Diego de Urbina and Don Diego de Cordova—I care but little for. I rather hold it an advantage, as we know now what sort of men they were. . . . Lastly, because a ship sinks in a storm, is that a reason men should never put to sea again? Because a crossbowman misses his aim, is that a reason crossbows should be laid aside?"[1]

Quesada was a lengthy speaker, as befits a lawyer; but, as in the case of Xenophon upon a similar occasion, he did not make the least appeal to sentiment. His harangue appears to have been what in North Britain, in speaking of a sermon, is called a "cold morality"—merely an appeal to honour and to common sense. After his examples and his apothegms so dear to Spaniards, he went on to say that:

"It would be an infamy to return with nothing done. Therefore (he said) I order all to be ready by the first streak of dawn, for I intend to start as soon as it is light."

An admirable address if he did make it, and, if he did not, he who wrote it well caught the spirit of the man. Certainly it attained its object, for all night long the camp rang with the din of preparations.

Armourers sharpened swords, crossbowmen looked out new strings for their weapons, lances were pointed, horses shod for the last time, and stores packed carefully in canvas to resist the damp.

At the smile of dawn[2] an altar was set up, and Father Antonio de Lescano said Mass at it. That first Mass on the banks of the Magdalena must have been a moving sight. The soldiers knelt on the wet grass, girt with their swords, their lances and their crossbows in their hands. The thin white vapour that envelops everything at that hour on the Magdalena shrouding the forest in its mysterious folds, making the trees look ghostly, and the swirling stream a very Styx or Periphlegethon; the dewdrops falling from the great leaves of unnamed trees, the cries of the nocturnal animals

---

[1] The translation is not literal, but gives the sense of what Quesada said.

[2] Al reir el alba.

returning from their prowlings to lie hidden in the woods must have made an impression on those fierce and fervent Christians not to be effaced.

Out in the river lay the fleet, the Lions and the Castles of Castile hanging down limp against the masts in the damp morning air, heavy and dank with dew. Upon their decks the sailors knelt bareheaded, straining their eyes towards the priest who knelt before the altar on the bank, striving to hear the words of comfort in a tongue unknown, and therefore doubly sacred to them.

Quesada, with his rapier by his side, dressed in his buff coat, and with the helmet in his hand that every son of Bogota should revere, just as an Englishman reveres the armour of the Black Prince at Canterbury, knelt just behind the priest.

Turning towards the kneeling ranks, Father Antonio gave the benediction, making large in the air the sign of their salvation, under whose ægis they were about to carry death and destruction through the land. The soldiers crossed themselves, first on the breast, and then in Spanish fashion, on the mouth. Quesada, rising from his feet, mounted his horse, gave a brief order, and the expedition set forth again upon its Calvary.

The instant that they left the river they found themselves once more in the impenetrable woods, for it was quite impossible to march upon the actual banks, as they were swampy and often swept by floods.

They had again to cut their way through the tangled mass of vegetation. Captain Inza, at the head of the axemen and the macheteros, set manfully to work, opening the way through solitudes never before trodden by human foot, for the Indians' only highway was the river that they travelled in canoes. The paths they made served for two purposes. In the first place, as it was opened, the army followed it, and in the second, as they blazed the trail,[1] it remained to guide them, just as to-day the telegraph stretches

---

[1] To blaze a trail is to cut large pieces of bark off the trees at intervals.

through the selfsame woods and points the way for the rare travellers.

The difficulties of road-making were so great that it often took a week for the pioneers to open up a path that the expedition traversed in a day. The long-expected fleet had relieved Quesada of his sick men, of whom he had a large contingent, and it was lucky for him that he could disembarrass himself of them, for the route in front of him daily became more difficult and dangerous. Rain fell incessantly, and the poor soldiers' clothes rotted and went to pieces on their backs. The wasps and hornets, sandflies, mosquitoes, and reptiles of all sorts, made their lives miserable. By night the vampire bats fixed on their feet or legs, if they were in the least exposed, and sucked their blood, fanning their victims all the time so gently with their wings that they were unaware of anything, till in the morning they awoke weak and exhausted from the loss of blood.[1]

The misery the expedition underwent must have been almost impossible to estimate.[2] The provisions soon turned mouldy in spite of all precautions, and, as game is scarce and hard to find in the forests of the Magdalena valley, starvation stared them in the face.

So great was their necessity that no one would help even

[1] Their horses also must have suffered terribly from the attacks of bats. Nothing is more common than in those portions of America, between the tropics, to find a horse that in the evening you have left, active and strong, munching his maize under a tree, in the morning weak and languid and scarcely fit to move. If you are a " baquiano," you lift his mane and find his neck clotted with blood, from a small puncture that the bat has made. A horse seems never to feel the bat; nor does a sleeping man.

[2] Castellanos (Juan de), " Elegias de Varones Ilustres de Indias," has a passage describing the wretchedness of the soldiers:

> Cubiertos van de llagas y de granos
> Cansados de las dichas ocasiones
> En vida los comian los guisanos
> Que nacen por espaldas y pulmones.

As Castellanos had been a soldier in the expedition, he knew what he was writing about. In after years he took holy orders and for many years was a priest at Tunja.

his greatest friend. Through the deep mud, torn by the thorns, starving, covered with boils from head to foot, the wretched soldiers staggered on, looking like an army of the damned. When a man found he could not keep up with the rest, he crawled into the thickest of the jungle to die alone, after the fashion of a stricken animal. Along this Via Dolorosa Quesada led his men, sharing their hunger and their misery.

So weak the soldiers got at last that, when a man felt his strength ebbing, he confessed himself to one of the two priests and received absolution. Then he marched on until he fell. As the expedition struggled on, a fleet of Indian canoes followed just out of range of the crossbows and harquebuses, and when they saw a soldier fall out of the ranks they pounced upon him like a vulture pounces on a piece of carrion, and drove their spears through him. Thus, as several of the historians of the time lament, not only was a soldier lost to Spain, but an unshrived soul doomed to perdition, and upon that account they hit upon the plan of receiving the confession of all those who felt that they were doomed.

If the Spanish soldiers died like flies, the Indian carriers' fate, bowed underneath the weight of the provisions and the baggage, was harder still to bear. There is no record that Quesada treated them with cruelty as did Ambrosio Alfinger, the Venezuelan general, who, as his carriers were all chained together, when one of them was ill, straightway cut off his head and let the body drop out of the chain; but for all that their lot must have been hard to bear. The Indians, born as free as the wild deer, were quite unfit for sustained work of any kind. Confinement usually proved fatal to them, and chains and labour they never could endure. So that by the time Quesada had been two months on the road most of his carriers were dead. The soldiers, then, were forced to carry both baggage and provisions, for, though they piled a good deal of them on the horses, a horse was far too precious to them to risk his strength by overloading him.

After three weeks of forced delays in camp, to give the

pioneers time to cut a path for them, they reached " a valiant river, whose waters were like blood."[1]   Upon this river they were constrained to camp, to await the arrival of the fleet to ferry them across.   Some slung their hammocks in the trees, and some built little shelters,[2] thatching them with leaves, for they had not sufficient tents for all.

In the first watch they heard a voice calling out: " Help, friends, a tiger is carrying me off; for God's sake help !" The whole camp stood to arms, and when the tiger saw the torches he left his prey wounded and bleeding on the ground.

They hung the hammock up on a higher branch, thinking to make the wounded occupant of it secure from all attack. However, in the morning watch,[3] the tiger silently returned, and carried off the man so noiselessly that the whole camp slept on, and no one was alarmed.

They missed the soldier in the morning, and found his hammock empty, blood-stained, and torn, hanging down against the tree.   Then they went out upon the trail, but never found a vestige of the poor soldier, whom probably the tiger had dragged deep into the woods.

As the man's name was Juan Serrano, they called the " valiant river " after him, and it still bears his name.

After this agitated night the army passed the river next morning in the brigantines.

If anything, upon the other side, their march was still more arduous.   In the various rivers that they had to cross they often lost a man or two.   In one of them an alligator seized a soldier, one Juan Luengo, and made off with him, in spite of everything that his companions tried to save him.   His death, and that of the poor soldier Serrano whom the tiger carried off, were but individual calamities.

---

[1] Un valiente rio que echa el agua una sangre bermeja.   " Valiente " in this sense means " great."

[2] Such a shelter, thatched with leaves, used to be called a " wickey-up " in the Western States of North America.

[3] "El cuarto de la modorra"—literally, the drowsy watch.   Those who have kept it in similar circumstances know how hard it is to keep awake at that hour in the drenching dew of the tropics.

A universal danger now began to menace everybody. Provisions had become entirely exhausted, and the soldiers had to support themselves on the rare game that they could find—on palm shoots and on any fruits that appeared edible. As few of them had any experience of the flora of the country, many of them lost their lives by eating poisonous berries, and died in agony. Their salt had all run out or had been melted by the continuous rains, and they had nothing with which to season anything they ate. So hard did hunger press them, that they devoured rats, mice, and frogs, and boiled pieces of their buff jackets and devoured them greedily.

The army that at the passing of the Rio Serrano had been reduced by hunger, fighting, and fevers, to two hundred and nine men all told, now marched along like living skeletons.

On several occasions, when a man dropped dead, his starving fellows dragged his body into the woods and fell upon it like a pack of wolves.

Lastly, one or two of the horses disappeared mysteriously. This was more than Quesada could endure, for he well knew that in his horses consisted his main strength. After severely reprimanding all his followers, he added that any horse that died should instantly be thrown into the river. This saved the rest of them, for it was of no use to kill a horse to feed the alligators.

Quesada now was at his wits' end what to do. The forests seemed interminable, the rains incessant, and nearly every other man was sick with fever and could scarcely hobble on.

Each day the horsemen were sent out to look for game, armed with their lances only, for they could not afford to use the little powder that remained. Even the crossbowmen dared scarcely use their bolts. Luckily for them all the horses had not suffered, for grass of some kind always was plentiful, and they were fat and strong.

A strange adventure happened to Captain Juan Tafur one morning early, as he was looking out for game. Having come suddenly on an ant bear whilst riding with another soldier called Palacios, they charged it instantly. Though the ant bear is slow upon its feet, its strength and its enormous claws make it an adversary not to be despised, and this the soldiers found out to their cost. Tafur wounded it with his lance, and, thinking it was dead, approached it carelessly. As he was looking at it, it sprang upon his horse's quarters, wounding them terribly. The horse plunged violently, but the ant bear clung tightly to its seat. Its mouth was right against the rider's shoulders, so close he could not even use his sword or the ant bear its claws. This was most fortunate, for had it but had space it could have killed him in an instant. Its weight pressed him down on the horse's neck and broke a stirrup leather, and he would probably have fallen a victim to it had not Palacios pierced it with his lance. It fell upon the ground and grasped the horse firmly round the two forelegs, completely hobbling him. Luckily a well-directed kick that the horse, after having shaken off his enemy, planted on its head, dispatched it, and the two soldiers returned to camp in triumph with the ant-eater packed upon the horse.

The soldiers devoured it instantly, though it most certainly is not an inviting-looking animal to make a meal upon. Moreover, an ant bear could not have been much of a meal for more than a hundred men.

All this time the fleet had been steadily fighting with the difficulties of the navigation of the unknown river, of which they had no soundings or the least idea of how the current ran, or of the position of any reefs or rocks.

For the most part the banks were uninhabited, as they appear to be to-day, for Indian hamlets in such gigantic vegetation are scarcely visible. Whenever it was possible the Licentiate Gallegos sent out boating parties to explore the creeks and search for any tidings of a considerable town.

Days passed, long days of agony and of starvation, and still the endless forest stretched to the horizon on both sides of the stream, and still the river seemed interminable. Hope was abandoned, and had it not been for the indomitable will of their young leader the soldiers would have given up the quest. Quesada suffered doubly what his men endured, for he shared all their hardships and their meagre rations, and was held responsible for all their miseries. Yet, even in that dreadful pass, he showed his iron nerve. A miserable horse soldier, pushed by extremity of hunger, having killed his horse to eat it, Quesada ordered him for instant execution. So great was the ascendancy he had obtained over his followers that no one murmured at the execution, and all held that it was just.

From that day forth the horses all were safe, and by his act of firmness Quesada, without doubt, rendered the future conquest possible, for without horses it could never have been carried out successfully.

After the execution, the army slowly began once more to struggle on, dragging their weary, fever-stricken limbs along, what must have seemed to them, the very road to hell.

Another day, or two days at the most, and they would all have perished; but as they painfully limped onward, towards the evening came a signal from the fleet. The lookout man at the masthead of the leading brigantine, in the last rays of the fast-setting sun, had seen a town perched on a high, red bluff. So great their need was of provisions and of rest that Quesada, half mad with grief at the plight of his expedition, determined instantly to go himself, though it was nightfall, to explore the town. He would not even send his brother Hernan Perez de Quesada, in whom he had great confidence; but, ordering three canoes to be equipped, started with his brother, Captains Lebrija and Maldonado, Ensign Olalla, and three other chosen men. A negro was the pilot, and in the falling darkness they set out, in the fierce current, upon the unknown stream.

The situation must have been wellnigh desperate to make Quesada embark on such a step. He must have known that, had the frail canoes been overturned and he himself have lost his life, the expedition would have returned to Santa Marta in a miserable plight.

All night they paddled, and as they struggled on under the light tropic sky, the mystery of the scene, the noises rising from the forests on the banks, the flight of night birds, the splash of fish that jumped and fell into the water, the myriads of fireflies lighting the trees and flitting to and fro as if they were nocturnal humming birds; the alligators floating past like logs; the heads of tapirs and carpinchos[1] swimming like little hippopotami, must have impressed Quesada, as something magical.

No doubt he sat wrapped in his cloak, with the dew running off his helmet, in the stern of the canoe, under the unfamiliar stars, without the solace even of divine tobacco, to pass the hours away. At times he may have paddled for a spell in the cold chill of the approaching dawn, for seated in an Indian dugout, cramped and obliged to keep the same position in the crank craft, the cold, wet mists soon numb one to the bones.

Had he but known it, his first stage was over, and his great conquest well within his grasp.

Of this he neither knew, or even could have guessed at it, and the night must have been interminable. Gradually the sky got lighter, streaks of faint colour broke across the dark, blue heavens. The mists shrouding the trees appeared —before they only had been felt—looking like veils of muslin, and the voices of the wild animals grew fainter at the approach of day.

Herons and cormorants flew past, and fish in myriads appeared, some leaping and some swimming with their backs awash, looking like silver in the dawn. Quesada may have observed such things, or wrapped in his reflections, seen nothing but the course of the canoe. When at last day broke, he found that the canoes were within a bowshot of the town. Composed of about thirty houses, it was built in a large clearing that overhung the river at an elbow in the stream. Quesada and his companions, their lances in their hands, girt with their swords and covered with their bucklers, landed below the bluff. Good Spanish

---

[1] *Hydrochœrus capybara.*

courage[1] and necessary precaution supplied the want of friends.

The town was empty; the inhabitants, having descried the ships, had fled into the woods.

Although they found no gold in the deserted houses—and, starving as they were, their first thoughts seem to have run on gold—they found what was worth more than all the gold of the Americas to hungry men, some fields of ripening maize.

Quesada put a guard over them, and when the fleet came up, later in the day, distributed his share to every soldier with his own hands. Had he allowed them in their ravenous state to eat their fill, the greater portion of them would have died.

They found that the town was called La Tora, as they were told by several Indians they had taken prisoners.

Three reasonable islands[2] stood in front of it, and formed some passages known as Las Cuatro Bocas. To-day the place is called Barranca Bermeja—that is, Red Bluff—and underneath the bank, just at the elbow and below the islands, the stream forms several whirlpools that are dangerous for canoes.

After six days the army reached the place. The men rejoiced to find provisions, and the horses ate their fill of maize.

Eight months had now elapsed since the expedition sailed from Santa Marta, and so Quesada determined to encamp to rest his horses and his men, and to explore the upper reaches of the stream.

[1] "La buena prevencion y esfuerzo español suplian la falta de compañeros." How unpleasing, patriotic phrases sound, except in the mouth of one's own countrymen! In fact, "No es la miel para la boca del asno" (Honey is not suited for the mouth of the ass).

[2] Tres razonables islas.

CHAPTER V

THE Indian cornfields were soon exhausted, and once again starvation stared the expedition in the face. The men began to die so fast that their dead bodies were thrown into the river overnight; perhaps because the survivors had not strength to bury them, or perhaps because Quesada did not wish to let his losses become known to all.

Once more he sent the fleet upstream to prospect, and to find out if there was any open country or more Indian villages. After twenty days they came back exhausted and discouraged, reporting that the farther they advanced the denser were the forests, and that the river seemed interminable. Moreover, they had come upon no settlements nor any cultivated land.

This time Quesada's position was more desperate than before. Provisions were exhausted, and the starving men, tormented by the insect plagues, their clothes rotten with rain and sun, their arms all rusted and hunger claiming its victims every day, had grown so weak that Quesada had to forbid them from going to the river either to drink or wash their clothes, for several had been carried off by alligators as they strayed tottering on the bank.

The return of the fleet, with nothing to show for all their suffering, but the loss of several men, completed their discouragement. For the first time the soldiers murmured against their general, saying they knew not where they were going to, and he was leading them to death.

Things came to a head when, even men broken to hardships and to war such as were Quesada's two best captains, Cespedes and San Martin, despaired entirely of success.

So, as the delegate of the officers and men, San Martin laid before Quesada what they had to say.

Things must have looked wellnigh desperate before Captain San Martin took such a step, for he had always been the first in every enterprise.

Standing before his general he represented that they had now been eight months on a journey that seemed endless, and that appeared likely to end in failure and in death to all of them. He spoke about their hardships and their difficulties, recounting all that they had suffered, telling Quesada that his soldiers had obeyed his orders in every particular since the first day when they set out, in circumstances of peculiar danger, both by sea and land. He said that the opinion of the soldiers was that to go on was rash, as they had no provisions and no guides. Therefore, he urged they should return to Tamalameque for the present to rest and to refit, as it was a country rich and well cultivated, where at least they could find food. He pointed out that Quesada had already lost more than half his men. From Tamalameque they could send to Santa Marta for new ships and reinforcements, and in the meantime found a settlement that in the future would serve them as a base.

This proposition was not unreasonable, for they had suffered much. Luckily for them Quesada was a man who, when he had put his hand to the plough, never looked back again. He at once answered San Martin, who may have been a little ashamed of his position, for Fray Simon says that he went unwillingly, and but to please the soldiers who were murmuring. Quesada's speech showed him the man he was.

He did not argue with his captain, nor reproach him for having made himself the mouthpiece of the rest. He spoke no word of sentiment and used no rhetoric.

Carefully, quietly, and as sedately as if he had been once more in the Chancery Court of Cordoba, he gave his reasons, even sententiously, saying that to retreat was to court disaster, for the vessels were too small to take them all aboard, and that those who would have to march must of necessity perish in the woods. He pointed out that the Adelantado had exhausted his resources and spent his last doubloon to fit the expedition out, and to abandon it with nothing done would be a treachery. He showed them certain linen mantles of superior make that they had found in the village of La Tora, where they were encamped, and said, as they could not have been the work of the rude savages that dwelt there, they must come from a country much more civilized. The little gold that they had found in the past eight months in Indian villages, they had been told, came from the interior. Hence, to the interior they must go, if they hoped to discover gold.

Then, in a lighter vein, he said that those who felt discouraged were like men who, as the Spanish adage has it, are drowned in little water,[1] and told them that if they turned back now, discoverers more courageous than themselves would reap the fruits of all their toil.

He finished with the nearest attempt at rhetoric that he indulged in, by saying, " An army of slaves with a lion as a leader is better than an army of lions led by a slave."

He knew he was the lion, and that the Spaniards always like an allegory or an epigram.

His speech concluded, he gave his orders as if nothing had occurred out of the ordinary.

" I command," he said, " this murmuring shall cease, and that Captain San Martin shall start at once upon another expedition, to explore the country farther afield."

Neither San Martin nor any of the soldiers said a word, but went about their duty instantly. Throughout his manifold adventures and hardships in the future, Captain San Martin was Quesada's right-hand man, and never again did he complain, or make himself the mouthpiece for complaints.

Quesada's influence with his men must have been great for them to acquiesce, so patiently, in his commands, after the sufferings they had undergone. Few men can ever have been placed in a more difficult position than he was at La T ra, on that eventful day. He crossed the Rubicon once and for all, and, like his prototype, was followed cheerfully by his men to victory.

---

[1] Se ahogan en poca agua.

Had he but faltered for an instant he was lost, and the honours of the conquest would have been reserved for a more worthy conqueror.

From where they were at the little hamlet of La Tora, in the far distance they could see a range of mountains, and not far up the river the mouth of a large affluent. This was the Rio de Opon that runs right through the valley of the same name. After deliberation Quesada, judging it must lead up to the mountains, ordered Captain San Martin to enter and explore its course. He set out in three small canoes, accompanied by twelve well-chosen men.

On the first day of this eventful voyage they saw nothing worthy of remark.

Upon the second they met a large canoe manned by three Indians. The moment that they saw the Spaniards they abandoned their canoe, plunged into the stream, and sought the shelter of the woods. In the canoe San Martin found some finely woven cloths, dyed a fine purple colour. He also found what raised his spirits higher than they had been raised on the whole voyage. Packed in banana-leaves were several cakes of hard, white salt, quite different from the salt got by evaporation on the coast. This was the first salt from the mines of Zipaquirá that European eyes had ever looked upon. Naturally, San Martin knew nothing as to where the salt had come from; but for all that, the sight of it sealed the fate of the Chibcha kingdom on the plains of Bogotá.

A soldier, one Bartolomé Camacho, was the first man to plunge into the water and swim to the canoe, being a mighty swimmer.[1] Thus, almost by accident, was the secret of the Indian kingdom revealed, just as the secret of the existence of the New World was first revealed by floating reeds, seen by another Spanish sailor from Colombus's ship two or three days before they reached the land.

The blocks of salt in the canoe justified Quesada's faith and his tenacity of purpose, for they saw that in front of

[1] He may have been the ancestor of the Camacho family of Velez. At any rate he was " gran nadador."

them some country must exist, more civilized than that in which they had toiled and suffered for so many months.

Joy filled all hearts, and San Martin, seeing some huts a little way ahead, landed and searched them. They proved to be all full of cakes of salt of the same kind that they had found in the canoe. He saw at once that the three huts were used as a store, for on the river bank in front of them were several posts for tying up canoes, and a well-beaten path led from the huts into a little plain.

Leaving three men to guard the huts and their own canoes, he pushed on rapidly with the remaining nine. After four leagues of march he came out on a larger plain with a well-defined track across it. This track he followed for nearly forty miles, until the mountains became clearly visible. Far off in front, he saw columns of smoke ascending as from houses and observed cultivated fields, and pushing on a little farther two large villages.

Then, judging that he had too small a force to advance into what he saw was a well-populated land, he entered several deserted huts, and having found them full of salt and cotton cloths, took some of them to show his general as proof of all that they had seen.

Knowing he must have been observed and reconnoitred by the Indians, though he had not seen any of them, he marched all night and camped at the first light beside a little stream.

They had hardly set their watch before they were attacked. Indians appeared to rise as if by magic from the reeds. Striking their hands upon their mouths they uttered war-cries, and advanced in what no doubt they thought were overwhelming numbers to the attack. Their arms were bows and arrows, spears, and clubs called " macanas " made of heavy wood.

Through the Americas, both North and South alike, Indians choose the grey interval between the dawn and day for their attacks, whenever possible. This was the first of many onsets of the kind just between dawn and day, when you can scarce distinguish a black thread from a white one, that San Martin had so far experienced. He met it bravely, his men standing together covered with their bucklers, their swords and lances in their hands.

The fight was fierce; but when the Spaniards, after a volley from their crossbows, advanced to the attack, the Indians fled, leaving several of their number dead upon the ground. Some of the Spaniards were wounded, but none severely, and San Martin seized and held fast an Indian who is described as having been "intelligent and agile."[1] A curious combination, for the two qualities as seldom go together, as honour and profit are found in the same bag.[2]

This Indian proved a most important capture, and in the future was of great service to them, though more because of his intelligence than his agility. The Spaniards named him Pericon, just as, in old times, in the Southern States of North America, they called a negro Sambo or Quashy, or merely Uncle, if he happened to be old.

Pericon was well treated by his captors,[3] and became a great friend of the Spaniards. They asked him by signs about the country, and he replied that farther on there was a thickly populated land. They showed him a thin plate of gold, and asked him if there was much of the same metal in the country of the hills. Poor Pericon said " Yes," perhaps only to please them, or perhaps because he did not understand their pantomime, and judged it better to say something of a conciliatory kind.

Laden with cakes of salt and with the Indian cloths that they had found in the deserted huts, holding the bows and spears that they had taken from the dead Indians in their hands, and with their feather crowns upon their heads and leading Pericon with them, they made a triumphal entry into Quesada's camp. As they advanced they broke into a rude chant, that Castellanos in his rhyming chronicle has

[1] Agil é inteligente.

[2] Honor y provecho no caben en un saco.

[3] Con el regalo y buen tratamiento que todos le hacian vino á hacerse grande amigo de los Españoles, á los cuales, luego preguntandole por señas, les decia que alla arriba de aquellas sierras habia muchas gentes.

preserved.[1] In it, they celebrated their discovery, after the fashion of the Roman soldiers at a triumph, vaunting the country they had seen—its openness, its coolness, and the abundance of provisions and of gold that it contained. The gold, indeed, as yet, only was vouched for in pantomime, by Pericon; but he turned out a true and veritable prophet, and all his gestures were verified by facts.

Quesada's camp received the news, as it were, on their knees, for heaven seemed to have opened for them after the hell they had endured. Men clasped each other's hands, and staggered to and fro like drunkards in an ecstasy of joy. They said, " Heaven has spoken by the general's mouth." In fact, it may be said to have so spoken, for though in every age brave men abound, men like Quesada, of stern moral courage, and a determination such as his, are very pearls amongst mankind. Out of their miserable shelters made of reeds and palm-leaves the fever-stricken men emerged, leaning upon their swords, or upon sticks cut from the trees, and all demanding to march on at once.

The night was passed in cleaning up their arms and making ready for the march. At the first streak of dawn[2] Fray Domingo de las Casas said Mass, and then, standing before the little altar that he carried with him, he blessed the soldiers as they passed in front of him.

A moving scene, and one fraught with consequence both to Quesada and his men, and above all to the Indian countries beyond the mountains, to whom his advent brought so much misery and pain.

[1] . . . Tierra buena, tierra buena,
Tierra que hara fin á nuestra pena.
Tierra de oro, tierra bastecida
Tierra para hacer perpetua casa.
Tierra con abundancia de comida,
Tierra de grandes pueblos, tierra rasa,
Tierra donde se ve gente vestida

 * * * * *

Tierra de bendicion, clara y serena,
Tierra que hara fin á nuestra pena.
   (Castellanos, " Elegias de Varones Ilustres de Indias," Madrid, 1748.)

[2] Al rayar el alba.

After the Mass they once more set out towards the mountains on the left bank of the Opon, the " macheteros " as before opening a road for them and the brigantines entering the river, fighting the current by rowing and with poles, for the Opon was far too narrow for a vessel to use sails.

All went well for a day or two, and then one night without the slightest warning the river rose in flood, most probably from heavy rains in the interior or the melting of the snow far away in the hills. It is not certain which of the two rivers—the Opon or the Carare—that form the valley of the Opon district the brigantines were in, for the various chroniclers name both the rivers indiscriminately. At any rate the army followed the banks of one or other river, and when the flood descended on them they had to flee for refuge to the trees, leaving the baggage to be swept away. Clinging to the trees like monkeys, they remained two miserable days, reduced for rations to forty grains of roasted maize per man. The horses were up to their backs in mud and slime when at the last the flood subsided and ravenous for food, having subsisted on a few leaves of canes that were as hard as leather and about as nutritive.

Once more Quesada found himself in desperate straits. All the provisions had been lost, their precious powder spoiled, and even the strings of the crossbows so damaged by the wet as to be hardly fit for use. In this extremity they once more boiled their scabbards and their bucklers, belts, and the leather articles they had, and cooked a nauseous broth. It made a mixture more like glue than food for human beings; but they were all so famine-stricken that they devoured it greedily.

It took them twenty days of suffering to reach the two huts where San Martin had found the cakes of salt, and when they got there the fields of maize that he had found on his voyage of discovery had been cut down and the corn carried off. Luckily they found an Indian dog or two and boiled them whole, not stopping even to take off their skins, and ate them as if they had been lambs reared in La Sagra de Toledo[1] or in the plains of Bogotá.

Another day or two and they would have died of famine, or been obliged to kill their horses; but this Quesada would not consent to, thinking it better that they all should perish than to destroy the chiefest arm they had. His resolution was rewarded by the appearance of the brigantines that had encountered serious peril in the flood, and been delayed by the swift current of the stream. When they arrived their worst necessities were soon relieved, for they had plenty of provisions in their holds.

As it was impossible for the vessels to push farther on from want of water, the river shoaling rapidly as it drew near the hills, Quesada's greatest difficulty, after the want of provisions, was the increasing number of the sick. After the exposure that the men had undergone in such a climate, the only wonder was that any of them escaped malarial fever; but the Spanish race is extraordinarily well fitted to endure every kind of hardship, especially those born in Castile, where the cold of winter is Siberian and the heat of summer almost as severe as that of Africa. After a consultation with the Licenciado Gallegos, the commander of the fleet, it was agreed that the latter should return to Santa Marta with the sick men, who numbered nearly half of the expedition, and that Quesada should push on into the hills with the two hundred that remained.

They agreed to meet again on that day year, in the same spot; but subsequent events rendered their meeting impossible, and by that time Quesada was the master of the country and possessed better ports.

Gallegos set out full of hope, for the worst seemed finished, and all he had to do was to report to the Adelantado[2] and then return with reinforcements. Quesada, always the soul of honour in these matters, promised that the sick should have their share in the gains of the conquest that

[1] Como corderos de la Sagra de Toledo.

[2] Neither he nor Quesada knew that the Adelantado was dead.

he looked forward to achieve. Once again circumstances beyond his control rendered his offer nugatory.

From the first start Gallegos had bad luck. Aboard his ship he had taken with him an Indian recently baptized under the name of Alonso; but who was still a chief. This new Christian[1] had been taken up the river, greatly against his will, from Tamalameque, where his father had been king. Either the rite of baptism had been forced on him against his will, in which case it may not have taken, or he had asked for it himself, hoping to seek revenge upon his enemies. In any case he seems to have been a subtle plotter, and to a great extent his treachery succeeded in bringing ruin on the fleet.

This bastard—or, at the least, misbaptized—Christian, from the first seems to have had great influence with Gallegos. Quesada had expressly enjoined upon him to lose no time upon the way in looking for provisions, but to push on to Tamalameque, where they abounded.

Alonso, who thought he saw a chance to bring off a great coup, in passing a large Indian village, asked leave to go ashore to bring off fresh meat for the fever-stricken men.

Once there he got together all the Indians he could influence, and told them that the Spaniards were few in numbers and many of them sick. This, he said, is the occasion to be rid of them. All his friends joined him, except a chief called Lopatin, who came by night and told Gallegos what was being planned. Gallegos would not listen to him and still clung to Alonso, perhaps because he was baptized, and not remembering the Spanish saying, that an old Moor makes a bad Christian.[2] However, Captain Chamorro, who had known Alonso a considerable time, told Gallegos that the Indian was a false Christian and a traitor, " a stealer of the sacrament," and a most dangerous man. Still, as Alonso

---

[1] Christiano Nuevo, was the name given to Moors, Jews, Heretics (as Englishmen and Hollanders), Pagans, or others who had been initiated into the hope of salvation, more or less by force.

[2] Moro viejo hace mal cristiano.

always came back to the fleet with fresh provisions and now and then with gold, Gallegos still believed in him, although he ordered that a canvas screen should be stretched over his ship's deck to keep off arrows if he were attacked.

He himself never left the ship, and issued orders that nobody should go ashore. This he did at the advice of the Chief Lopatin, who came again to warn him of the plot. Had but the order been obeyed, all would have been well; but to give orders to the Spaniards of those days was not the same thing as to have them executed.

One day most of the sick had gone ashore to pass the siesta underneath the trees, when suddenly the Indians fell upon them, moving as softly through the woods as cats.

Thirty sick men were taken prisoners, horribly tortured, and dispatched. Canoes swarmed out of every creek, arrows fell thickly on the ships, and Gallegos, standing on the deck directing the defence, was hit and lost an eye.

Captain Rincon, who had been sleeping in a hut, cut his way with his sword through the thickest of the Indians, lopping off hands and arms at every stroke. He did such acts of valour that Fray Simon states he was afraid to write them, " leaving them to the courtesy of each one "—that is, each reader of his book.[1]

Captain Chamorro ran his ship aground, and instantly as many Indian canoes beset him as beset Cortés upon the narrow causeway that led from Mexico to Tacubaya, on the retreat known as La Noche Triste, of which Bernal Diaz writes.

The Spaniards fought their way downstream through the hordes of canoes, with arrows falling on their decks, though it was night-time, as the Indians had lighted fires upon the banks. Men fell by dozens, and, when at last they had got clear, only one ship remained afloat. Gallegos finally arrived at Santa Marta with but twenty men alive,

[1] In this he did not follow the example of the Adelantado of Castile, who, Perez de Guzman, in his " Generaciones y Semblanzas," tells us, was accustomed to relate " cosas dificiles de creer, que habia visto en tierra de Moros."

and most of them disabled by their wounds. His reputation suffered heavily, through his credulity in listening to the false converts' treacherous advice. Nearly two hundred men had lost their lives. Two ships had been abandoned, and he himself had lost an eye. His evil fortune caused all the Indian chiefs, who had been friendly, to rise against the unlucky colony.

Seeing that he would not be trusted any more in Santa Marta, he set out to join the celebrated Licenciate La Gasca, in Peru, and did good service there, fighting in the rebellion of the Pizarro brothers upon the royal side.

The pseudo-convert Alonso disappeared, and was no longer numbered with the dusky catechumens that it was the delight of the good friars and priests to bring into the fold, having no doubt returned back to the woods and his ancestral faith.

CHAPTER VI

QUESADA, after a week's rest, set out to cross the little plain that San Martin had traversed on his scouting expedition. So far, the road was known, and as the Indians had felt the force of European arms in their attack on San Martin they had judged it better to retire. Quesada found the country quite deserted, and a considerable quantity of crops ungathered in the fields.

In two short days they reached a range of hills. They found them shrouded thick in mist—a new experience for them, after the tropic sun. Rain soon fell heavily, and turned the Indian trails into a sea of mud.

Quesada chose out all those soldiers who were most fit for the hard work he saw he would encounter, and left his brother, Hernan Perez de Quesada, with the horses and the weaker of the men.

He himself went on in front to try and find a practicable path by which the horses might ascend the hills. Such footpaths as they found were merely trails winding amongst the rocks, used by the Indians to bring down the salt, that San Martin had found in the deserted huts at the head waters of the Opon.

The country that he had to traverse has remained some of the wildest in the Republic of Colombia. Along the banks of the Opon there still roam Indian tribes, refractory to any sort of civilization and hostile to the whites. They live just as they lived when first Quesada saw them—wearing no clothes except a breech-clout, and armed with spears and clubs. They still use poisoned arrows, and no one ventures up the Opon, the Lebrija, or the Carare, except well armed

64

and in sufficient numbers to resist any attack from the wild tribes.[1]

When the trail enters the dense forests of the foothills, the scenery is beautiful, with a strange wildness and aloofness of its own. Great wreaths of moss hang from the trees, dripping with moisture, so that the traveller is in a perpetual shower-bath. Orchids of every kind—Oncidiums, Cattleyas, and many others of the tribe—cling to the branches, and flocks of great, blue butterflies[2] flit across the path, as silently as woodcocks float through a northern wood. Huge tree-ferns stand up starkly, looking like little palms, and flights of brilliant-coloured birds are ever in the air. Toucans and humming birds, egrets, cranes, curassows, trogons, bush-turkeys, cardinals, orioles, and half a hundred others, with flocks of chattering macaws and parrots, flash past like jewels in the sun. On the high peaks eagles and condors soar, describing circles as they scan the firmament for prey.

Through all these marvels of the flora and the fauna of the tropics Quesada's followers marched along, probably marking none of them; but still feeling their influence without knowing it.

As the rough Indian trail, gradually mounting, wound in and out by rocky, open glades, and through the dark recesses of the woods where Tegua palms,[3] with their umbrella-like foliage and slender stems, towered high above the other trees, and clumps of giant guaduas[4] stood about here and there as if they had been planted by design, the track daily became more difficult. In fact, it more resembled a trail for cats[5] than a path made for men.

Still they pushed upwards almost without provisions, drenched by perpetual rain and by the moisture falling from

[1] In the year 1891 they attacked and slew with poisoned arrows one of the companions of Albert Milligan, the Orchid-Hunter, shooting him with poisoned arrows so deadly that he expired within an hour ("Adventures of an Orchid-Hunter," p. 167. London, 1891).

[2] *Morpho cyprius.*

[3] This palm produces the vegetable ivory nut.

[4] "Guadua" is the name given in Colombia to the bamboo.

[5] Arcades de gatos.

the trees, their armour rusted, and the leather of their saddles and their shoes rotting away, turned to a pulp by the devouring damp. On the sixth day after they had begun to climb the mountains, with tremendous toil and such fatigue as would have daunted any but themselves, they reached some opener country, in which at a great distance they descried some villages and several fields of maize.

There, quite exhausted, Quesada with his chosen followers rested, sending back three soldiers to his brother, who had remained behind with all the horses and the greater portion of the men. They immediately set out, leading the horses after them, for the paths soon became too mountainous and broken for them to dare to ride.

The soldiers stumbled upwards, shivering with cold as they ascended, and drenched by the clinging mist that hung so heavily about the trees that they could hardly see more than a yard or two ahead.

As in the eight months they had spent within the tropics most of their clothes had fallen away in rags, and they were dressed either in such Indian cloths as they had come across or in the skins of animals, their sufferings were severe in the keen cold that they had now to face.

Many of the men were sick with fever, and dragged themselves along painfully, leaning on branches torn from the trees or on their swords. For the first time Quesada had a sharp attack of fever, and now and then had to be carried in a litter by his men.

So starved and tired they were that many of them became delirious, and one, Juan Duarte, ran raving mad, and even when their perils all were past, never was really sane.

Another soldier, Tordehumos by name, they had to leave behind, as they thought, at the last. They left him seated with his back against a tree, his sword beside him and a few pieces of dried meat, all they could spare in their necessity, having prayed over him and " tried to make his peace with God."

How long he sat against the tree, awaiting death with his sword by his side like a true conqueror, he never knew in after days. Feeling himself, as he thought, in extremity, he prayed most fervently, commending himself most specially to the Madonna, for he was a good Christian on all four sides.[1]

His prayer was answered, as it was fit it should have been, seeing he was the first true Christian that ever prayed upon those mountains, and in such desperate straits. A beauteous lady[2] stood before him bathed in celestial light. She spoke to him, telling him, in the words her Son so often used during his sojourn upon earth, to rise and walk.

He did so, and by degrees, struggling along, oftentimes falling on his knees, but always cheered and comforted by the celestial vision he had seen. After two days of struggling and of agony he reached the camp.

All his life long no one believed his story, although Fray Simon, who alone of all the chroniclers refers to it, must have had some suspicion as to who the " beauteous lady " was.

If the foot soldiers fared badly amongst the mountains, the horses, upon which so much depended, suffered even more. Since the days of the conquest, no horse has ever climbed the precipitous Sierra de Opon by the same road Quesada used.

The track, only intended to be trodden by barefooted Indians, went up the mountain face. At certain places it became so steep and ran so perilously near the edge of precipices that they were obliged to haul the horses over the worst spots with ropes made from lianas cut down from the trees.

How they survived such treatment is difficult to understand, and still more difficult when it is remembered that the horses numbered sixty and the men not two hundred, and most of them weakened by fever and the want of food. Still they pushed on, vanquishing every danger, with but the loss of a single horse, who rolled down and was killed.

Their progress naturally was extremely slow, and so

[1] Cristiano por los cuatro lados—*i.e.*, a man with no admixture either of Moorish or Jewish blood.
[2] Una bellísima señora.

Quesada, as he waited for them, sent out the ensign Antonio de Olalla to explore in front of him.

Olalla soon returned saying the mountains were impossible to scale, though he had followed up a valley to the end. This valley Quesada named El Valle del Alferez,[1] a name it still retains.

Quesada, who, though brought low with fever, still remained just as determined as he ever was, then sent out Captains Cespedes and Fonte with a detachment to prospect. With them they took the captive Indian Pericon as an interpreter. Quesada told them if when twenty days had past, they had not yet returned, he would consider them as dead.

Fonte and Cespedes pushed on into the land, and found each day new towns and villages; and to Quesada's camp Indians arrived, who told him of cultivated country when once the hills were crossed.

This raised his spirits so much that he shook the fever off and said he counted all the hardships he had undergone upon the river as a mere nothing, now that success seemed sure.

The captains, Cespedes and Fonte, though they heard constant tidings of a rich country on the other side of the hills, could get no word of any road across. Just as they had begun to lose all hope of finding out a pass they took an Indian prisoner. This poor savage, thinking he would be killed and eaten by the fierce-looking strangers, refused to speak a word. When through the offices of Pericon his fears were calmed, he talked quite freely, and undertook to show the way across the hills by a road that he said the Indians used to bring down salt and other merchandise from a well-peopled country that he professed to know.

Captains Cespedes and Fonte followed it and camped close to an Indian village, and there they learned that the

[1] Alferez = ensign. It is a corruption of an Arabic word " el-farez," that means " the horseman." So we may suppose that in old times ensigns were mounted officers in Spain.

Chief Opon[1] was in a town hard by celebrating his marriage with a new wife. The captains set out and surprised the place, and made the newly married chief a prisoner. To conciliate him, they gave him various presents of things he must have wanted—such as hawksbells, glass beads, and knives, with other trifles from Castile.[2] In fact, they gave him what the conquistadores used in all their conquests as current coin, on the occasions when they paid the Indians for their gold.

The chief was not deceived by their attempts to gain his friendship, having perhaps no use for hawksbells, or having heard of the exploits of the German General Alfinger who had passed near the valley of Opon.

As the two captains and their men were resting from their fatigue and making sandals out of aloe fibre,[3] for all their shoes had been worn out upon the stony paths, Opon sent out to gather all his followers to fall upon them.

Luckily for them, just as it happened with Cortés[4] in Mexico, an Indian woman gave them information of the plot. In the attack upon the village of Opon the Spaniards had taken prisoner an Indian woman. This lady showed great affection to the Spaniards,[5] and it was well for them she did. As they marched on, guided by Opon himself, this captive Indian lady told the Spaniards that the chief was leading them into an ambuscade. Opon, of course, denied the charge, until a soldier[6] gave him so rude a blow

[1] The Spaniards called the valley after the name of the chief, as happened so frequently all through this conquest. It is curious that the custom does not seem to have been often followed in their other conquests, either in Peru or Mexico.

[2] Bujerias de Castilla.

[3] The *Agave mexicana* is known as " fique," in Colombia.

[4] The story of Cortés and La Malinche, the Indian princess who fell in love with him, is told by Bernal Diaz del Castillo in his " Conquest of New Spain," in full detail and with the picturesque handling that places the old warrior in the first rank of writers on the conquest.

[5] " Mostró gran aficion y amor á los españoles ": Fray Simon, cap. xxx., p. 185.

[6] This soldier was far advanced in comprehension of the Indian character (" Estaba adelantado en la condicion de los Indios ").

with the flat of his sword that it stretched him on the ground. This gentle method of dealing with a hypocrite convinced Opon that honesty was the best policy, though he, after the fashion of so many others, only recurred to it in the last resort.

However, once convinced, he saw the best thing he could do was to allay suspicion, so he sent in such store of fresh provisions that all the camp feasted for several days. Well fed and rested, they set out in spirits into a desert[1] that lay in front of them that, according to Opon, would take them several days to cross. They took good care that the chief should not relapse into perversity by putting a stout leather collar round his neck. A rope was fastened to the collar and a soldier held it in his hand, being assured his life would pay the forfeit if the chief should escape. The path ran on the edge of precipices, but Opon, no doubt assisted by his stout collar and the rope, guided them faithfully right through the hills.

As the twenty days that Cespedes had promised to Quesada he would not exceed had now elapsed, he led his followers back towards the village of Opon. Upon the way Cespedes entered an Indian hut to rest, and found in it some emeralds of little value,[2] the first that had been met with in the New World.

Upon arrival at the chief's village, they were so much pleased with his conduct as a guide that they restored him to his liberty, and gave him some trifling presents from Castile—no doubt amongst these were the familiar hawks-bells and glass beads; but one may hope that for remembrance they bestowed upon him the collar and the rope. It would have been a fitting parallel had he hung them up in his reed hut, just as Columbus always carried about with him the chains that were his chief reward for the discovery of a world.

Thus, through the guidance of Opon, Fonte and Cespedes first found the path out into the plains, and the con-

---

[1] " Un despoblado "—literally, an unpeopled place.
[2] Esmeraldas de poco valor.

quest of the Chibcha empire merely became a work of time.

Lazaro Fonte was left with a few men to guard the corn the Spaniards had accumulated in the various Indian villages, and perhaps to keep an eye upon the chief. Cespedes returned to where Quesada had remained encamped guarding the horses, for he would never trust them to any but himself, knowing by the experience of the conquests of Peru and Mexico how valuable they were.

Quesada knew that the paths he must ascend to emerge finally upon the plains were difficult to pass. Even to-day a trail in the Colombian mountains owes little to the steep, rocky staircases of the Atlas, or those amongst the hills of Ronda, away across the straits. All of them are more fit for partridges[1] than men.

In the days of the conquest no four-footed beast had ever travelled the Colombian trails. They proved so difficult that Quesada ordered the horses to be turned loose to find their way, without a halter upon any of them. The idea was fortunate. During the twelve days Quesada took to rejoin Fonte and Cespedes at the village of Opon only one horse was lost.

Quesada having passed a night with all his forces in the valley of the Alferez, and another in the valley of the Shouting[2]—so called because when Cespedes and Fonte first passed through it the Indians kept up their war-cries all the night, during an attack they made—he entered into the path Opon had led the scouts along and emerged upon the open plains.

He had now achieved the first part of his conquest and vanquished nature herself in her most powerful entrenchments in the miasmic marshes of the Magdalena, and from henceforth had but to struggle with the ill-armed Indians of the high plains of Bogotá. He must have felt success was in his grasp, and certainly he had displayed such gifts of

[1] Camino de perdices = road for partridges, is a common term in Spanish for a steep hill road.
[2] El Valle de la Grita.

leadership, so much tenacity of purpose and diplomatic gifts, that he was certain to succeed. When one surveys the record of his nine months' struggle in the wilds, his passage right across the Andes by paths that from his day to ours no horse or even mule has passed again, far easier modes of access having been found, it is most difficult to give the palm, whether to the dauntless leader struggling with the unknown or to the endurance of his followers. Each age brings forth its special qualities.

To-day the soldier stands in a hell of noise and fire. Shells pass over him with shrieks, as of a million damned souls in pain. Shrapnel tears up the earth; Greek fire is belched upon him, whilst suffocating gases poison the air and stretch him gasping on the ground. Artillery fires with such rapidity as to seem a continuous roar of flame and death, and from the heavens destruction drops upon his head. He must stand firm and brave it all, for there is no-where for him to go to, to escape it; nowhere to hide, even for those whose nerve has failed them in the terrible ordeal. There he must stand with thousands of his fellows, mere dumb, heroic, cannon fodder, with heads and arms and legs and entrails scattered around on every side of him. In his mute, glorious thousands he gives up his life, without a chance of recognition or of making himself known. Glory comes seldom to the modern warrior. Even his general hardly has an iota of a chance of it. Should he by merest hazard emerge from the ruck of the commanders he receives a peerage, and all his triumph is to be huddled through the streets with two or three more of his fellows in a hired motor-car.

Yet modern warfare has its compensations. Food is good and plentiful. Few soldiers of to-day have felt the pangs of hunger, almost none of thirst. Long and con-tinuous famine is unknown to them. Their clothes are strong and warm, their boots well greased and adequate. If they are wounded they are conveyed as soon as possible to hospitals, and receive all the attention that modern science has at its command. They do not leave their homes without a chance of ever hearing from their friends and those they love, and, above all, they fight, suffer, and die, in the main, in surroundings that are familiar to them. Houses and trees they know, the lowing of the cows, a windmill on a hill, a tall church tower, speak to them of things they love in their own native lands.

In Quesada's days, men, when they crossed the seas, crossed them for ever. There was no return, except in rarest instances. Skies, plants, trees, seasons, animals, men, human habitations, the birds and fishes, all were strange to them. Often they had not the least idea where they were going to; for the seas that they sailed were all uncharted, the lands they trod unmapped and unsurveyed.

Hunger and thirst were always with them. Disease they had to fight without a doctor and without medicines. For surgery, they had the actual cautery; hot grease poured into wounds, and if a limb seemed to be gangrened or was shattered, a comrade severed it with his dagger whilst three or four of his companions held the sufferer on the ground. When their clothes rotted off their fever-stricken bodies, they went naked till they got the skin of some wild beast to cover them. Certainly they did not face a thousand deaths hurled at them by mechanical appliances; but they faced poisoned arrows, and the privations of an earlier world, with certain torture if they were taken prisoners by their enemies.

Their sufferings also had their compensations. They lived a healthier and more natural life. They were not, as are those modern fellow-victims of the universal folly of mankind, mere cogwheels in great machines, whose evolutions they can neither make nor mar, nor even hinder, protest they as they may. The soldiers of Quesada were not caught so irrevocably in the hand of fate. At least, they could preserve some individuality. Their chances of distinction were far greater. The records of the conquest teem with accounts of poor, illiterate men who rose to eminence. Pizarro was a swineherd; Almagro a bricklayer's labourer; Sebastian de Belalcazar only a donkey-driver; Bernal Diaz del Castillo a page to the great Cortés; and Pedro Cieza de Leon, the best historian of the conquest of Peru, a common soldier. Yet most of these died governors of provinces, with titles and with honours showered upon them.

Each age brought out its different qualities, by reason of the different sufferings its prototypes were called on to endure. Suffering is the mother of the virtues, and every age has endured so much, that the majority of men should all be virtuous.

In one thing, and one quality alone, the soldiers of Quesada's time joined hands with those of yesterday. Both were as patient as an Iona Cross under the Highland rain. Death, hunger, thirst, wounds, neglect, the criticism of dullards and of fools, left both of them unmoved. Let him who can or dares award the palm to either age. They were all men.

CHAPTER VII

QUESADA now had brought to an end successfully one of the most extraordinary marches that the world has known. In all the annals of the conquest it has no parallel, except that of Cortés from Mexico to Honduras; but then Cortés was at the acme of his fame and set out with a large and well-appointed army, and had at his disposal all the treasure of Montezuma, the last Aztec king, whereas Quesada had but little money, and was practically unknown—certainly quite unknown in Spain.

His resources were but few and he had no chance of receiving reinforcements, for the colonists of Santa Marta all thought that he was dead, as they had received no tidings of him for nearly a whole year. " He and the whole army were grateful to the Lord for having brought them safely through so many dangers. Especially because He had allowed the ' sun of the Gospel '[1] to shine for the first time in those neglected valleys, to lighten the darkness that the devil had spread over the souls of those poor ' naturals.' "[2]

The Gospel sun is " awfu' easy carried," as Highlanders say of the Gaelic tongue. Still, few would have suspected that Quesada's soldiers had a great deal of it. They had the grace, however, to come and thank him in a body, and specially to give their thanks because he had not listened to them when they had wanted to turn back. Thus he was justified of faith as well as works, a conjunction that but seldom gratifies a man, here in this vale of tears.

As from the reports he had received from the Indians he had captured, he knew that he was now close to well-

[1] El Sol del Evangelio.
[2] " Naturales." This shows that we were not the first to use the endearing term of " native."

peopled districts, Quesada naturally was anxious to ascertain how he stood as to numbers and in regard to the condition of his men.

So he determined to review his army, and at the muster, found that of a thousand men who had either left Santa Marta with him nine months ago, or had been sent to him in the shape of reinforcements, only one hundred and sixty-six remained.[1] Not a large force with which to conquer an extensive empire, and smaller, by a good deal, than were the expeditions, either of Pizarro or Cortés.

Most of those who had died had not been slain in battle; the sea, the river, fevers, the deadly climate, wild animals, snakes, alligators, the perpetual rain, the want of every necessary and all comfort, had by degrees, as it were, melted them away. Their bones must have been almost in sufficient numbers to serve as landmarks on the death journey they had undertaken; just as the skeletons of baggage animals actually mark the path across the deserts of the East.

Those who survived must indeed have become case-hardened, immune to the effects of climate, real " baquianos,"[2] fit to face any odds and conquer or to die in the attempt.

Luckily the horses had suffered less in proportion than the men, for at least they usually found grass, so that they reached the plains in tolerable condition, able and fit to work.

Thus once again was Quesada justified in his great care of them, and in the severe but necessary step he took in executing the poor wretch who in the pangs of hunger killed his horse for food. Had but the horses all been lost, or even only a few remained, the expedition might have been rendered impotent to face the serried forces of the Indians that they were destined to encounter, before that Bogotá was won.

Fortunately for Quesada he was relatively stronger in

[1] The actual number of those who had been with him was one hundred and eighty, as twenty sick men had arrived at Santa Marta with the Licentiate Gallegos.

[2] Seasoned soldiers.

horses than was Pizarro or Cortés, for sixty had survived. More fortunately still, the Chibchas were not the warlike Mexicans with whom Cortés had to contend. Moreover, he had got into a country that had a climate in which Europeans did not suffer from the rigorous cold that they endured under Pizarro on the high plateaux of Peru.

Upon the plains of Bogotá the thermometer seldom or never rises above 66 degrees[1] or falls below 50 or 52.

The actual place where the memorable review of the scant forces occurred was El Valle de las Turmas.[2]

All passed quietly on the day after the review. No doubt the men remained in camp, cleaning their arms, exercising the horses, resting after their manifold fatigues, and talking over what fate still held in store for them. It was almost their last day without fighting, alarms, or adventures of one kind or another, till they had made themselves the masters of the land.

Early next morning they were attacked in force. From every point of vantage: from behind rocks and trees, appearing as it were from nowhere, till the whole valley seemed to boil with Indians,[3] enemies appeared. After a desultory battle that raged all day and the greater portion of the night, Quesada found himself forced to break camp and set out farther into the plains, so as to have the benefit of his cavalry. Captain Inza with his band of " macheteros "[4] led the advance. The Indians, trusting in their superior numbers, tried to get to close quarters with the Spaniards, thinking to overwhelm them with a rush. Captain Inza, seeing at a glance the danger of their tactics, jumped on his barebacked horse, having no saddle, as it had probably either been eaten in the days of famine or had been destroyed by the continued rains.

Followed by one Rodriguez Gil he charged into the

[1] Fahrenheit.

[2] " Turmas de tierra " are truffles.

[3] Pues no habia valle, ni cerro, cumbre ni ladera que no hirviese con Indios.

[4] These were the pioneers who had opened the paths through the forests in the low country.

thickest of the foe. Naturally, they made a terrible destruction of the Indians with their lances, and must have been good horsemen, as it is difficult to use a lance effectively upon a barebacked horse.

After God, indeed, Quesada owed this victory and many others to his horses, although most of the men had lost their saddles and their bridles, and had to fight with halters of lianas run through their horses' mouths or tied beneath their jaws.

Powder was very scarce amongst his men and had been rendered almost useless by the damp. The crossbows were in somewhat better state; but even they had suffered, for the strings were so weakened by the wet as to lose half their power. Their swords were rusty, and as their scabbards had long rotted and been thrown away or boiled for soup, the men had made new sheaths of snake skins, and the fresh grease of these had spoiled the temper of the steel so that they broke at the first stroke. They had some lance heads, cane-knives,[1] and daggers; but in the main they fought with clubs and javelins that they had taken from the Indians, and spears of Guaduas[2] hardened in the fire.

The charge of Captain Inza on his barebacked horse had shown the Indians what a horseman could accomplish, though bridleless and saddleless, and in the future, when they saw horsemen issuing from the ranks, they turned and fled for refuge to the rocks.

This skirmish left the road open to Quesada, who marched on, and in the month of January, 1538, encamped in the district of Chipatá, where now the town of Velez stands.

He had been more than ten months wandering in the wilds, not in the least knowing where he was going to, till he came out upon the plains after his adventurous passage through the hills. He knew that he had arrived at the country of the Chibchas; but only had the vaguest notions obtained from the captive Indian Pericón of its extent, its population, or its capacity for war. Pericón was of the greatest service to him as an interpreter.

---

[1] Machetes. [2] Guadua = bamboo.

Quesada naturally was anxious to learn all he could about the different tribes, with whom most probably he soon would have to fight.

Pericón, who seems to have been well disposed to him and intelligent, told him that there were many tribes—some subject to the great Chibcha chief Bogotá, and some at war with him.

Each tribe had its own chieftain called an Usaque, and Bogotá himself was called the Great Usaque—that is, Chief Paramount. His chief town was known as Muequetá. This place the Spaniards never called by its right name; but renamed it Bogotá,[1] following their usual custom in this conquest of naming all the places that they took after the reigning chiefs. At the conquest the term Nuevo Reino de Granada, only was applied to Bogotá and the surrounding plain. By degrees it was extended to what is now Colombia.

The place near Velez where Quesada had encamped was the headquarters of a chief called Sacre, whose name the Spaniards, as it happened, never used to designate the town. Here, once again, Quesada drew up his ragged host and once more spoke to them.

Of all the speeches that are recorded of the conquerors, this one in some ways was the most remarkable that has come down to us. After congratulating his men for having escaped so many perils, by the aid of God, he said:

" We are now in a settled and well-populated country. Let no one show violence to any man. We must have confidence in God, and carry matters with a light hand.[2] Thus shall we gain the sympathy of those we meet, for after all they are men like ourselves, if perhaps not so civilized,[3] and every man likes to be treated with civility. So will these Indians. Therefore we must not take from them that which

---

[1] It is said that even to-day, when talking amongst themselves, the Indians use the name Muequetá.

[2] La mano blanda (Fray Simon).

[3] "Industriados " may be rendered by civilized, as it would appear that was what Quesada wished to convey. Whether the " industrialized " man is really more civilized than the Australian black, in essentials, is a question for commentators.

they do not want to give. By following this plan, they will give us what we require, whereas by harsh treatment we shall force them to withhold even necessities. After all, even the ground we tread upon is theirs, by natural and divine right, and they allow us as a favour to be here, and owe us nothing."

No other conqueror, with the possible exception of Alvar Nuñez Cabeza de Vaca,[1] seems to have dreamed of taking up such a position towards the Indians.

The whole speech was instinct with a spirit of justice and humanity, that it would have been wise in him to have followed to the end.

Quesada without doubt had profited by his study of the law, as it appears laid down in books, as distinct from its practice in the courts. Fray Simon says the speech was pleasing both to the captains and the soldiers. If this was so it must have pleased them as a speech dwelling upon the evils of intemperance is often pleasing to a drunkard.

Such speeches seem to act as anodynes to conscience, stilling it as curari paralyzes the nervous system; but at the same time, unlike curari, leaving the will full strength. Quesada must have known, and if he did not know, the inexorable logic of facts soon showed it to him plainly, that his soldiers primarily were on the lookout for gold. To do him justice, except on one occasion when he was overborne by threatened mutiny, he strove to carry out his theories That in itself is to his credit, and places him above almost all conquerors of North and South America and those of Africa to-day. Not one of these seem to have had the least perception that a mere " native " had inherent rights in his own land.

[1] Alvar Nuñez was the conqueror of Florida. Throughout the conquest he treated the Indians well. Subsequently he made a wonderful march from Santa Caterina, in Brazil, to Paraguay, and became the first governor of that country. His interference on behalf of the Indians gained him the hatred of the colonists, who sent him a prisoner in chains to Spain. After years of litigation he was set free, and all charges against him disproved. Colonial governors in all empires, even to-day have to walk warily in regard to " natives."

After this homily they set out, as we may presume, refreshed in spirit, and not confiding in their few rusty arms, but in their valiant hearts.

As they pursued their way across the plains, with Quesada and his captains riding at their head, the terror that the horses wrought on the poor Indians was so great, they threw themselves with their faces flat upon the ground so as to avoid the sight of the awe-inspiring beasts. Others remained like statues, rooted to the ground, afraid to move a limb.

The expedition, though it had emerged out of the Magdalenian wilds, was still in the hot country,[1] though every mile they marched brought them towards a cooler temperature.

They reached a town close to the River Sarabita, from which the Indians all had fled on learning their approach. This town—or, to be accurate, the place where once a Spanish town existed—is known to-day as Mariquita. From it they came to Sorocotá, and found some vegetables unknown to them, though some of those who had been in Peru said that their name was " papas "—that is, potatoes, for the potato is indigenous to Bogotá.

From Sorocotá Quesada marched to a town known to the Indians as Tinca. It is now called Honda, a delightful old Spanish town situated on a rocky eminence that overlooks the rapids of the Magdalena, and was for years the place where travellers left the steamboats and rode on muleback, up the old trail to Bogotá.

Quesada followed the same road by which so many thousand travellers have jogged along in modern times. The Spaniards after the conquest made a narrow paved track, arched in the middle like a Roman military road. Now it is left deserted since the railway has been opened from the town of Girardot. It ran by Guaduas, a town Quesada halted at; now, broken into holes and quite forlorn, it yet remains, worn slippery by the passing feet of countless mules, to mark an epoch in the history of the country, as

[1] Tierra Caliente.

it once served Quesada to mount the last ascent into the plains.

After he had passed Guaduas he held another muster of his soldiers in the valley of Marquira, and found that since his last review they had not lost a man. This muster took place on the 12th of March, 1538 or 1539, according as we take the date given by Fray Simon or by the other chroniclers.

It was just eleven months since they had started from Santa Marta, and as it was St. Gregory's Day Quesada called the place San Gregorio, a name that it still bears.

As they marched up the valley they found, as they advanced, well-populated villages on every side of them, with all the houses grouped round the habitation of the chief.

Just as in Mexico, the Indians took the Spaniards for Children of the Sun, and offered sacrifices to them. They were with difficulty persuaded that the Spaniards were not cannibals, and threw young children down the rocks for them to feast upon.

Luckily Quesada took an old man prisoner, and having given him a red cap and other trifles,[1] sent him back to his countrymen as an ambassador. Being convinced at last that the supposititious Children of the Sun did not eat children, the Indians sent a deputation to the camp to see Quesada and to talk with him. The opportunity was too good to be missed, especially to one bred to the law as was Quesada; so he at once took up his parable.

Speaking through the interpreter Pericón,[2] he told the Indians that the Spaniards had come both for their temporal and their spiritual improvement. How it did not appear; but in a sermon that, following the example both of Pizarro and Cortés, he preached, he laid before them all the mysteries of our faith. What they thought of the dogma is not recorded; but it may have been beneficial to them, in some way not yet made plain to us. At any rate, in all the villages they passed, the Indians came out peacefully[3] to

[1] Chucherias.

[2] " Por boca de ganso "—that is, speaking by a goose's mouth, as goes the Spanish phrase.   [3] Salieron de paz.

welcome them. This was a source of great astonishment to the Spaniards, as on the Magdalena they had always been attacked.

At a place known as La Peña Tajada,[1] where a mountain stream has cut a passage through the living rock, Quesada found writings and pictures on the stones. As the writings and the figures were at a great height upon the rocks, some of the chroniclers seem to have thought that they were put there only to mystify.[2]

That Quesada's speech to his soldiers was not mere rhetoric seems to be established by the fact that in the town of Tuesca, not far from the place where he had seen the writings on the rocks he hung a soldier for plundering. The charge was subsequently proved false. Still it serves to show what a hold he had upon his soldiers, that no one murmured at the act.

After the execution he again issued strict orders against plundering, knowing how important it was for him to keep on good terms with the Indians.

The next important village that he passed bore the name of Nemocon.[3]

However, peace was not long destined to endure.

The Cacique[4] Bogotá, who is described by several of the chroniclers as a " barbarous tyrant," fell upon Quesada's rearguard, chiefly composed of sick and wounded men. They resisted valiantly, until Quesada had time to send back reinforcements under Captain Cespedes. These charged the Indians upon horseback and made a fearful slaughter of

---

[1] The Pierced Rock.

[2] An ingenuous, or perhaps ingenious, hypothesis. Near the Mesa de Carduján, in the State of Nuevo Leon in Mexico, there are similar pictures and writings at a great height upon the rocks. In the days when I passed through the valley, the Mescalero Apaches made things unhealthy for archæologists. Quesada himself has left no comment upon these Indian writings, though as a lawyer it may well have struck him that they were a specimen of Indian conveyancing.

[3] In the Chibcha language it is said to have meant " The Lament of the Lion."

[4] Cacique = chief.

them, thus opening up the way to the town of Zipaquirá. As they were now well into the Sabána[1] de Bogotá, that is as flat as a billiard table, the cavalry could act with great effect. Quesada thus was justified in the severe measures that he had been compelled to take to preserve his cavalry at any cost.

The people that Quesada now found himself amongst were semi-civilized. Fray Simon says they " gave divinity to the sun amongst the other brash of idols that they had."[2] The temples that they erected to the sun were very different from the great stone edifices that the conquerors found to the same deity in Cuzco, Quito, and in Mexico. They would appear to have been but mere straw huts.[3] In them were hung up offerings of thin gold plates, fine cotton cloths, emeralds and coloured beads. They also burned a perfume to their gods, made of a fruit called moque, that gave out a most abominable stench.[4] Children were sacrificed in their temples, and their bodies left out on the hills for the sun to devour. In no other part of America does it appear that human victims were offered up to the sun, though certainly in Mexico the God of War was thus propitiated. Generally the Sun-god appears to have been rather an abstraction, a sort of summing up of the powers of nature, rather than a finite deity. Amongst the Muyscas, for the Chibchas[5] appear to have had two names, this was far from the case.

The Muyscas certainly had made some progress towards civilization and a settled polity. Although they had no

[1] " Sabána " is the word generally used in the north of South America for a plain. It literally means " a sheet," though, when used in that sense, it is pronounced " sábana " and not " sabána."

[2] " Daban deidad al sol entre los demas idolos de toda broza que tenian." " Broza " literally means " rubbish." I have ventured to translate it by the Scottish word " brash."

[3] Tenianle al sol hechos unos templos no suntuosos, sino acomodados buhios (huts).

[4] Que su olor quemada es tan abominable que no se puede sufrir.

[5] Chibcha may have been the term used to designate the kingdom of the Muyscas; the name by which the people called themselves. Muysca, or Muisca, is said to have meant " a man."

stone buildings, and the pictorial arts were little developed in their kingdom, they had a calendar of an extremely complicated kind. The moon was the chief object of their adoration, so their calendar was framed upon her phases. Twenty moons made a year, and, curiously enough, although they counted on their fingers and had names for the numbers only up to ten, they had a word for twenty, for it appears to have had some sacred signification for them, and thus the numbers 5, 10, 15, and 20 were used by them for the carrying out of business, agriculture, the times of sowing and of planting, and generally throughout their lives.

The interpretation of the calendar was left entirely in the hands of their wise men and chiefs, who prophesied or calculated the times of sowing and of reaping, foretold droughts, famines, triumphs, and everything connected with their state, making the Indians their dupes, and being held themselves as little short of gods.

Thus, though barbarians, they were far from savages, and many times removed from the rude tribes upon the Magdalena, amongst whom Quesada and his men had wandered almost for a year.

Quesada probably first met the Indians who had come under the influence of the Muysca civilization in the town of Zipaquirá, for it is well within the plain of Bogotá.

CHAPTER VIII

At Zipaquirá it must have been manifest to Quesada that he had a conquest nearly as important as those of Peru and Mexico, almost within his grasp. On all sides he had evidence of a state that had some of the attributes of stability and power.

The very fact that at the place he was encamped the Indians obtained sufficient salt, not only for their own consumption, but for export to the tribes upon the Magdalena, must have impressed a man whose powers of observation were so keen. Trained as he had been to the law, well educated, and with his mind rendered more acute by all the sufferings of the past years, and made more confident by his success in the new profession he had embarked in, he saw no doubt that he was destined for great things. From his experience of Indian fighting, he must clearly have perceived that the mere numbers of the Indians would make no difference to his success, so long as he was able to preserve his cavalry intact. His popularity amongst his followers had never stood so high. It has been well said that the world goes out to meet the conqueror; but he must conquer first. This in a measure Quesada had already done. None could have doubted that he was, by far, the man of the best education in the host. Still soldiers, especially when faced with hunger and with danger, are not generally inclined to make too much of education, unless the qualities of leadership are joined to it, as they were most undoubtedly in Quesada's case.

The Spaniards of those days, just emerged as they were from eight centuries of warfare with the Moors, and for the first time masters in their own country, esteemed but two professions—the Church and arms. To the first they gave the blind devotion and respect so frequent in all martial nations; but to the second their affection, and affection usually is stronger than respect. Thus men, such as were Charles V., Gonzalo de Cordoba, he whom his countrymen styled " the great Captain,"[1] the Marquis of Peschiera, with Pizarro and Cortés, were national heroes for their success in war. All were the victims of the jealousy and the neglect of Charles V. and his son Philip; but none the less the Spanish people almost worshipped them.

Each expedition, such as that Quesada led, always set out buoyed up with the hope of finding another Mexico or a Peru; nor was the hope entirely without foundation, as so much of America was still unknown. In spite of Prescott and of Robertson and other Protestant historians biased by their religion against Catholics, and blinded by their belief in Anglo-Saxonism to the good qualities of the Latin race, pride in the addition of more territory and power to the Spains[2] must have weighed greatly with the conquerors.

The love of gain certainly was strong in them, as it is strong in all mankind; but it could not have been the only motive that induced the Spaniards to endure such hardships and such perils as they suffered in their quest. Base motives never yet have set men on to do great deeds. Not five per cent., nor twenty, nor yet the illimitable wealth of Potosi, could have been the only power that sent men in a vast tide to the New World. Besides the hope of planting their religion, that, be it not forgotten, they believed in steadfastly and with enthusiasm, no doubt adventure and the hope of glory bulked largely in their minds.

That they were cruel is a truism; but not more cruel than were other conquerors at the time when they lived, or than are conquerors to-day.

One thing is certain, and it stands to their credit and should not have been forgotten by their critics who in their comfortable armchairs wrote of the deeds of men, far away from their native land, beyond the usual restraints of civilized opinion and amongst myriads of foes.

[1] El Gran Capitan.   [2] Las Españas.

When the first fury of the conquest had spent itself, and when men such as the great Las Casas, the Apostle to the Indians, had denounced the infamies that had been committed, the Spaniards stayed their hands.

In most of the republics they left Indians who to-day are citizens, and who have risen in some instances to the highest offices of state.[1] How many, the Indians in the United States or Canada ? In what Valhalla suitable to them are the inhabitants of Tasmania, or the Australian blacks ? An enlightened Anglo-Saxon Protestantism has allowed them to be exterminated, thus at one blow solving the problem of their duty to an inferior race. What does it matter ? After all, they wore no trousers.[2]

Quesada had made manifest to all his little world, that microcosm of his fatherland, soldiers, camp followers, and priests camped at Zipaquirá, that he could suffer with the most enduring, and that his courage was superior to that of all his followers, for he alone had never once despaired.

He had the confidence and the admiration of the expedition, and by his speeches it is clear that he had comprehended his position in relation to the natives of the land more clearly than any other of the conquerors. That he was led away—perhaps by circumstances, perhaps by weakness, or perhaps by love of gain—from his position, and fell into most of the usual practices of the other conquerors, is but to say that he was human, liable to err, and that his practice, just as does our own, did not square truly with the thesis of his life.

Before Quesada marched from Zipaquirá a picturesque incident occurred, that must have reminded some of the older soldiers of tales that they had heard in youth of the wars with the Moors.

[1] Benito Juarez, the Liberator of Mexico from the French invasion, was a pure-blooded Indian. Porfirio Diaz, for thirty years the president of Mexico, had at least three parts of Indian blood in his veins.

[2] " Mais quoi ! ils ne portaient pas des haults de chausses !" (Montaigne).

An Indian advancing from the ranks challenged any of the Spaniards to single combat.[1] Captain Lazaro Fonte, always ready for a fight, sprang on his horse barebacked, having no saddle probably, and charged full speed upon the foe, brandishing his lance. The Indian bravely waited his assault, that must have seemed tremendous to a man who had never seen a horse. Dropping his lance, Lazaro Fonte, as he passed by the Indian, seized him by his long hair and dragged him back a prisoner into the Spanish ranks. After this incident the Indians fell back, and Quesada, who had remained with the vanguard at Nemocón, advanced, and, looking out over the plains, for the first time had an uninterrupted view of the territory fate had placed within his hands. As he beheld the Sabána dotted about with Indian towns and villages, bounded by the Andes, their walls of rock cut here and there by tall, white cones such as El Ruiz and El Nevado de Tolima, and the distant peaks of Suma Paz, he must have felt that the past years of suffering had not been passed in vain.

The Sabána de Bogotá was not, as nowadays, unbuilt upon and given up to pasture, with but a few haciendas and their corrals and outbuildings surrounded by tall poplars, at rare intervals; but set so thickly everywhere with towns and villages that Quesada, after gazing over it, gave it the name of " El Valle de los Alcázares."[2]

The towns were all surrounded by high palisades. The streets were at right angles, after the fashion of the towns to-day in South America.

At every square were fixed high poles, daubed with a red

[1] This was a common occurrence in the long wars between the Spaniards and the Moors. The Moor (for the Moors generally seem to have been the challengers) used to advance and shout, according to the Spanish chroniclers, " Hay Mobariz ?" (Is there a champion ?). The Spanish chroniclers' knowledge of Arabic was usually as slight as the Moorish chroniclers' acquaintance with Spanish. Needless to say, the same combat often has different endings, according to the nationality of the chronicler. Historians and chroniclers have the same customs, for both are very often human beings.

[2] The Valley of the Palaces.

varnish[1] made of " bija." These poles, that had a sort of top, like the tops of a sailing ship, upon them, marked the houses of the chiefs.

Quesada, who was a martinet, was far from pleased that the advanced guard had entered Zipaquirá before he had had time to back them up. As he but seldom lost a good occasion for a speech, he gathered all his men together, and addressed them on the value of strict discipline. Much did he tell them of Epaminondas, who must have been unknown to most of them by name—except, of course, to the Italian soldier,[2] who in the affair of the donkey Marobaré talked about Olympus—that is to say, if he was still alive. Possibly the fact of the unfamiliar name impressed the soldiers, although the inference that Quesada drew from the sacrifice of his own son by Epaminondas for a breach of discipline could not have been too reassuring to them in case they fell into the same fault.

Neither Pizarro nor Cortés ever seems to have ventured upon speeches of the sort; but Quesada's men, as usual, took his address as if it had been gospel, and promised to comply with all he said.

After his defeat the Cacique Bogotá had taken refuge in a town called Cajicá. Quesada instantly laid siege to it, and it must have been well held, for it took him eight days to subdue.

On this occasion he was helped by a large band of Indians who are said to have accompanied him, partly by fear and partly through goodwill.[3]

---

[1] " Un barniz de almagre y bijas." Bija was made from the berry of a small tree called Achiote. It is still used to colour and season stews with in Colombia. The tree is the *Bija orellana* of botany. The Indians at the time of the conquest used it to paint their faces a bright red.

Fray Simon says they used to paint their cheeks at feasts, just as our Spanish women use rouge (" Se tiñan las mejillas cuando se ponen de gala, como nuestras españolas, el arrebol !").

[2] See Chapter I.

[3] "Medio por fuerza, medio por gusto." It reads ambiguously, and it is to be supposed that the Indians' goodwill only became manifest after the application of some force.

In the town Quesada found the litter in which Bogotá was carried by his followers, as were Atalhualpa and Montezuma in Mexico and in Peru. The chief had fled, after having buried all his treasure, both in gold and emeralds. The Indians said it was immense; but Quesada had to content himself with the litter, which had heavy ornaments of gold. So well had Bogotá concealed his treasure, and so faithfully have the Indians kept the secret, that it remains undiscovered down to the present day.

The fact of the gold-ornamented litter and the treasure serves to show that the Chibchas, though less well organized and far less civilized than were the Aztecs and the Incas, were rich and powerful, and without doubt the third in importance of the states the Spaniards found in the New World.

Their territory has been computed to have measured about six hundred square leagues.[1] It extended from Seruiza to the north, in latitude six degrees, to Suma Paz in four degrees— that is to say, it measured about five and forty leagues by fifteen, more or less, according to the phrase used by the chroniclers.

The population, Colonel Acosta estimates, was dense— approximately two thousand to the square league. If he is correct in his surmise, few European countries at the time were so well populated.

The greater portion of the inhabitants lived in the Tierra Fria—that is, fairly high up on the hills.[2]

As they had no beasts of burden, even the llama of Peru being unknown to them, their agriculture was extremely laborious. Still it supported them in comfort, even in abundance, for they exported several articles as salt and cotton cloths, exchanging them for gold dust, hot country fruits, and fish.

[1] " Descubrimiento de la Nueva Granada " (Colonel Joaquin Acosta, Paris, 1898), cap. xi., p. 187.

[2] Colombia is divded into three climatic zones, called respectively Tierra Caliente, Tierra Templada, and Tierra Fria. These zones depend entirely upon the elevation in which they lie. Thus, Bogotá in latitude four degrees is far cooler than Cartagena in latitude nine degrees, on account of its great altitude.

The Chibchas marched to the west with the Musos, Colimas, and Panches, wild and fierce tribes with whom they lived in a state of perpetual war. To the north they had as neighbours the Laches, Agateas, and the Guanes; and to the east the wild and scattered nations across the Andes, who dwelt in the great plains that stretch along the Rivers Meta, Casanáre, and the Orinoco. With the last the Chibchas had but little contact, as they were far away. At the time of the conquest, more or less the same political conditions prevailed that Pizarro had encountered in Peru—that is, one race of chiefs had not long mastered all the rest. Three chiefs ruled the whole territory. The greatest of them was called the Zipa. At the time of Quesada's coming, he was that Bogotá, whose name the Spaniards gave to the town they founded near to the site of the Indian town in which he lived, called by the Indians Muequetá.

The second chief was called the Zaque, and had his seat of government in Tunja.

The third was the chief of Iracá,[1] who had a half-religious character, as the successor of Nemterequetaba, the semi-mythical founder and civilizer of the land.

Little by little, after the fashion of the Incas in Peru, the Chibchas at the coming of the Spaniards were slowly conquering the rest. The chiefs of various towns—such as Ubaque, Guasca, Fusagasugá, and Ebaté—had only recently been conquered by the Zipa, Bogotá. His policy was, after subduing them, to leave the conquered tribes their own jurisdiction, reserving to himself the power to appoint a chief in case the succession in the local chief's family should fail.[2]

[1] At the time of Quesada's arrival on the scene the representative of this chief was called Sugamuxi. This name the Spaniards altered to Sogamoso, and conferred on the town in which the chief dwelt. The town still bears the name, as does a river that, rising near it, falls into the Magdalena.

[2] Amongst the Chibchas the succession was through the nephews, not from father to son (" L'Essai sur l'Ancien Cundinamarca," Ternaux-Compans).

In this case Bogotá always appointed one of his own military officers, known as Guechas.

The Chief of Tunja also had his tributaries; but all the time he was losing ground before the pressure brought to bear by the Zipa, Bogotá, whose troops were better disciplined than were his own, on account of being usually employed against the savage Panches on the frontier. Had not the Spaniards appeared upon the scene, it is most likely that the Zipa, Bogotá, would have soon risen to supreme power, as for the last sixty or seventy years his ancestors had all been conquerors.

The early history of the Chibchas, like that both of the Incas and the Aztecs, is wrapped in mystery. The Spaniards who arrived in 1539 only found records that reached back to 1470, in which year the first historic Zipa, Saguamachica, first began to reign.

He reigned for twenty years, and was succeeded by Nemequené, whose name is said to have signified "Bone of a Lion." This chief was killed in battle, leaving his son to fill his place. He it was that the Spaniards found in power.

The Chibcha heaven was as well populated as Olympus, and their deities little inferior to any deities of whom history has preserved the attributes and names in general dignity. Their theory of the creation of the world may well take its stand beside most theories of nations more civilized than they were, and, without doubt, was just as satisfying to them as the creation in the Book of Genesis has been, and is, to most unreasonable men.

In the beginning light was shut up in a great thing that no one could describe, which they called Chiminigagua —a word that signifies Creator. From it there came a flock of birds as black as jet that, flying through the air, launched from their beaks a continual stream of light, to illuminate the world. It is evident the Chibchas, after the fashion of the Jews, thought of a being, for Chiminigagua is merely but Jahve writ large, who, tired of darkness, said, "Let there be light." After the creator of light, the Chibchas venerated the sun and moon.

Their story of the population of the world is quite as worthy of our credence as any other story of the same kind. A little after the first day—that is to say, after the creation of the light—a beautiful woman called Bachué came out of the lake of Iguaqué leading a boy of about three years of age. When the boy grew up he married Bachué, and from that marriage all the human race began.

The Chibchas venerated Bachué, and adored her in little images of gold, representing her with the boy whom she married afterwards, at various stages of his life.

Spiders were sacred to the Chibchas for a curious reason, that appears one of the most imaginative that has occurred to any people in connection with the soul. After death the Chibcha souls made their way by various dark and tortuous passages to the centre of the earth. Before arriving at their destination they had to pass a river, and this they did on rafts of spiders' webs, as by no means they could have crossed the river without these rafts, and thus must have remained in a perpetual limbo. No one was known to kill a spider, for to have done so would have been to kill a soul.

Curiously enough the Chibcha heaven does not appear to have had a single harp within its precincts, nor was there any psalmody, for these poor Indians could not conceive of happiness in sloth. Their idea of felicity was in cultivating the Elysian fields, and not in straying in them in perfect idleness.

So every soul that entered into the abodes of bliss found gardens ready for cultivation, in which one may suppose the work was easy, crops certain, and neither hailstorms, drought, or locusts ever molested the celestial cultivators.

Before this idyll, for it was but a continuation of Theocritus, the Happy Hunting-Grounds seem a crude barbarism. Even Olympus, with its nectar and ambrosia, becomes a sort of Monte Carlo translated to the skies. Chibchacum was the tutelary god of the whole people, and had under his care sowing and harvest, and also metal workmanship, and seems to have stood next in their estimation to Bochica, the deity who brought goodness to the world.

Nemcatacoa was the patron of the cloth-workers, and had the duty of presiding at their feasts. He also was the god of idleness and sloth, and as he mingled with them at their drinking bouts, dancing and singing with the best, they held him but in scant respect, and never offered up to him the presents that they gave to other deities more self-respecting than himself. They held he was sufficiently repaid with all the chicha[1] that he drank at their banquets, and seem to have considered him a merry sort of god—half Bacchus, half Silenus, with a dash of the buffoon.

The rainbow they adored under the name of Cuchavirá, and this deity appears to have enjoyed some of the attributes of Venus, although not all of them. Women prayed to her during childbirth, as they did to Lucina under the Romans; but Cuchavirá never seems to have demeaned herself after the fashion of her Grecian prototype in matters amatory.

The Chibchas' first acquaintance with this deity embodies portions of the legends of the deluge mixed with the tale of Atlas holding up the world.

God Chibchacum, their tutelary deity, being enraged at the excesses of the people of the plains of Bogotá,[2] he determined to destroy them, but he chose water for his instrument. Turning two rivers loose upon the plain they soon produced a lake.

The remnant of the Chibchas that escaped took refuge in the mountains, and, finding they would die of hunger on their peaks, prayed fervently to Bochica, in the same way

---

[1] Chicha is a beverage made of maize, and was drunk both by the Chibchas and the Inca population. It is thick, and to the profane has a nauseating smell. If taken to excess it produces a kind of idiocy and general paralysis. It was formerly prepared by the old women masticating the grain and spitting it into a bowl. Nowadays, either through degeneracy of the race, increasing civilization, or the advance of mechanical appliances, the grain is generally pounded in a mortar. " Tout lasse, tout passe."

[2] Evidently Bogotá was the Gomorrah of those days.

that any other people would have prayed to their own deities in the same circumstances.

Bochica, seeing their belief, was touched at it, for the best way to propitiate any kind of god is by believing in him. Being of the same nature as most other gods of whom the world has any cognisance, or not forgetful of the adage " Noblesse oblige " that should be ever in the mind of every deity, Bochica stayed his hand and, having repented of his hastiness, appeared one evening on the rainbow. Then he convoked the Chibcha people and told them that he had changed his mind, and had determined to turn the rivers he had sent to overwhelm them for their sins into calm, fertilizing streams.

Through suffering they had attained to love, for those whom Bochica loved he evidently chastised. Throwing down the golden rod that he held in his hand, it cut a breach through the rocky wall that hitherto had bounded all the plain. This break became the world-renowned waterfall of Tequendama, and exists to the present day to show Bochica promised no more than he was able to perform.

Not satisfied with this manifestation of his power he punished Chibchacum, the tutelary god, for his affliction of the Chibcha nation, by making him hold up the earth. Hitherto it had been supported upon posts of guayacán.[1]

Unluckily Bochica's plan has brought some inconveniences into the lives of the inhabitants of Bogotá.[2] Chibchacum now and then is forced to shift the world from his right to his left shoulder when he feels tired. This is the cause of earthquakes, and they no doubt serve to remind the Indians how the sins of their ancestors so nearly wrecked mankind.

To this wealth of deities the Chibchas erected temples,

---

[1] Lignum vitæ, the *Guaiacum officinale* of botanists.

[2] " The best-laid plans of mice and men gang aft agley," as Poet Burns pawkily observes.

It is said that the great popularity of St. Christopher amongst the descendants of the Indians arises from the fact that he is often portrayed holding up the earth. Thus they connect him with their ancient divinity Chibchacum (" Descubrimiento de la Nueva Granada," Colonel Joaquin Acosta, note 2, p. 196).

that seem to have been but hardly worthy of them. As a general rule, they were great houses made of canes and thatched either with straw or palm-leaves, and in them lived their priests.

The offerings that were given to their gods were usually vessels of various coloured clay, not much unlike those vessels that are found in the Inca burial-places of Peru and known as " huacas " to the Peruvians. These vessels were often filled with gold dust or with little images, beads or thin plates, and animals of various kinds carefully wrought in gold.[1]

The priests were brought up to their functions from their boyhood, and prepared themselves for what may be described as their matriculation, by a series of fastings and of penitences.

They were the repositories of any abstract knowledge that the Chibchas may have had, and most unfortunately, just as in Mexico and in Peru, they were ruthlessly extirpated as a class, by their fanatical or illiterate conquerors. Thus perished most of the Chibcha records and antiquities.

Of all their deities, to the sun alone they offered human sacrifices, contrary to the custom of most races of America, for whom the sun was generally a deity of peace and plenty. These human sacrifices had a direct relation to their calendar, and the division of the time, for at them the priests used to announce to the assembled people the result of the calculations they had made in reference to sowing and to planting and the time for harvesting. As they took place but once in fifteen years, they marked their epochs for the Chibchas, who estimated time from the solstitial sacrifices,

[1] So great was the belief in their own gods that for a long time after they had all become official Christians the Spaniards used to come upon " adoratorios secretos " of the Indians, in which they carried on their ancient rites and heathen ceremonies. On one occasion in Zipaquirá one of these secret oratories was found that had, amongst the offerings to the idols in it, the cap of a Franciscan friar, a rosary, a priest's biretta, and a book of " Casos de Conciencia." The last, others who are not Indians might gladly offer up (" Descubrimiento de la Nueva Granada," Colonel Joaquin Acosta, note 1, p. 197).

and thus they served in some degree for them, the uses that the picture writing served for the Aztecs, and the " quipos " for the Peruvians.[1]

Although the temples of the Chibchas were not remarkable as edifices, either for size or architecture,[2] it is not to be forgotten that they were only second in importance to what may be styled the sites of pilgrimages—such as the tops of mountains, sacred groves and lakes—to which they were accustomed to resort to worship and make offerings to their gods.

Nearly every town of any size had its sacred lake, to which the people went in pilgrimage. A path led down to it, and at the intersection of two ropes to form an angle, the sacred raft was moored.

Commonly, each lake had its own legend attaching to it; but the most usual myth was that a mysterious lady and her daughter lived underneath the waters of the pool. These were propitiated by prayers and offerings of vessels made of clay filled with gold dust, or with golden images and charms.

Of all the lakes, the Lake of Guatavita was the most celebrated in Chibcha times, and has continued so down to the present day. In a deep valley of the same name as the lake a mountain rises, and at its top lies a round tarn, much like the Lake of Nemi, deep and desolate. Down to the water's edge still lead remains of a stone causeway used in the ceremonies. In the days when the Cacique of Guata-

---

[1] The quipos were an elaborate system of knots on coloured woollen strings, that served as records to the Peruvians.

[2] The only Chibcha chief who seems to have projected the erection of a stone temple was the half-fabulous chief Garanchacha, who, having given out he was the miraculously conceived son of a virgin, by the sun, killed the Zaque of Tunja and usurped his power. This Garanchacha got together stones and marble at a place a little to the north of Tunja, where they can yet be seen. Most of them still are lying on the ground. Señor Manuel Velez Barrientos, somewhere about 1846, came on the remains of a large edifice, in the valley of Lina, whose use he could not understand. He wrote a curious description of it in the Journal of the Geographical Society of Paris in 1847.

vita was an independent chief, he used to go once every year, accompanied by a procession, to make a ceremonial offering to the spirits of the lake, and then to bathe in it. On the appointed day he was anointed well with turpentine and then rolled on a bed of gold dust that, sticking to his flesh, converted him into a golden statue as he stood naked on the raft. Then, when the sun shone full upon him surrounded by his nobles on the raft, he offered up his prayers, and after having cast offerings of gold and emeralds into the depths, he plunged into the waters like a great golden fish. As he emerged the assembled multitude broke into cries of joy and of applause, for by his action the cacique was supposed to have ensured the goodwill and the protection of the mysterious ladies of the lake.

The ceremony over, the young men engaged in running and in jumping, and then when night set in, to the flickering light of myriads of torches, the people sat down to a banquet by the water's edge that ended usually in universal drunkenness. During the banquet two old Indians, naked but for fishing-nets wrapped round their loins, and with their faces daubed with mud, played dirges on a flute made out of a cane.[1] The fishing-net they wore as a Memento Mori, as amongst the Chibchas it was a symbol of mortality, worn ceremoniously at feasts. This picturesque and curious ceremony of the Golden Man (el Dorado) was distorted by the tales of the first conquerors into a legend of a Golden City (El Dorado), that proved an ignis fatuus[2] to all sorts and conditions of men, including Sir Walter Raleigh and

[1] Sometimes these ancients sang so sadly that the whole assembly was dissolved in tears, thus proving that the Chibchas took their pleasures sadly, or at the least had " le vin triste " at their rejoicings.

[2] From the first days of Quesada's expedition, when Captain Lazaro Fonte and a rich merchant, one Antonio Sepulveda, constructed a canal to drain a portion of the lake, and actually succeeded in fishing up gold to the amount of five or six thousand ducats, there have been countless schemes to dry the Lake of Guatavita and retrieve the gold thrown into it at the annual ceremony of the Golden Man. The lake was said to have been sixteen fathoms deep at the time of the conquest. Since then, it has fallen a good deal in depth.

Gonzalo Pizarro, who nearly lost his life during his quest of it, in his celebrated journey over the eastern mountains of Peru.

All civil power amongst the Chibchas was vested in the Zipa, who promulgated all the laws, administered justice, and was commander of the troops. The veneration that his subjects had for him was so great that no one dared to look him in the face.

Though he had only one legitimate wife, he had several hundred ladies called Thiguyes, a word that perhaps may be interpreted, coadjutresses. His heir was the eldest son of his eldest sister, who at the age of sixteen was taken to a palace in the town of Chia, and for several years instructed in the duties that he would some day be called on to perform.

The Zipa himself generally lived in Muequetá, but he also had a country house in Tinansuca, and another in Theusa-quillo, where now stands Bogotá.

Homicide, rape, and incest were punished with death.

Defaulting debtors had a tiger cub sent to them by the Zipa. This animal they were obliged to rear and keep tied up before their doors, until the debt was paid. Women suspected of adultery were forced to eat red pepper. If they confessed under this torture, they gave them water and then executed them. If they endured the torment for some hours they were judged innocent, and straightway liberated.[1]

Their marriage ceremonies were to the full as sensible as any others; except perhaps those of North Britain, in which country an asseveration before witnesses binds man and wife for life.

Amongst the Chibchas the two contracting parties appeared before the priest, who linked their arms together, and asked the woman if she would promise always to love God (Bochica) above her husband, and to esteem her husband

[1] Either there was no punishment for male adulterers amongst the Chibchas, or else the chroniclers have failed to discover it, or perhaps suppressed it for the honour of their sex. The universal experience of mankind would seem to point to the fact that adultery is not the exclusive pastime of the female sex, although perhaps on the plains of Bogotá, in those days, it may have been the case.

more highly than their sons; lastly to swear never to eat if her husband wanted food.   Then, turning to the man, he told him to declare in a loud voice that he took the woman for his wife.

This simple ceremony joined the woman and the man in holy matrimony. Only one wife, and that the first, was held legitimate, although a man could have as many other wives as he was able to support.

Wives amongst the Chibchas had the privilege of beating their husbands when they did wrong, especially the wives of chiefs, as the chiefs could not be punished by their subjects for anything they did, and, being men, were sure to do wrong at times.   In the lost " Memorias " of Quesada, from which Fray Simon occasionally quotes, he says: " Being upon a journey one day I came to a chief's house, and found him tied to a post with his wives beating him for drunkenness."[1]

Most of their chiefs and nobles after death were rendered mummies by a peculiar process that seems to have been lost after the conquest.   Some of the mummies have been found with their insides stuffed full of gold and emeralds; but very few of them, so well the Indians contrived to hide their burial-places.

Maize, potatoes, and the quinoa[2] were their chief crops, and these they cultivated with rude stone and wooden instruments, for iron was unknown.   Their cultivation must have been extensive, for even to-day, upon the plains of Bogotá, are to be seen ridges turned up before the conquest under the Indians' hoes.

Potatoes gave two crops a year, and maize but one, in the cool climate of the Sabána de Bogotá.   In the hot valleys they cultivated manioc;[3] but the banana, now so universal in the land, seems to have been unknown.

[1] This little incident throws a sidelight on polygamy, often lost sight of by monogamists.

[2] *Chenopodium quinoa.*

[3] Captains San Martin and Lebrija, in their Report to Philip II., speak of the fertility of the country, and that it seems fit to produce all the fruits of Europe, as the climate is fresh and temperate.   They

Besides the manioc they cultivated the *Arracacha esculenta*, an umbelliferous plant, that has long, yellow roots about the size of carrots or of parsnips.

Their most important article of commerce was the salt that they got from the mines of Zipaquirá. With it they purchased all the commodities that their own country did not produce in any quantity, as gold and gold dust, for, though the precious metal seems to have been abundant with them, it was brought from other provinces.[1]

The Chibchas were the only nation that the Spaniards found in the Americas who had a monetary system, consisting of thin plates of gold, about the size of pennies, that they used in their affairs.

Their measures of length, were the pace and the palm; but they do not seem to have had measures of weight or of capacity.

Fairs were established regularly at convenient places, one being held every three days at Turmeque, where vegetables, fruits, and in especial emeralds were always upon sale.

Their most important fair was held at Coyaima, near the Magdalena, in the country of a tribe called Poincos. To it they took their salt and emeralds, their painted cotton cloths, and the gold objects that they made out of the gold they purchased from the other provinces. At this fair, known to the Spaniards as Yaporogos, from the cacique who was in power at their first coming, the Chibchas bought quantities of parrots and macaws brought from the Magdalenian woods. After the birds had learned to speak they

---

also remark on the abundance of eggs and of a kind of rabbit, called curi. The eggs must have been those of partridges or some other birds, for domestic fowls had not been introduced at the time they wrote. Their prediction *re* the fruits of Europe has been amply fulfilled, for fruits and flowers of Europe grow with great luxuriance in the Sabána of Bogotá. The Report of the two captains is rare and difficult to come at. Ternaux-Compans has preserved it in his " Recueil des Documents sur l'Amérique," Paris, 1845.

[1] Most likely from the Chocó and from Antioquia.

sacrificed them to their gods, thinking they made the fittest substitute for human sacrifices.[1]

In regard to architecture, the Chibchas seem to have been greatly behind either the Mexicans or the Peruvians. Quesada did not find a single building made of stone on the Sábana of Bogotá. In general their houses were mainly built of wood and mud, and thatched with palm-leaves. The roofs were conical, and the houses generally round. Their doors were made of mats that they hung loosely at the entrance, although in houses of the better sort they were of wood with wooden locks, such as are still in use in remote villages in Colombia.

The high stockades, the patios, and the tall painted poles, with their " crow's nest " upon them that they used for observation, gave to their towns, seen from afar, an appearance of being more important than they actually were, and caused Quesada, when he first saw them from a distance, to give the name of " Valley of the Palaces " to the whole district of the plains.

The Indian nobles of the plain of Bogotá had country houses,[2] from which streets stretched out like a fan. These streets the Indians used for their dances and processions on their feast days.

The roads and streets were then the theatres in which they celebrated their feasts with comedies, games, and dances to the sound of their rustic pipes, and showed their riches in the wealth of feathers, skins, and golden diadems they wore.[3]

[1] The idea was not a bad one, although it almost seems a pity to have sacrificed the birds when they had learned to talk, as there must certainly have been so many scoundrels far less innocent than they, fit for no other object in the world than to talk, and to be sacrificed.

[2] Piedrahita (Doctor Don Lucas Fernandez), " Historia General de las Conquistas del Nuevo Reino de Granada," Madrid, 1688, p. 138.

[3] Piedrahita, " Historia General de las Conquistas de la Nueva Granada," p. 139:
" Estas carreras ó calles estan entonces los teatros en que celebraban sus fiestas con entremeses, juegos y danzas, al son de sus rusticos caramillos, ostentando cada cual su riqueza en el aseo de plumas, pieles de animales y diademas de oro."

What a description of Arcadia, and how happily they passed their lives, in spite of human sacrifices and the barbarities that seem incidental to all primitive communities! Eden perhaps was still more innocent; but not Arcadia, for in that land beloved of poets they had wars and crimes and shed the blood of animals, just as the Chibchas killed their prisoners at the feasts Piedrahita tells of in his Chronicle. Still, they were happy in their own way, and every man must make his heaven for himself, for heaven made by another's hand would be a hell.

The Indians of Bogotá lived under a sort of feudal system, for though the Zipa had supreme authority he was obliged, like other autocrats, to delegate some of his power to his nobility for purpose of government.

Thus an old historian[1] compares the chiefs known as Usaques to the Spanish dukes, the Guiqcaes to marquesses. These chiefs had great power over the Indians, though they themselves were subject to the Zipa in everything.

The Indians were forced to dress after the fashion that their lords dictated. No Indian under the rank of a chief was allowed to eat venison.

Rodriguez Fresle says of them that they were vicious, and though they had a multitude of wives, yet they committed many and great incests, not sparing even their mothers or their daughters in their lusts. " In fact, they were barbarians who had no law, nor any knowledge of God."[2]

[1] Juan Rodriguez Fresle, author of the celebrated " Carnero Bogotano." This curious production was so called, either because it was written on parchment or bound in sheepskin. " Carnero " means a sheep. Though long known in manuscript in New Granada (Colombia), it appears to have been first printed in 1859 at Bogotá. The editor was Don Felipe Perez, a well-known man of letters in Colombia. His son Don Enrique Perez follows in his father's footsteps in the fields of literature. Don Felipe Perez was first cousin of the late Don Santiago Perez Triana, minister at the Court of St. James for the Republic of Colombia, and so well known for his speeches at the Hague Conference, for his books, for his extraordinary linguistic powers and his great geniality.

[2] "Con ser viciosos i tenir muchos mujeres i cometer grandes incestos, sin reservar hijas ó madres; en conclusion, barbaros sin lei, ni conocimiento de Dios " (" El Carnero Bogotano ").

Fresle no doubt speaks as one having the knowledge of the true faith; but it seems improbable that what he says about the Indians' morals can have been true to any great extent, either in Bogotá or any other portion of the world.

The Spaniards found amongst the Chibchas a somewhat similar tradition to that they found in Mexico and in Peru. In all these countries a legend existed of a man or men coming from the east, bearded and fairer than the inhabitants of America, who introduced such civilization as they enjoyed. Amongst the Chibchas he was an ancient man, with a long beard, who appeared under various names, but whose chief name was Chinzapagua, which is supposed to have meant " the Envoy of the Lord." He found the Chibchas sunk in barbarism, dressed but in cotton loin-cloths, and without the least idea of laws or government. He taught the Indians how to weave and spin, and for a considerable time wandered from town to town preaching and teaching both by his example and his words. Then suddenly he disappeared near Sogamoso and was never seen again.

This missionary was accompanied, the legend says, by a strange animal of great bulk and size.[1]

The priests and friars in their simple piety were certain that the mysterious " Envoy of the Lord " could have been none other than the Apostle Santo Tomas, and the great quadruped that accompanied him they imagined to have been a camel, an animal[2] that passes easily enough through the eye of any needle if its possessor has but sufficient faith.[3]

[1] In the town of Bosa, one of the animal's ribs was found after the conquest by the Spaniards: " Conquista de la Nueva Granada," Colonel Joaquin Acosta, p. 209.

[2] The rib found, Colonel Acosta thinks (p. 208), was probably that of a mastodon, for bones of that creature have been found both near Bosa and Suacha. In that case the miracle must have been still more striking, for St. Thomas need not have brought the mastodon across the seas, as there were native specimens ready to be tamed.

[3] Fray Simon says, in reference to the tradition: " Ni apruebo, ni repruebo solo, la refiero como la he hallado admitida como cosa comun entre los hombres graves y doctos de este reino." Fray

Such, more or less, was the state of the Chibcha State, when first Quesada and the Spaniards broke into the secluded plain of Bogotá. It must have been well peopled and set thick with villages and towns, whose appearance, at least from a distance, was so picturesque that Quesada, who had been brought up at Granada, was enchanted with it.

As a State, the mountain kingdom or confederation had made some progress on material lines.

Some of the arts, as gold working and weaving, had made some progress with them.

As regards science they seem to have been able to foretell eclipses, and their calendar and method of computing time was most ingenious.[1]

Their laws and the system of their government were not, upon the whole, more foolish than such systems seem to have often been in other and much better constituted States, and, though inferior to those of Peru under the Incas, equal or perhaps superior to those of Mexico before the Spaniards' time. Their architecture was the art in which apparently they had made least progress, judging by the somewhat scanty records that the conquerors have left us.

Fray Simon, the Bishop Piedrahita,[2] and Caste-

Simon was a Franciscan, although his dictum savours more of the diplomacy of the saint who sleeps in the Basque Provinces, hard by the villages of Azpeitia and Azcoitia. Dr. Don Lucas Piedrahita, Bishop of Santa Marta and " Calificador del Santo Oficio de la Inquisicion," might have been a native of North Britain by his answer to his own question, for he says: " Digame, curioso lectoro, de quien otro que de un apostol, pudieran referirse entre gentiles, las que tenemos dichas." The careful reader is constrained to answer, Who indeed ? Padre Zamora, of the Order of the Predicadores, is of opinion that Santo Tomas was " un abismo de la predicacion." Therefore, " as one abyss calls to another abyss, this abyss of preaching was obliged to carry the truths of the Gospel to the abyss of the New World." That seems to clinch the matter.

[1] The entire system is preserved in the curious " Disertacion sobre el calendario de los Muyscas, por el Dr. Don José Domingo Duquesne de la Madrid, Cura de la Iglesia de Gachancipá de los Mismos Indios," año de 1795.

[2] " Historia General de la Conquistas del Nuevo Reino de Granada." (Madrid, 1688.)

llanos,[1] the ex-soldier who took holy orders and became a priest, have many references to the Chibcha houses; but they are sparing of details.

Most of what is known about the Chibchas is to be found in these three authors, and without the curious and interesting " Disertacion " of the priest, Dr. Don Jose Domingo Duquesne,[2] and the scattered observations to be found in the " Carnero Bogotano,"[3] almost nothing would have come down to us of their lives and policy. It is fortunate for posterity that these two writers preserved and recorded all they could, and most unfortunate for Colombia that at the conquest there were no writers of the calibre of Cortés himself and Bernal Diaz del Castillo in Mexico, or Pedro Cieza de Leon and the Inca Garcilasso de la Vega in Peru.

Quesada's own account of the whole conquest, believed to have been contained in his manuscript, " Los Ratos de

[1] Castellanos, " Elegias de Varones Ilustres de Indias." First part, in Madrid, 1589.

[2] See Appendix.

[3] Juan Rodriguez Fresle. His book, though known as " El Carnero Bogotano," had, as was normal in those days, a long title: " Conquista y Descubrimiento del Nuevo Reino de Granada; de las Indias Occidentales del Oceano y Fundacion de la Ciudad de Santa Fé de Bogotá." Fresle was a farmer, and as he says himself, was born in Bogotá—" natural de esta ciudad y de los Fresles de Alcala de Henares, en los reinos de España." His father was one of the first conquerors and settlers. The book was dedicated to Philip IV., and contains the lives of generals, archbishops, and an account of the civil wars of his time, together with " algunos casos sucedidos en este reino, que van en la historia, para ejemplo, no por imitarlos, por el daño de la conciencia." He was seventy years of age when he began his book. In his youth he had made a journey to Spain. His book was written in the character known as " Letra Pastrana." As he was a great personal friend of the Cacique of Guatavita, he was able to obtain most valuable details from him of the Chibcha customs, that had already been abolished or fallen into disuse. Upon this head, he says, " It appears to me that some impertinent fellow [algun curioso] may point his finger at me and ask, How did it come about I knew these ancient affairs?" He then explains that he was born in Bogotá and was the friend of the Chief of Guatavita. He finishes this matter by saying, " I am now seventy years old, which age I have atained to as I sit writing . . . on the 25th of April and the day of our lord St. Mark of the year 1636."

Suesca," is unfortunately lost, although portions of it are thought to be incorporated in Herrera's Decadas, and others in the Chronicles of Castellanos and Piedrahita and in the work of Fray Simon.

Unluckily, the Spaniards, animated by the lust of conquest and religious bigotry, burst like a devastating cyclone upon the country, destroying everything, partly from ignorance and partly of a set purpose to stamp out idolatry. The following incident shows to what extent their religious bigotry went, even some years after the fury of the conquest should have spent itself. In the year 1636, a hundred years after the conquest, in an open space near one of the long streets that stretched from the dwelling of the Zipa towards the mountains, there was a tank that had been made by the Kings of the Chibchas before the Spaniards came. Beside it stood two tall and feathery palms. These trees were looked on with great veneration by the Indians. The Archbishop, Fray Cristobal de Torres, thinking that the Indians looked on them as relics of their old religion, had them cut down, " ad majorem Dei gloriam," it is to be presumed.

Although our English withers are not quite unwrung in matters of the kind, a heretic may be allowed to hope that for his vandalism the archbishop had an additional ten thousand years of purgatory written against him by the recording angel in his book of pains and penalties.

CHAPTER IX

As Quesada with his expedition was encamped at Cajicá, news was brought to him that the Cacique of Chiá, a man whose affairs were destined to have an important bearing on the conquest, had also fled, and buried all his gold and emeralds in a safe hiding-place.

In order to make the hiding-place more secure, the Cacique of Chiá had all his valuables loaded on the backs of slaves commanded by several well-tried officers. When the treasure was all buried and hidden so securely that it has never yet been found, the officers butchered all the slaves so that they never could reveal the secret. They then returned to the cacique and asked for their reward. The chief, who must have been a man of a grim humour, said they had earned it, and he would give it to them. Then drawing out a knife he cut their heads off with his own hand, thus making certain they could never tell the Spaniards where the buried treasure was concealed.

As during all his stay at Cajicá Quesada had abundance of provisions, so much, in fact, that upon one occasion each soldier had a deer apiece, he must have seen that he had come into a country, if not exactly civilized, still pretty far advanced upon the road. Of course, he had no knowledge of the internal life and policy of the Chibcha State; but at the same time the abundance of good food, the relatively quiet condition of the country, and the clothes that the Indians wore,[1] so different from the nakedness of the Magdalenian savages, must have been certain indications to a

---

[1] The Indians of Bogotá did not at that time wear the poncho—or, as it is called in Colombia, the ruana—but had mantles that tied across their shoulders in a knot. The poncho was introduced from Peru, either by the Spaniards or by Peruvian Indians, who came and went between Quito and Bogotá.

man of his good education, that he was destined to achieve a conquest little inferior to that of either Pizarro or Cortés. Spain was all ringing with the fame of the riches they had brought from their respective conquests, and they had both been created marquesses.[1]   Although no thought of a title could have crossed Quesada's mind at that time, yet in after-years it was once promised to him, and considering all he did for Spain should not have been withheld.

The policy of both the Emperor Charles V. and his son Philip was niggardly in the extreme towards the conquerors to whom they owed so much.

In regard to the Indians, the Code known as the Laws of the Indies shows how liberal-minded and how fair were nearly all the Kings of Spain to their new subjects, had they been able to have the laws they promulgated, fairly carried out.

All seemed propitious in the camp at Chiá, but for the attitude of the Zipa, Bogotá. He still, in spite of all Quesada's efforts to attract him to his camp, refused an answer to the messengers. Although the cacique sent Indians every day to the camp with fresh provisions, he himself took refuge in the woods with his chief officers and his wives.

Easter being now at hand, Quesada determined to pass Holy Week in quiet at Chiá. A soldier, to commemorate the fact, cut on a stone an inscription which might have lasted to the present day, and should have been preserved as a memento of the conquest.

The inscription ran as follows:

" In this place, at this camp, the Licentiate Quesada passed Holy Week; this year of 1538."[2]

Unluckily, a missionary priest after the conquest took the stone and used it for the doorstep of a new church that he

[1] This was before the days when the title of marquess became so common in Spain as to give rise to the saying, " There is not a town, wood, mountain, or river, in Spain, that has not got its corresponding marquess."

[2] En este sitio y cercado tuvo el Licenciado Quesada la Semana Santa este año de 1538.

was building in Chiá, and naturally the inscription was effaced and the stone broken up or lost.[1]

All during Holy Week Quesada renewed his efforts to open up negotiations with the Zipa, offering him peace, and behaving with the greatest moderation and diplomacy. Had but the chief taken advantage of Quesada's instances he might have saved his life, and the whole course of the conquest might have run on different lines.

Of course, Quesada was the invader of a peaceful country, whose inhabitants not only had no quarrel with him or with his men, but never in their lives had heard the name, either of the Spaniards or of Spain. However, we ourselves, who have behaved just as Quesada did, have not the smallest right to criticize him. He had his horses and his crossbows, his swords of tempered steel and iron-shod lances, and we our arms of precision and our artillery. In either case, neither in Africa, in Asia, or America, were the rights of the natives ever considered for a moment either by England or by Spain.

Just at this juncture a very curious case arose as to the chieftainship of Chiá. The Zipa, Bogotá, who it seems was a born diplomatist, seized on it to make friends of Chiá against the Spaniards.

It was the custom, as we have seen, amongst the Chibchas that the nephews, not the sons, succeeded to the chiefs in their hereditary power. The chief, however, also had the right to name as his successor a member of one of the numerous noble families other than his own.

Bogotá, having invited Chiá to a conference at Cajicá, met him in the presence of his sister, who was about to be confined. Bogotá named Chiá as his successor to the dignity of Zipa, with remainder to the sister's child if it should prove a son. He added as a provision of the pact that Chiá should renounce the chieftainship of his own people if he succeeded to that of Bogotá. A curious and interesting

---

[1] Fray Simon describes this missionary priest as " bien poco curioso," but then the world is so full of careless vandals, that no one need be surprised.

arrangement, and one that, as it proved, gave an infinity of trouble to Quesada after the death of Bogotá.

Quesada, owing to the abundance of provisions, remained in camp at Chiá longer than was prudent, hoping to make peace with the various chiefs, and in especial with the Zipa; but it proved impossible.

During his stay, the first voluntary instance of conversion to the Christian faith that had occurred during Quesada's expedition happened to take place. True, there had been conversions; but they had not been exactly voluntary, as, for instance, in the case of the Indian Pericón, who showed the way over the mountain paths on to the plains. Pericón had been made prisoner, so that his conversion probably was of the same nature as the freedom of the Indians who were made " naborias," but not for that enslaved. Oviedo, in his " Natural History of the Indies,"[1] explains that a naboria is an Indian who is not a slave, but has to work, although against his will. The distinction is a point for casuists, and probably in the religious field applied to Pericón.

This was a different case, and it appears quite genuine,

[1] " Naboria es Indio que no es esclavo, pero tiene que trabajar aunque no quiere: " Historia Natural de las Indias," Oviedo.

Juan Bautista Muñoz, in his " Historia del Nuevo Mundo," 1713, says that " Oviedo fué muy corto en punto de humanidades, é incapaz de interpretar y usar diestramente los autores clasicos " (Oviedo was little learned in the humanities, and incapable of skilfully interpreting classic authors). Muñoz goes on to say: " Observaba, preguntaba, escribia sin cesar, corregia y aumentaba lo escrito con una diligencia digna de imitacion. Lastima que tanta industria y curiosidad no hubiera caido en sujeto de mas letras " (He observed, questioned, and wrote without ceasing, and corrected and added to what he wrote with a diligence worthy of imitation. It is a pity so much carefulness and industry should not have fallen to the lot of a better educated man). Muñoz must have been a learned fool himself. Oviedo may not have been a classical scholar, as he had passed his youth and middle age in fighting and discovering. He had, though, what is far better than mere book learning—an observant mind, as his great work, " The Natural History of the Indies," shows. The definition of the word " naboria " shows that he had humour, a quality that neither Salamanca nor Oxford can impart. *Quod natura non dat, Salamanca non præstat.*

although the brand snatched from the burning lived for too short a time in grace to prove his steadfastness.

Quesada, having heard that the Cacique Suba was a man likely to accept his overtures of peace, went to his village, and found him willing to submit. Peace was declared between the high contracting parties—Charles, by the grace of God, Emperor of all the Spains, and the Chief Suba—with great rejoicing. Quesada was delighted, and Suba, no doubt, made happy with the usual gifts of hawksbells, a scarlet cloak, and other goods of a like nature, calculated to impress him with the might, majesty, and power of his ally and friend.

All was rejoicing, when suddenly a cloud darkened the horizon of their joy, though destined, as it will appear, to finish in a sunset, brilliant beyond relief. The Cacique Suba (by the grace of God)[1] was taken seriously ill, so ill, indeed, that the two priests who accompanied the expedition saw that the only way to save his soul was by the way of baptism, and that without delay. Straight they commenced to catechize[2] him and to prepare him for the rite. Grace touched the infidel, and having understood that there were many things he must believe in order to avoid eternal condemnation, he did so cheerfully,[3] accepting everything, and asking earnestly to be admitted to the fold.

The priests at once baptized him, seeing that he was acting from conviction, and there was little time to lose. The new-made Christian shortly yielded up the ghost, quite confident of his salvation, to the great joy of everyone concerned.[4]

[1] Por la gracia de Dios.

[2] Comenzaron á catequizarle.

[3] Con mucha alegria.

[4] " Perdieron los Castellanos á su buen amigo el Cacique de Suba que falleció de una breve enfermedad, recibiendo antes el bautismo y fué el primer cristiano de estas regiones ": " Descubrimiento de la Nueva Granada," Colonel Joaquin Acosta, p. 218. The regions of which Colonel Acosta writes have, indeed, produced many good and fervent Christians. As regards the Cacique of Suba, without questioning his faith, that certainly was all-embracing, he had but little time to show by his good works much friendship to the Castilians.

Quesada at last saw that he was being played with by the Zipa. So he determined to march on Muequetá, the chief town of the Chibcha Kings. The chroniclers relate that the reason why Bogotá refused to meet Quesada was through the interpretation of a dream. It seems doubtful whether the chief himself had the dream and his medicine man interpreted it, or whether it was the medicine man who had the dream and told it to the chief. At any rate the impression that the dream made upon his mind must have been very deep.[1] The soothsayer or medicine man was called Popon, and was the chief of the valley and the town of Ubaque. The dream was of a bath of blood which, being interpreted by Popon, signified that Bogotá would lose his life at the hands of strangers who should invade his lands. The really interesting point about the dream is not preserved by any of the chroniclers, for none of them tells us whether the dream took place before or after the strangers came into his life. As nothing shook the chief's determination not to meet the Spaniards, Quesada marched to Muequetá, and found it almost empty, as everyone had fled.

In Muequetá they found considerable booty[2]—some gold and emeralds; but far less than they had expected, as the Zipa had carried most of his treasure off into the hills. The soldiers murmured, and were disappointed not to have found the riches of Peru.

Unluckily, none of the conquerors have left us any description of the Zipa's capital, Muequetá. We know it stood not far from where Quesada founded Bogotá, but there was no Cortés, no Bernal Diaz del Castillo, to preserve any description of it, and, alas! no Unknown Conqueror,[3] to draw any of the buildings, as in Mexico.

From what Quesada says incidentally, and from his having given the name of the Valley of the Palaces to the whole

[1] Un sueño que le habia declarado un famoso jeque . . . dicho Popon.

[2] Un buen rancheo.

[3] The brief account of Mexico by the Unknown Conqueror and his sketch of the Great Teocalli are preserved in Ramusio's " Voyages " (" Colecciones de Viajes y Navegaciones ").

plain, there must have been some buildings, even if made of perishable materials, of important size.[1] Their situation was almost that of Bogotá as it now stands, backed by its twin hills, and with the brawling river running through the streets. The sun must then, as now, have fallen in clear weather on the eternal snows of El Ruiz, turning them rose-coloured, and the deep shadows of the hills behind the city at sundown have been projected over the Sabána until the town lies buried as in a shroud, only the towers of the churches standing up like lighthouses.

Quesada and Cortés destroyed, the first a rancheria built of wood and straw; the second, one of the most curious prehistoric-looking cities that the world has known. Luckily, in both instances, they founded other cities, and had the luck to found them at a time when architecture, though it had lost its glory, was not entirely debased.

The cities that they founded perhaps owe more to their position than to their architecture, but they remain to show us that the Spaniards of those days (the men whom Protestant historians use, to point their morals, upon all occasions), when they destroyed at least built up again something that we ourselves could hardly imitate. Although the soldiers were discontented, Quesada still had so much authority[2] over them that he stopped all plundering.

The Spaniards were not allowed to remain in the town peacefully, for Bogotá attacked them every day. Thinking to make them leave the town, the Indians shot arrows into it, wrapped up in blazing straw, to set the roofs alight. All was of no avail; Quesada working beside his men put the fires out, and drove the Indians back into the hills. Though fighting went on continually, Quesada still kept sending

[1] The Captains San Martin and Lebrija, in their " Relacion," speak of it as " one of the finest cities " in the Indies. This it could not have been, as Mexico, Quito, and Cuzco must have been immeasurably superior to it.

[2] " Su reputacion era tanta con los soldados por sus virtudes y su valor que con mansedumbre le oian y con valor le obedecian ": Herrera, " Decada VI.," libro i., p. 3.

messages to Bogotá, offering him terms of peace. What were his motives, only he himself could have explained. He scarcely could have thought that it was possible the Chibchas would submit to him, accompanied as he was by but a handful of Spanish soldiers. It may have been that he put faith in his own powers of persuasion, and hoped, by bringing Bogotá to a personal conference, to persuade him to submit. However, though his Indians were daily being killed in their attacks upon the town, the chief was still defiant, so that at length Quesada, finding himself baffled, determined to set out and track the Zipa down.

By this time many of the soldiers had learned a little of the Chibcha language, and many of the Indians who had come from Santa Marta[1] with the expedition, a good deal of it.

By degrees the Indians became familiarized with the Spanish soldiers; whilst Quesada still delayed his march to track the Zipa in his retreat, an Indian who was a celebrated runner challenged the Spaniards to run with the best horse that they could bring against him.

Lazaro Fonte, the best horseman in the expedition, at once took up the challenge, and buckling on his spurs mounted his " zaino "[2] and prepared for the race. At a given signal the Indian started off like a stag, his feet scarcely appearing to touch the road in his career. Lazaro Fonte kept just alongside of him, at a hand gallop,[3] and the Indians all thought the race was theirs. Touching the zaino with the spur, Fonte flew past the Indian, and either by accident or by design brushed up against the runner, who fell, measuring his length upon the ground.[4] Lazaro Fonte does not seem to have acted as a good sportsman should, for being, as he was, a first-rate horseman, he must

[1] Fray Simon thinks this was an account of " el mas comun trato que tenian con algunas Indias." As the Spaniards had all been baptized, this source of information was not open to them.

[2] " Zaino " in Spanish America usually is used to designate a dark brown horse. In Spain, for a black, without a white hair about him.

[3] A media rienda.

[4] Barriendo la tierra con el hocico.

have acted by design. The Indian, when he recovered from his fall, expressed his resolution never to run again against such beasts.[1]

Quesada still was delayed by the impossibility of finding any guide to follow Bogotá in his retreat, and not desiring that his men should remain camped in idleness, began to look about for something to employ them on. For a long time the Chibchas had been at war with a wild tribe upon their frontiers, known as the Panches, who passed for the most formidable warriors with whom they had to deal.

Although Quesada had been unable to find guides to show the way to where the Zipa, Bogotá, had taken refuge, he had no such difficulty as regards the Panches. This was but natural, as Bogotá was their hereditary and almost sacred ruler, whereas the Panches were their enemies. No doubt the Chibchas believed, as men in their position have so often thought, that their two enemies might destroy each other. Without doubt the Panches had always been a thorn in the side of the Chibcha kingdom. They lived upon the frontier beyond the towns or villages of Fosca and of Cienaga. These Indians were cannibals, used poisoned arrows, and were generally tall, well-made men, whereas the Chibchas were short and squarely built. Their appearance was designed to enhance their reputation for ferocity, for their hair was long and hung down from their flattened heads—a conformation they obtained by pressing them between boards in their childhood. The Chibchas always were obliged to keep bodies of picked men upon the Panche frontier, and even these were sometimes not strong enough to counteract their raids. These frontier troops were known as Guechas, which is said to have meant warriors or champions. They wore their hair short, so as to present no hold in single combat, and kept strict discipline.

Quesada, having obtained guides, sent out Captains San Martin and Cespedes to reduce the Panches to obedience. Having heard so much of their ferocity, the little expedition entered their country with their swords drawn, lances in

[1] Con tales bestias.

rest, and with their crossbowmen and the few harquebusiers that they had all ready for the fray. The soldiers and the horses all wore their quilted cotton armour.[1] Even the bloodhounds that accompanied them all had their quilted coats.

At the last frontier post they found a body of the Guechas, who pleaded with them not to adventure into the Panches' country in such small numbers, alleging that they would have but little chance against the hordes that they would meet. Little enough the captains cared for a disparity in numbers, relying on their arms. They crossed the river that divides the valley of Fusagasugá from those of Pati and Apulo, following a mountain trail, narrow and tortuous, on which only a single man could pass. As they wound down the pass into the valley of Apulo, the Panches fell upon them, about five thousand strong. Their arms were clubs and lances, and as they advanced, they rained a shower of poisoned arrows and of darts upon the Spaniards. Situated as they were without reserves—for the Guechas who had followed them at first had halted higher up the mountain path—thinking the Spaniards would soon be overwhelmed, they could not be reckoned on for help. Captain San Martin, being an experienced Indian fighter, and knowing he would soon be overpowered if he remained on the hill trail, pushed down into the plain. There he could bring his horsemen into action, and once again to them (after God)[2] the Spaniards owed the victory. Had they been surrounded by the Panches on the hills their fate would surely have been sealed, for the Panches were a far more formidable foe than the unwarlike Indians of Bogotá.

The Panches resisted the unknown elements they had to face like heroes, and though the horsemen cut bloody lanes through their ranks, they were filled up at once by their reserves. At last they broke and fled, but sullenly, turning repeatedly to launch their poisoned arrows and their javelins. So hot the combat was at times, the issue of the fray so doubtful, that many of the Guechas posted on the

[1] See Chapter II.   [2] Despues de Dios.

hills behind the Spaniards went back to tell the Zipa that the Panches were victorious. Only ten Spaniards and six horses were seriously wounded, and all of them were cured, owing to the care they took to cauterize their wounds.[1] A somewhat radical proceeding, the actual cautery, but it was all they had.

After the battle the two captains returned in triumph to Quesada's camp. Upon their homeward march one of those curious incidents took place so characteristic of the conquest of the Americas. Upon a little eminence, a Panche warrior of great stature appeared and explained by signs that he wished to avenge in single combat the death of his companions, as he had not been able to arrive in time to fight the previous day. A Spanish soldier went out to meet him, and though overthrown at the first onset regained his feet, and at one stroke cut off the Panche's head.

Captain Cespedes wished to have taken the man prisoner, as he admired his courage, but the Indian gave him no time, bounding like a tiger on the soldier who advanced to meet him, and running on his fate.

As they resumed their march after this incident, they were again alarmed to see six Indians advancing towards them on the road. As they drew near they saw they carried with them a rudely fashioned cross, and had a paper in their hands. It proved to be a letter from Quesada to Cespedes or San Martin, or anyone who had survived, and evidently had been written in alarm upon receipt of news of a defeat spread by the Guechas who had run away during the action in the hills.

Quesada, who was anxious to find out from what part of the country the Indians procured their gold, carefully

---

[1] " No habieren peligro de la muerte por el cuidado que se puso en caldearlos con hierro ardiendo, remedio eficaz contra la herida de hierba."   " Hierba "—literally, a herb—was the word all the chroniclers of the conquest employed for the poison the Indians used for their arrows.   In point of fact, though the juice of some plants was used, the chief ingredients seem to have been either powdered ants or putrescent animal matter.

questioned the messengers who came and went between the interior and the coast, and who by this time had acquired some little knowledge of Castilian,[1] or Christian, as the chroniclers usually styled it in their books. These told him, as it is believed at the instigation of the Zipa, Bogotá, that they lay to the west. This was in the direction of the Panches' country, and it may be the Zipa wished to involve the Spaniards in further trouble with the warlike tribe. At least, such is the opinion of Colonel Joaquin Acosta,[2] Piedrahita, and others of the best authorities. Whether this was the case or no, one thing is certain, that the emerald mines were in the direction that they went.

Quesada sent an expedition out under Captain Valenzuela, guided by the men whom Bogotá had sent, or perhaps only indoctrinated, to find the emerald mines. They set out full of hope, and after having slept at Bojacá went on to Guatavita, and camped beside the celebrated lake, where the strange ceremony of the El Dorado[3] was accustomed to be held. From there they passed on to Chocontá, the last town of the Zipa's territory. The night that they arrived there, forty of the Spanish soldiers went mad from eating the berries of a tree, to which on that account the Spaniards gave the name of borrachera—that is, the drunken tree, or perhaps more accurately the tree that makes men drunk.[4] Quesada is reported to have said on this occasion: " They soon got over it, but remained madder than before, for they went on endeavouring to carry out the madness of taking the property of people who lived two thousands leagues from Spain."[5]

[1] "Hablar en cristiano " (to speak Christian—that is, Spanish) was an ancient euphemism in Spain.

[2] " Descubrimiento de la Nueva Granada," Colonel Joaquin Acosta, p. 222.

[3] See Chapter VIII.

[4] It is the *Datura arborea*.

[5] " Descubrimiento de la Nueva Granada," Colonel Joaquin Acosta. Colonel Acosta does not say where he discovered this passage of Quesada's writings. It may probably be incorporated either in Castellanos or Piedrahita. If these were his real sentiments, it is a pity that he fell from grace.

Quesada had now entered the territory of a rival king, the Zaque of Tunja, a mortal enemy of Bogotá's. For some reason or another Quesada had not found this out, either because of the loyalty of the Indians to one another against the common enemy, or because he was not well served by his interpreters. Thus he missed the opportunity of playing the two chiefs against each other, after the fashion that Cortés played the Tlascalans against Montezuma, when he first invaded Mexico. He therefore had to fight each chief separately.

As Captain Valenzuela and his expedition slowly marched along, the Indians came out to meet them, bringing provisions, under the impression that the newcomers were Children of the Sun. As the same superstition or idea prevailed at the first conquests both of Mexico and of Peru history might have been written differently, and some of the discredit that attaches to every European nation in its dealings with less advanced races been removed, had but the Spaniards known how to take advantage of the picturesque idea, and bear themselves in a manner more befitting to their supposed lineage and state. The world might then have seen great Indian kingdoms in Peru and Mexico gradually inducted into European ideas, but with their own strange customs and religions still preserved. We must not lay the flattering unction to our souls that we, as Englishmen, would have behaved in the least better than the Spaniards had we been placed in the same situation as they found themselves. Facts are against us. Nor is it to be thought that all the Spaniards of those days did not lament the conduct of their countrymen and even criticize it.[1]

[1] Dr. Don Lucas Piedrahita, Bishop-elect of Santa Marta, has the following passage, that clearly shows his opinion on the matter, and how much he resented all that had been done: " The motive that inspired all these enterprises from Castille was the preaching of the Gospel and the conversion of the infidel to the true faith; well, then, here (in Bogotá) the concourse of the infidels who were to participate could not have been more numerous " (" Historia General de las Conquistas del Nuevo Reino de Granada," Piedrahita,

Although, as is plain by his speeches, Quesada criticized not only the motives of the conquest, but his own share in them, no one can suppose that all or any of his captains had any special qualms. It is not very likely any of them imagined that they had left Castile to preach the gospel or to convert the infidel.

Madrid, 1688). The bishop is writing of the expedition under Captain Valenzuela to the emerald mines. The good man may have thought that the motive of the conquest was to preach the Gospel, but " Uno pienso el bayo, y otro el que le ensilla."

CHAPTER X

THE next stage was to a place called Turmeque, described as great and populous. Quesada sent on Captain Valenzuela to report upon the emerald mines, and Captain San Martin to see if he could reach the plains of which they had just heard. The Spaniards not unnaturally thought, coming as they did from Europe, that if the mountains were so relatively thickly inhabited the plains would be more thickly populated still. They had not the least idea that the plains were then, as they are still to-day, one of the wildest and least populated portions of the globe. The climate, the wild animals, the difficulties of the road, the marshes, the countless rivers and the insect plagues, that make life miserable upon the Llanos of the Orinoco, were all unknown to them.

Quesada, with the bulk of his expedition, remained to rest at Turmeque. As he found that the Indians were terrified by the sound of the soldiers' trumpets whilst he was resting in the camp, he ordered them to take any old pails and kettles[1] that they had and beat them with warlike instruments. Thus did he reverse the adage of the sword being beaten into a ploughshare, though how his men cooked their provisions without kettles no chronicler has told. The soldiers called the place the Valley of the Trumpets, a name it may still have preserved, for nearly all the names given at the conquest have become permanent.

Captain Valenzuela in three days reached Somondoco, where the emerald mines were situated, but they turned out to be difficult to work. Having with great labour got out some few emeralds he returned to Turmeque. He brought the news, however, that from the top of some high hills near Somondoco he had seen vast grassy plains in the

[1] Pailas y peroles de cocina.

123

far distance, stretching out like the sea.   Captain San Martin immediately set out to report upon them.   At a place called Lengupá they passed the frontiers of the Chibchas, and soon began to descend a mountain path towards the plains. The road was terrible, winding along the edge of precipices.   The rain was constant, and the few Indians that they met were wandering savages.   The expedition suffered every kind of hardships, being reduced at one time to eat cakes made of cazabe flour, cooked on the embers, and seasoned with a kind of ant that the Chibcha guides who accompanied them devoured quite greedily,[1] being accustomed to eat ants.

The march made by Captain San Martin, struggling along with his horses driven in a band before them in mud up to their bellies; the saddles carried on the heads of the Chibchas who had accompanied the expedition; the soldiers starving and in rags looking like a band of gipsies, was truly wonderful as an example of what the Spaniards of those days were able to endure.   Even to-day it is a serious undertaking to travel down from Bogotá into the Llanos of the Casanáre, over Andean trails.

Only one incident seems to have relieved the suffering and the monotony of hunger and hard work.   On one occasion they took prisoner an Indian maiden.   She was " so beautiful and modest and so well-behaved that she could have competed[2] with the Spanish women who were most adorned with these qualities."   As she was very like a girl

---

[1] " Los Indios de Bogotá crian hormigas para comerlas ": " Historia de las Indias," Fray Francisco de Gómara, p. 66.

[2] " Era tan hermosa, modesta y grave que podia competir con la española mas adornada de estas prendas y porque se parecia á una que los soldados habian conocido de Santa Marta, que la llamaban La Cardeñosa, le ponian á la India ese nombre ": Fray Simon. Piedrahita, who was a bishop and therefore less likely to take notice of such a carnal trifle as an Indian girl, says: " Una India que en cualquiera parte del mundo pudiera señalarse en hermosura (tan prodiga andaba la naturaleza en la disposicion de perfecciones de que dotó el sujeto), que de aspecto grave, achaque de que adolecen todas aquellas que tienen confiança de su beldad, y no la aplican á empeños ilicitos " (p. 138).   Though a Churchman, Piedrahita shows a good knowledge of the subject.

the soldiers had known in Santa Marta, called La Cardeñosa, they gave the same name to the Indian girl. Quesada had specially enjoined on Captain San Martin not to be absent more than ten days. This period was now completed, and San Martin, although he had not reached the Llanos, had received reports about them from the wandering Indians far from encouraging. However, he in company with all the Spaniards of his time did not believe them; holding that probably the Llanos, instead of being the wild unpopulated tract they really were, concealed illimitable wealth. Somehow or other, even as early as in Quesada's day, the story of the Golden Man[1] had got transformed into the legend of a Golden City, that, as it never could be found, all thought was situated somewhere on the great plains along the Orinoco's banks.

As San Martin knew by experience that Quesada was not a commander to be played with, the ten days having run out, he returned back on the same road. He arrived safely at Lengupá, without the loss either of a soldier or a horse. From there he sent a messenger to Quesada saying that it appeared impossible to reach the Llanos by the path he had taken; but that the Indians told him there was another road from Sogamoso, and that he intended to attempt it after a little rest.

He was now upon the proper way, for from the town of Sogamoso there runs a trail that has been used from immemorial times down to the Llanos, by which to-day cattle are driven from the Casanáre up to Bogotá.

Before San Martin started for Sogamoso he sent back two horse soldiers[2] to Quesada with five hundred dollars' worth of gold and some large emeralds. When these two horsemen found themselves at a place called the valley of Boganipe, to their surprise they came upon fresh tracks of horses on the sand. These proved to have been made by the Alferez, Vanegas,[3] who had been sent out by Quesada to gather news of San Martin.

---

[1] El Dorado.   [2] Dos de á caballo.
[3] Vanegas subsequently founded the town of Tocaima and became the second Marshal of New Granada, after Quesada's death.

Besides the horsemen San Martin sent out two foot soldiers, thinking Quesada might be still at Cienaga. When these men arrived at Cienaga it was just nightfall, and as they heard no sound and saw no lights they thought the camp had been abandoned. For fear of being taken prisoners by any band of Indians that might be in the neighbourhood, they hid themselves in some thick bushes and waited for the day. At midnight they were surprised to hear the braying of an ass, an unfamiliar sound in New Granada at the time. As they well knew there was but one specimen of the race in the whole country they were overjoyed. At once they knew it must be Marobaré, the "asno conquistador."[1] His voice seemed to the shivering soldiers like a safe-conduct,[2] and in the morning they came into the camp. They found that Quesada with about half his men had marched to Tunja, a great and populous place of which he had just been informed. There both Vanegas and San Martin rejoined him and gave in their reports. Captain San Martin had to confess his expedition had been a failure, except so far as the five hundred dollars of fine gold and the large emeralds went. Vanegas, who had been sent to search for tidings of him, had journeyed through the valley of Boganipe, and then come upon a temple in the woods. This temple was of considerable size, and in it were many images of eagles and of snakes, all of pure gold and " reasonably well made."[3] The whole was worth six thousand dollars, and Vanegas, thinking it was a sacrilege to offer gold to a false deity, appropriated it, thinking, no doubt, that he knew better gods in greater need of it.

Quesada and his men had now been sixty days in the territory of the second of the great Chibcha chiefs, the King of Tunja,[4] and so well had the Indians guarded the secret that he was entirely ignorant of the fact.

[1] See Chapter I.

[2] Un salvo conducto.

[3] Razonablemente labradas.

[4] His Indian title was El Zaque, as that of the King of Bogotá was El Zipa. The chroniclers often refer to them, sometimes by their Indian titles, at others as kings, and sometimes they merely

For how much longer the secret would have been preserved no one can say; but one day an Indian presented
himself before the Alferez, Vanegas, alleging that he had
been ill-treated by his chief and vowing vengeance on him.
He promised that he would show Vanegas where a great
chief lived, who was immensely rich. All the conditions
that the Indian made were that his hair should be cut off
and he should be disguised. At once Vanegas sent to tell
Quesada of his discovery.

After interrogating the Indian, Quesada hastily chose out
the fifty best men that he had, half of them mounted and half
infantry. Then he set out to surprise the Chief of Tunja.[1]
This potentate's title was that of Zaque, and his own name
was Quemenchatocha.

Quesada, though severe enough with his soldiers about
plundering and full of wise saws in his speeches about
justice and the like, seems to have had no scruples as to
appropriating the Indian's treasure, as it were, under his own
hand and seal. This is not to say that he was cruel or
bloodthirsty, as were most of the other conquerors. He
had, however, to justify his position as leader of the expedition, both to his immediate chief, the Adelantado Don
Pedro de Lugo, who he believed was still alive, and to the
Emperor in Spain. In one way, and in one way only,
could he do so; that was by sending gold to them; firstly,
to pay the Adelantado what he had advanced to equip the
expedition, and secondly, for the imperial fifth.[2] Placed
as he was, most of his theories of justice and humanity
vanished before the pressure of stern facts. Such is the
usual fate of theories in this vale of tears, and possibly is the
best reason why it deserves the name.

The Zipa of Bogotá having escaped him and having buried

---

call them caciques (chiefs). Cacique was a Carib word from Santo
Domingo, but was introduced and used by the Spaniards all over
South America.

[1] Tunja is said to be corrupted from Hunsa, the original Chibcha
name.

[2] In all the conquests, a fifth part of the gold had, by a special
clause in the generals' commission, to be sent to the king.

all his treasures, Quesada was determined that the Zaque of Tunja should not have time to escape as did his brother king. So he pushed on at a smart trot, the infantry running beside the horsemen, holding to their stirrup leathers. For all their haste, they did not arrive before the gates of Tunja till about two hours before nightfall. A deputation met them at the gate, entreating them to wait till morning, and not by a violent entry at night to alarm their king, who, they explained, was old and in ill-health. It was of no avail, and through the middle of the crowd of Indians Quesada and his men passed on towards the centre of the town. As they advanced the tumult always grew greater, the Indians blowing their war whistles, shouting, and brandishing their arms.

In the last rays of the fast-sinking sun a wondrous spectacle broke on the Spaniards' eyes. From nearly every house, swinging lightly in the breeze, hung plates of gold, beaten as thin as sheets of paper, that gave out sounds like an Æolian harp. The houses were well built, although of slight material, and the tall poles of the chiefs' residences, all brightly varnished red, gave a fantastic look to the strange city that was so soon to be destroyed.

When they arrived at the king's house, they found the way into the stockade that surrounded it secured by cords, and packed with Indians all armed to the teeth. Quesada threw himself from his horse and cut the cords; then, with his drawn sword in his hand, followed by only ten of his adherents, he passed into an interior courtyard, leaving his mounted men outside to guard the gate.

There, in the middle of a patio, he found the king seated upon a wooden throne,[1] and with his courtiers standing in order round about him, all armed, and wearing golden breast-plates and diadems of plumes.

So did the Roman senators await the entry of the Gauls into the senate house in Rome. The attitude of the King of Tunja was to the full as heroic as was that of the senators;

---

[1] " Sentado en dutro." Dutro, according to Castellanos (" Historia del Nuevo Reino de Granada "), was the Chibcha for throne.

all that he lacked in history was a larger theatre and a favourable historian. Though old and stout, the Zaque was of imposing stature. His presence showed he was a man accustomed to command. His glance was fierce. His face was wide; his nose was large and twisted; his nostrils open; so that he had a formidable appearance. He looked, in fact, with his great stature and his fierce look, as if he had been the successor of the devil.[1] Although this was the way the King of Tunja struck the Spanish chroniclers, they were forced to admit that he was reputed of good judgment, sagacious and astute, diligent in his office, and keeping all the strings of government in his own hands.

This potentate was not dismayed by the abrupt incursion of the strangers; but sat quite quietly regarding them, with his feet resting on a fine piece of matting three or four inches thick. His face was quiet and composed, his bearing dignified as he remained immovable upon his throne, with all his courtiers standing about him waiting his commands.

Quesada, who was a gentleman, at once recognized the king, and by the mouth of an interpreter addressed him in the usual style of all the conquerors. He told him, as Cortés told Montezuma, that he himself was the vassal of a mighty king, who had sent him out to help the Indians, and to ensure them in the possession of their lands[2] and for the salvation of their souls. He offered him an alliance with the mysterious potentate who had dispatched him to America, and told him he could rely on equitable treatment.

Quesada did not, as did Cortés, explain the dogmas of our faith to the Indian potentate, and tell him that he must accept them instantly or perish in hell flames.

Considered in relation to the other speeches of the conquerors on similar occasions, Quesada made a reasonable harangue. It was the speech of a man who knows he has the necessary strength behind him to enforce his words, but yet contains no statements that anyone could reasonably

---

[1] " Succesor del diablo ": Fray Simon.
[2] There seemed no great necessity for this assurance, as the Indians' fixity of tenure had never been threatened.

challenge, for it was true he had been sent out by Charles V. As to the alliance, it was a proposition that a sensible man might take into consideration. For the assurance of possession of their lands, it must have seemed a madness to the Indian king, who naturally had no idea of the strength that the mere handful of invaders actually possessed. Fray Simon says that " the speech did not strike him badly."[1]

If this was really so, the Zaque must have been an extraordinary man. He answered with considerable dignity that, as what he had heard was new to him, he must have time to think about it. Meanwhile, he hoped Quesada would retire to a house that he had prepared for his reception, and come again to talk the matter over after a night's rest. Nothing could have been more reasonable, or more in keeping with the attitude of a prudent prince who had been offered an alliance with a foreign potentate by a handful of armed men, who had appeared without an invitation and might have dropped down from the skies.

The Zaque, who was both prudent and astute, may have been meditating treachery. Quesada thought so, and, situated as he was, accompanied but by fifty men, lost like a grain of sand upon the shore amongst ten thousand Indians, it is not to be wondered at. Still he could hardly have expected that the Zaque could agree upon so serious a matter as an alliance with a foreign and an unknown king without some consultation with his councillors. Quesada was not long in making up his mind, and, being convinced apparently that treachery was intended, determined instantly to make the king a prisoner.

Pizarro and Cortés had done the same in Mexico and in Peru, but, bold as were their coups, they were as nothing to the enterprise Quesada undertook. Both Cortés and Pizarro were at the head of considerable forces that, though inferior in numbers to their enemies, yet had superior strength at their command. The emperors of Mexico and of Peru had put themselves into their hands, and though this made the treachery of the Spanish generals still more odious, it

[1] No le pareció mal la platica.

gave them a command of the whole situation, out of Quesada's power to wield.

Quesada and his lieutenant, Antonio de Olalla, were perfectly alone in a great building, full of armed Indians devoted to their king. Outside there were but eight and forty men, half of them mounted, and obliged to guard their horses above everything. Thus only about twenty men were left available to assist their general.

Quesada and Olalla drew their swords and resolutely advanced towards the throne where the old king was seated, surrounded by a ring of his armed courtiers. When they put out their hands to seize him, for the first time he seems to have taken in what kind of men he had to deal with, and the danger that he ran. Rising up from his seat to his full height, his eyes flashed fire, and in a voice that shook the rafters he called upon his bodyguard to slay the madmen, and then to deal with those who had remained waiting outside the gate. All was confusion in an instant, the Indians closed like angry wasps round the audacious Spaniards, and, above all the tumult rose the voice of the herculean king encouraging his men. Had they been fierce warriors such as were the Mexicans, Quesada's fate had certainly been sealed; but, though the Indians clustered round him with their levelled lances pointed at his breast, all were afraid to strike. This gave time to the Spanish soldiers who had remained outside the courtyard to rush at once towards the palace, thinking their general was attacked, for they had no idea of what was going on inside. Some tried to ride their horses into the interior courtyard, and foot and horse all struggled in the gate. The noise was deafening, as the Indians in the town to the number of ten or twelve thousand all were alarmed and yelling their shrill cries.

What might have been a fatal moment for the Spaniards blocked in the gate, was averted by the coolness of Captain Gonzalo Suarez, who rode his horse right through the group of struggling men, and turning, shouted to them not to fall into a trap. They obeyed and formed their ranks. He placed a guard of mounted men across the gate, with orders to let no one pass either in or out. Then, with a few picked men, he went inside the palace and beheld a most astounding sight. Quesada with one hand held the king, and with the other menaced him with his sword, threatening him with death if he attempted to escape. The king, who was both well advanced in years and very corpulent, soon ceased to struggle, and when the Indians saw he was a prisoner, they quietly dispersed. No blow was struck in his defence by his armed bodyguard, and the ten thousand Indians in the town were overawed by the firm front the Spanish horsemen at the gate presented to them.

Fray Simon and other chroniclers see the hand of God in the adventure, and think the general's life was saved miraculously. That may be so; but, on the other hand, most deeds of arms and wild adventures undertaken with but scant chances of success are of themselves so great a miracle, that intervention from a superior power seems to destroy their merit and take away that element of chance that makes them admirable. No feat in all the conquest of America was more adventurous or undertaken in the face of such extraordinary odds. Had but the Indians rallied round their chief, the fate of the two Spaniards could not have remained for an instant in the scales. It is difficult to say who was most worthy of our admiration, the dignified old king seated upon his throne, quite undismayed at the incursion of the strangely armed, ferocious-looking men, mounted upon their terrible and unknown animals, or the two bold adventurers who faced such fearful odds.

Quesada, still holding fast the king, led him to the outer courtyard, and set a guard of soldiers over him, telling them to treat him courteously and let his servants and his councillors have free access to him. By this time night had closed upon the scene, the still, cold night of the Sabána of Bogotá with its deep purple sky that looks as if a velvet curtain has been drawn above the world, thick but translucent, pierced by a myriad stars. No doubt Quesada did not look at it, or at the Southern Cross that cast a soft effulgence on the wide plain, its beams seeming to transfix the earth in their intensity. His thoughts ran on far different matters, and probably he grasped for the first time that fate had raised him to an equality with Pizarro and Cortés, whose exploits he had always emulated. No single moment in the course of his adventurous life could have held more intense emotions for him, as he reflected on the success of his audacity.

His first act was to set horsemen to patrol the palace, and to prevent the Indians from rallying and overwhelming him when they saw what a small force had overpowered the town. Luckily for Quesada the Chibchas were so little warlike that when they fought and failed to get the upper hand, their practice was to supplicate the Sun to pardon them for having undertaken an unrighteous enterprise.[1]

From such kind of people naturally there was but little to be expected in such a crisis as they found themselves. Although the Spaniards had the advantage of their horses and such few pieces of defensive armour, crossbows, and harquebuses as had survived the rust and damp of the long months of wandering on the Magdalena, they were but fifty men all told. The best authorities estimate the armed Indians in the town at nine or ten thousand, and talk of the population being as innumerable as ants.[2] For all their numbers they made no attempt to rescue their old king from the invaders' hands. One thing they did do, that was to pack up as much of their emeralds and their gold as possible, in bags, and throw them over the stockade to those outside, who bore them off and buried them so safely, that the treasure never has been found.

Quesada was unable to restrain the soldiers, for all his power over them. Excited as they were, and for the first time loose in a town that seemed to them to be on a par with the cities they had heard of in the conquest of Peru,

[1] " Los Chibchas, si son vencidos, lloran y piden perdon al sol de la injusta guerra que començaron ": " Historia de las Indias," Gómara, p. 66.

[2] Innumerables gentes . . . como hormigas.

with lighted torches in their hands they searched the town for gold. Through the streets they rushed, brandishing torches at the imminent risk of setting the straw-roofed houses in a blaze. The shouting and the tumult of the Indians still continued, and the confusion was increased by the long lines of fugitives all loaded with what treasure they could carry, pouring out of the town. Around the outer stockade of the palace the Spanish horse soldiers patrolled all through the night, their armour and their stern faces lit up now and then by the gleam of a passing torch waved by some plunderer. The unlucky king remained under the guard of Quesada and a soldier. What his feelings must have been as he saw all his town ransacked are not hard to imagine, for he was a man of stronger character than either Montezuma or Atalhualpa, and his calamity had fallen upon him far more suddenly than theirs.

The first thing that the soldiers came upon was a bag containing eight thousand dollars' worth of gold. Their next find was a sort of reliquary containing bones, probably those of some old chief; but this is mere conjecture of the chroniclers, for almost every record (if there were any) of the history of the Chibcha race has been irrevocably lost. This reliquary weighed about six thousand dollars' worth of gold. Amongst their loot were an enormous number of thin plates of gold, known as " chagualas," that hung before the doors of the chief houses and the temples, either as charms or to make music by the action of the wind.

Bags full of emeralds and curious sea-shells the Indians used as trumpets, mounted in massive gold, and golden eagles that had adorned the roofs were thrown in a great pile before Quesada, as he sat guarding the captive king. As the soldiers threw down their loot, they cried exultantly, " Peru, Peru, Sir General; this is Peru !"

After making all allowance for their excitement, and though the riches found in Tunja have been much exaggerated, the fact remains that Captains Lebrija and San Martin, in their " Relacion " to the King (Philip II.), say that, united to a small sum that had been found in Sogamoso, the Tunja treasure amounted to one hundred and ninety-one thousand two hundred and sixty-four dollars' worth of pure gold, and more than eighteen thousand dollars' worth of silver, with thirty-seven thousand of gold more or less alloyed. In addition to all this, there were one thousand eight hundred and fifteen emeralds, some of considerable size.

The soldiers also found a quantity of beads of every colour made out of various bones, and beautifully worked, as well as beads of gold. Fine Indian mantles, shields, and arms adorned with gold, made a great heap before Quesada's feet, so great, say the chroniclers, as to tower high above his head.

Quesada, at the instigation of his soldiers, but apparently against his will, urged the old king to buy his liberty for a great sum of gold. He proved no Atalhualpa of Peru, promising to fill a chamber full of gold so that his life was spared; but wrapped himself in an impenetrable and scornful silence. Once and once only did he speak, to say, " My body is in your hands, do with it what you choose, but no one shall command my will!"

This touched Quesada, for he was no mere freebooter, caring for naught but gold. He instantly gave a strict order that the person of the king should be respected, and that his wives and servants should have access to him and serve him with his accustomed state. This order was obeyed, and Quesada to his credit soon set the king at liberty. He did not live to enjoy it many weeks, for the emotions of that eventful night, when in a few short hours he saw his kingdom, state, and power tumble down like a house of cards, proved fatal, and he died of a broken heart. The chroniclers all say he was a tyrant, violent, and sudden in his rage, and bloodthirsty.

Pay and appeal,[1] so runs the Spanish saying. The King of Tunja paid most certainly for all the crimes he may, or that he may not, have committed. His history, though written by his enemies, remains his best appeal.

[1] Pagar y apelar.

CHAPTER XI

THE Tunja Indians seem to have made no attempt whatever to recover their lost independence, for the country soon settled down quietly under Quesada's rule. Having in his practice refuted all his theories as to the injustice of coming seven thousand miles to rob, and of the Indians being in their own country, where the Spaniards[1] only were intruders, Quesada ruled the conquered Indians with moderation and with equity. Had he remained in power for several years after the conquest was achieved, conditions on the Sabána de Bogotá would have been very different from what they became under the rapacious governors who succeeded him. Events were destined to take him from the country he had conquered, and so the chance of a mild government by an educated man was lost. The reins of power fell into the hands of men sent out from Spain, whose sole idea was to get rich as soon as possible, no matter at what cost.

As the expedition was in camp at Tunja, news arrived of a great temple at a place called Suamos, famed for its riches and its sanctity. Quesada instantly set off to plunder it, having thrown all his theories to the winds. On the first night he rested at a place called Paipa, and was received by the chief inhabitants,[2] who brought a little present, and told him that the head chief was getting ready several loads of treasure for him. Quesada camped, and the Duitamas returned into their town and spent the night in hiding all their gold. When morning broke they all ascended several little mounds that overlooked the camp, and after a loud chorus of derisive yells disappeared into

[1] All of these phrases appear in his addresses to his men, as reported by the various chroniclers.

[2] These were inferior chiefs, known as Duitamas.

136

the hills. When the Spaniards advanced into the town they found it empty, without an ounce of gold.

Quesada pushed on rapidly to Suamos.[1] Near to it lay the sacred valley of Iraca, the seat of the third Chibcha potentate, and the theatre of the mysterious apparition of their lawgiver.[2]

The inhabitants attempted some resistance, as they looked on their temple with great veneration and respect. However, as the ground was flat, the Spanish horsemen soon dispersed them, and they advanced into the town just as night fell upon it. They found it solitary, deserted, but by an aged priest with a white beard, who told them that, as he had passed the whole of his long life in the service of the temple, he had remained to die. This was the first time that the Spaniards had seen a bearded Indian, and though the chroniclers referred to him as the minister of the devil,[3] to whom the Indians prayed, the more imaginative soldiers seem to have been touched at his appearance and used him with respect.

At the door of the great temple stood a row of mummies,[4] all adorned with golden ornaments and emeralds. These were the bodies of their chiefs and of the priests who served the temple, and were held highly sacred by the Indians.

The temple was of considerable size, built all of hard wood, brought on the Indians' backs from the hot country of the Magdalena, and wonderfully wrought. The soldiers, tired with their march, set down their torches in the temple without extinguishing them, and fell asleep exhausted on the floor. Either the torches caught the straw-thatched roof, or perhaps the old white-bearded priest himself set fire to the temple where he had passed his life. The sleeping soldiers

---

[1] This may be the modern Sogamoso.

[2] See Chapter VIII.

[3] Fray Simon, Piedrahita, and Castellanos always refer to the Indians' prayers as their " talking with the devil."

[4] " Y en una barbacon bien compuesta [the Temple] hombres difuntos, secos, adornados de telas ricas, y joyas de oro ": " Elegias de Varones Ilustres de Indias," Castellanos, Madrid, 1589, Canto Sexto, p. 183.

were awakened by the flames that soon devoured the wooden structure, though it is said the building smouldered five or six weeks[1] after the fire took place.

Although the fire consumed the temple and whatever riches it contained, and the Chief Suamos before he fled into the hills had concealed his treasure, Quesada took away about a thousand dollars' worth of gold.

The old, white-bearded priest lost his life in the flames—it was never known whether by accident or by design. His end was worthy of him, for after having passed his days in his beloved temple he perished with it. It is to be hoped that he received his due reward, in some Valhalla of the Indians, where temples cannot burn.

Fearing that the whole valley of Iraca would rise against him, for they had held their temple in great veneration, Quesada returned in haste to Tunja, by forced marches, making the Indians carry his plunder on their backs. So careful was he of his horses, knowing their value to him, that to have them fresh and ready for a fight if the necessity should arise, he made his soldiers all march on foot, with Indians carrying the saddles and the horses driven on in front.

At Tunja he received news that a chief called Tundama was preparing to attack him, having allied himself with several other chieftains, and raised an army of ten thousand Indians. Quesada's policy was that of any other conqueror in his position—that is, to detach some of the allies from the confederacy, under the pretext that the chief partner in the league was a mere tyrant pursuing his own ends. He sent an embassy to Tundama, telling him that he was the vassal of a great potentate, and had come to save his soul. The Chief Tundama seems to have been a man of humour, for he returned an answer that he cared little for his soul so that his body was in safety, and sent a message of defiance, telling Quesada to leave his territory. This, of course, he would not do, but advanced against Tundama

[1] Fray Simon says: " Some say for five years, but this seems too long " (Cinco años pareceme mucho).

instantly. Tundama, who had made good use of his confederacy, met him with the best disciplined and appointed army that the Chibchas yet had put into the field. The armies joined battle at a place called Bonza, and for a time the Indians maintained a stout resistance to the Spanish arms.

The Indians' weapons were long lances, clubs, and wooden swords, with javelins[1] that they launched with a throwing stick.[2] There is no mention of their using bows and arrows. Their generals wore tall headdresses made with the feathers of parrots and macaws. Quesada nearly lost his life on this occasion,[3] for, having charged almost alone into the thickest of the Indians, he received a blow from a club that felled him from his horse. He bounded to his feet and defended himself with his accustomed valour[4] against the Indian[5] who, after having brought him down, was trying to dispatch him with his club. Quesada would undoubtedly have lost his life, for the Indians were crowding round him, had not a Spanish soldier, one Baltazar Maldonado, fought[6] his way through the press and caught his horse, and aided him to mount. Never in his adventurous life was he in greater danger than in the Bonza fight.

The battle over, Quesada marched from Paipa, leaving the chief "tolerably well chastised."[7] From the dead Indians he took "a reasonable booty,"[8] composed of golden bracelets, chagualas, and circlets that the chiefs wore round their heads. Those Indians who had not been slain took refuge in some marshes that were near, into which the horsemen could not penetrate.

Quesada then marched to Suesca, not far from where

---

[1] Tiraderas.   [2] Estolica.

[3] " Estuvo muy á pique de ser muerto ": Piedrahita, p. 121.

[4] " Su acostumbrado valor ": Piedrahita, p. 122.

[5] "Gandul " is the word that Piedrahita uses to describe the Indian. Castellanos (" Historia del Nuevo Reino de Granada ") says the word was used to designate a grown-up Indian (adult). In modern Spanish it is often used for a vagabond.

[6] A grandes lanzadas.   [7] Algo castigado.

[8] Un razonable despojo.

now stands Bogotá, a place in which fate destined him to pass much time in his old age. There it is said he took his resolution to settle in the Sabána of Bogotá and build his capital. At first he had determined to build his capital at Tunja, either because of the fine climate or in remembrance of his bold exploit on the memorable night. It is said the superior beauty of the position of Bogotá eventually decided him, and he could not have picked a better site on which to found a town.

At Suesca he received information of the fertile vale of Neiva, in the hot country near the Magdalena, and, hearing it was rich in gold, set out to march there with about fifty men, leaving his brother Hernan Perez de Quesada to command the camp. This brother was a man of character, and, though inferior to Quesada in ability, was a good soldier; but he lacked his brother's tact.

Then began one of those arduous, fantastic expeditions that few men but the Spanish conquerors, without provisions and without the smallest knowledge of the country, could ever have survived. Quesada and his men were now accustomed to the high altitude of Bogotá, a climate so severe in its abrupt difference from the tropics that nearly every foreigner suffers from it upon his first arrival, and is unable to take exercise. Yet, Quesada and his men apparently entered and left it, and entered it again, without experiencing any bad effects. It may be that as they journeyed slowly, they became gradually accustomed to the abrupt changes, although even on muleback people to-day suffer severely from mountain sickness[1] in the high passes of the Andean chain. The reports he had received of Neiva were such as to influence his imagination, and the cupidity of all his men. Neiva, it was said, possessed a temple sustained on pillars of pure gold, and had a row of golden statues standing around a court.

The only road known to the guides was a mere track that ran by Pasca, over the desert plateaux, down to the valley

[1] Known as " soroche " in Colombia and Ecuador, and " puna " in Peru and Chile.

of Fusagasugá. These high desert plateaux, known as Paramos, lie at an altitude of ten to twelve thousand feet, and are inhabited but by a few miserable Indians, who cultivate enough potatoes to sustain existence, and possess some herds of goats. The winds are icy; magnetic storms of fearful violence break over them at frequent intervals, and but for the tall plant known to the inhabitants as Frailejon[1] and a short wiry grass, the pastures of the goats are absolutely bare. The hardships they endured upon these barren plains must have been most severe; but they emerged at length into the hot and humid valley of the Magdalena, where at once their Indian guides deserted them, fearing the tropic heat, as do the Indians of Bogotá to-day, who suffer just as much in the low country as do newcomers from the coast in the high altitude of Bogotá.

When they arrived upon the Magdalena, so far was Quesada from finding a temple held up on columns of pure gold, that there was nothing, but a few deserted huts. Such Indians as they were had taken refuge on the left bank of the great river, and all night long kept up a constant yelling at the invaders from their camp.

Quesada found the Neiva valley of incomparable fertility, as it still is, producing all the fruits of the tropics with a minimum of toil. Fertility of soil was not the first desideratum with the Spaniards of these days, so Quesada, discouraged by the lack of gold in the deserted huts of Neiva, though they contained a few " chagualas " and a few images, was preparing to march back to Bogotá. Just as he was about to start, to his astonishment an Indian emerged dripping from the river, carrying a bundle on his head. The Alto Magdalena is almost three-quarters of a mile in

[1] Fraylejon. " La resina de este nombre que nunca se endurece y es excelente para meter en calor, aun á los muertos, como dicen, y desencojer nervios entumecidos. Es planta baja que solo nace en las montañas mas frias cerca de la nieve. Es del tamaño y figura de un frayle vestido de blanco. Las flores son grandes y amarillas y dan un olor grave y displicente ": " Historia del Reino de Quito," por el Presbitero Don Juan de Velasco, año de 1789; edicion de Quito, 1844.

breadth in the valley of Neiva, and runs fiercely between its banks. Thus the poor Indian had performed no little feat in crossing it. His courage or his curiosity were great, for him to adventure unarmed and alone in the camp of the terrific strangers, whose feats of arms must have been known to him.[1] It turned out that his bundle was composed of thin gold plates, reasonably fashioned in the shape of hearts. This raised the spirits of the soldiers, who had been suffering with fever from the rapid change of climate, from want of food, and from the disappointment they had undergone. When the indefatigable Indian, after several journeys across the river, laid a considerable pile of gold at Quesada's feet, the soldiers, looking at it as in a dream, said, What use is gold to men about to die ? Their disillusion and their weakness through the perpetual attacks of fever were so great that they prepared for death, and this, too, after a year of the same climate lower down the Magdalena's banks. To remain where they were was to invite disaster, and to return, weak as they were, above their resolution, had not Quesada once more shown himself indefatigable. Two soldiers who were stronger than the rest, Pedro Salgar and Juan de Ovalle, carried the gold by turns. The miserable procession, leaning on sticks and tottering as they walked from fever and from lack of food, set out upon its *via crucis* through the hills. Quesada, desperately ill himself, went on in front leading his horse, for all the horses had been attacked by a mysterious illness, that rendered them almost too weak to bear their saddles on their backs.

The first cool night in the high Paramos revived the horses and the soldiers, and next day they made a tolerable march.

After five or six days of suffering they reached Pasca, with the loss of six of their companions, and rested from their toils.

[1] He was rewarded with some knives and scissors, but no mention is made of hawksbells, those tinkling symbols of European might, so perhaps the supply had become exhausted.

To the fair, fertile vale of Neiva they gave the title of " El Valle de la Tristeza," which in their case it certainly deserved. Since then it has become one of the healthiest of the hot districts of Colombia, and with the enchanting valley of the Cauca disputes the title of an earthly paradise.

From Pasca Quesada sent an express to his brother Hernan Perez to meet him at or near Bogotá.

His first act on arriving there was to appoint commissioners to divide up the treasure they had collected in emeralds and gold. The royal fifth amounted in this case to forty thousand dollars, five hundred and sixty-two emeralds, and a considerable quantity of alloyed and inferior gold. Each foot soldier received five hundred and twenty dollars' worth of gold, and every horseman a thousand. The officers were given two thousand dollars each. Quesada apportioned seven parts of the whole to himself, and nine to the Adelantado Lugo. Later on, when he received the news of the Adelantado's death, he adjudged the nine portions to himself. Though some have blamed him severely for so doing, it is to be remembered that the Adelantado's son was a complete and worthless scoundrel, who had betrayed his father and run away to Spain.

Upon the whole, for a man who had come out, as he told the King of Tunja, to save the Indians' souls, he had not done badly for himself. Some of the soldiers were discontented; but this, as Fray Simon observes with a pawkiness worthy of a North Briton, usually happens on occasions of the kind.[1]

After the gold they divided up the emeralds. The soldiers must have both trusted and respected Quesada far more than his men trusted Cortés in Mexico, for there they were always at issue with him as to the division of the spoil. On this occasion many of them came to Quesada, and giving him their share begged him to keep it for them, and lay it out on their account when he returned to Spain.

When all was satisfactorily arranged, Fray Domingo de las Casas asked for a contribution to found a chaplaincy,

[1] Suele pasar en tales ocasiones.

to say perpetual masses for the souls of those who had perished before they conquered Bogotá. To the honour of the soldiers, they subscribed willingly.

Whilst the conquest of Tunja had been going on, and during the unlucky expedition to the vale of Neiva, the Zipa, Bogotá, had never ceased from harassing the invaders to his best ability. Combats were frequent, and night and day he kept the Spaniards on the alert by his attacks. He himself had retired to a fastness near to Facatativá. This town stands, and stood in those days, just at the top of the high pass that leads up from the hot country of the Magdalena into the temperate plains. The old paved mule trail to the town of Honda, passing by Guaduas, breaks off from it. Upon one side it is backed with mountains. Upon the other, in Quesada's day, an extensive marsh, through which ran paths, known only to the Indians, stretched towards Bogotá. In an hour's march thick bushy country gradually extends down to the tropic forests, so that the position that the Zipa had retired to was impregnable, until Quesada found the path through the morass. The chief himself never directed his attacks in person, on account of the prophecy that he should die by the hands of strangers, a prediction that he managed to avoid. So it became of the first importance to Quesada to take a prisoner who could be compelled to show the paths to the Zipa's fastnesses. Captain Lazaro Fonte—always the most active of Quesada's scouts—happened one day to capture two Indians who had been lurking in the reeds. It turned out they were spies sent by the Zipa to get information as to the Spaniards' camp. Nothing, not even torture, could make the elder prisoner betray his king. He died without a sign; but the younger man, more careful of his own life than his king's,[1] promised to show the way.

This was the first time Quesada had allowed actual cruelty. Once more, and once more only in his long career, did he fall into the same error, and curiously enough the second instance brought him censure and a fine from the Council

[1] Fray Simon.

of the Indies, that never noticed the innumerable instances of cruelty that stained the names both of Pizarro and Cortés.

Following the poor caitiff, Quesada instantly set out with the best portion of his forces, hoping to surprise and take the Zipa prisoner. All night they followed paths through the morass, guided by the unlucky Indian who had preferred to save his life by turning traitor, and as day broke they found themselves before a strong stockade.

Although the Indians were in force to the number of several thousand, and their king was in their midst, they fled almost without resistance. The only attempt they made to give the king a little time to flee was by throwing firebrands on the Spaniards, so that the Zipa might escape under the cover of the smoke. One Dominguez, a crossbowman, seeing a principal Indian, but without knowing that he was the king, shot a bolt that pierced the escaping Zipa through the shoulder-blade. He fell into the arms of those about him, who bore his body to the woods.

Thus died the Zipa, the most powerful potentate of the Chibcha confederacy, who, had he lived, would probably have become the sole chief of the race. In one respect he was more lucky than was Atalhualpa or Montezuma, for at least he died free and amongst his friends. One of the chroniclers, with a complete neglect of the humour, so universal in the Spanish race, remarks of him, "He gave his life up, miserably bathed in his blood, though he could have had a better fate had he made friends with the Spaniards and bathed himself in the floods of Holy Baptism."[1]

He had a better fate than his successor, who voluntarily put himself into Quesada's hands.

The Spaniards never found his body; but it is said the Indians, after having sought for it in vain for many days, remarked a flight of vultures settling down, deep in the woods, and, going to the place, came on the body of the Zipa

[1] Fray Simon. The good friar seems to have forgotten how often these floods seem to have proved fatal to the adult Indian bather, by his own account.

and buried it. This fact was unknown to the Christians at the time.[1]

His palace, as the Spaniards styled it, was full of game—deer, rabbits, and birds of every kind. All kinds of cotton cloths were piled up in abundance; but there was but a single golden vessel,[2] and a few beads and images. This golden vessel proved to be full of gold dust of the value of a thousand ducats.[3] Curiously enough the Indians, who had attempted no resistance in the lifetime of their king, now attacked the Spaniards so continuously that Quesada was obliged to quit the marshes, and move on to the open plain, where he could use his cavalry against the Indian attacks.

It is supposed that the great energy the Indians displayed was inspired by the new Zipa, Sagipá, a valiant warrior and very much beloved. This warrior, who had been a captain under the late king, was in a difficult position, for the legitimate inheritor to the Zipaship was the Cacique of Chiá.

Thus Sagipá, after Quesada had retired to Bonza, found himself harassed on one side by the Cacique of Chiá, and on the other by the ferocious Panches, the hereditary enemies of the Chibcha race. The Panches were a ferocious race of Indians, whose country lay to the west of Bogotá. They are described by Herrera as going naked, armed with arrows and carrying shields[4] that covered them from their feet to their heads. The same authority says that their normal life is that of people, half reasonable, for they punish crime, especially homicide. There are many gallows in the roads

[1] " . . . y buscandole los Indios con gran cuidado, vieron que aquellas gallinas silvestres que llaman Urubues que comen todo genero de carroña, iban al monte, y sospechando lo que fué, las siguieron y hallaron muerto al señor Bogotá, de lo qual no tuvieron noticia los Christianos por entonces ": Herrera, " Decada VI.," libro xiii., p. 71.

[2] " Totuma de oro ": Colonel Joaquin Acosta, p. 235. " Totuma " is the Colombian word for a gourd.

[3] The gold ducat was worth about nine shillings.

[4] " Los Panches andaban desnudos, en carmes . . . y llevaban pavesas que las cubren de pies á cabeça ": Herrera, " Decada VI.," cap. vi., libro I.

of their territory.[1] Herrera dwells with some complacency upon these gallows, evidently holding that it was a sure proof of their semi-reasonableness.

With the fear of these savages, and the hostility of the Cacique of Chiá, Sagipá thought that the only course that remained open to him was to throw himself upon Quesada's generosity. He arrived in person at the camp and sought an interview with the Spanish general, telling him that at first he had determined to avenge the death of Bogotá at any hazard ; but that upon reflection he found the Spaniards were invincible.

The general received him with great affability, and both Quesada and all the Spaniards were astonished at his gallant bearing.[2] Sagipá expressed himself with grace and majesty,[3] and seems to have been in all his ways a prince. He was also rich, which helped him not a little, affable and courteous with everybody.[4] These qualities, although they do not of themselves ensure success in rulers or in statesmen, yet by their absence often ruin their careers. Sagipá had the silken glove, but most unluckily for him not the traditional iron hand inside of it. After the fashion of so many princes, either tottering on their thrones or not yet well established in their seat, he sought alliance with a stronger than himself, forgetting that there can be no real equality with a superior power.

He begged Quesada for his aid against the Panches, his savage neighbours on the west. Quesada answered, promising him protection and telling him that, as he was now the vassal of a mighty prince, the Emperor Charles V., he might consider himself safe.

[1] " Hay muchas horcas por los caminos . . . es gente tan bestial que no adoraban, ni creian, sino en sus deleites y vicios ": Herrera, " Decada VI."

[2] " El general le recibió con mucho gusto, acrecentandole á el y á los demas Españoles con ver su compostura, gallardia, gracia y disposicion de su persona ": Fray Simon.

[3] " Por la buena gracia y majestad de palabras con que se expresaba ": Piedrahita, 14, lib. 5°, cap. 6°.

[4] " Era hombre rico que le ayudaba mucho . . . afable con sus palabras bien criado con todos ": Fray Simon.

It is not to be supposed that Sagipá had any definite idea of what was said to him, or who was the great prince whose vassal he had become so expeditiously. Quesada, on the other hand, had by this time determined to found his colony, and, as he knew the Panches must be his neighbours, no doubt thought that the present was as good as any other time to make them feel his strength.

Sagipá went home to call his army up, and upon his return the new-made allies instantly marched against the common enemy. Sagipá's army numbered many thousands, all armed in Indian style, with lances, arrows, and with clubs. Quesada mainly took his cavalry, and so they marched, descending every mile into a hotter country, and following nearly the same track by which the railway now descends from Facatativá to Girardot. They must have passed by Zipacón, and by the plateau where now stands the station of La Esperanza, and then by Juntas de Apulo, to where the Panche forces were encamped at Anolaima, close to the river's[1] bank.

As they descended, passing from the open plains with their short wiry grass, their air of solitude and dearth of animals and birds, their hard, blue shadows and their scanty vegetation, the country changed insensibly, and cloaks must have been tied behind the saddles, helmets slung to the ends of lances, as round the marching column trogons and tanagers, and golden orioles with their black-and-yellow beaks, have darted overhead. Humming-birds must have hung poised above the flowers, and as the column, winding like a snake, entered the tropic forests, the rich, dank smell of the decaying vegetation hung on their nostrils, almost choking them, as bathed in sweat they struggled through the woods.

They found the Panches in a natural position at a place called Tocarema, not far from Anolaima, where they defended themselves so bravely and so well that they beat back the first assault, routing the Chibchas under their Cacique Sagipá completely, and wounding ten of the Spaniards with their poisoned darts.

[1] The Magdalena.

Quesada's situation was most critical. All night his soldiers stood to arms. They also cured their wounds in " the accustomed manner."[1] Quesada, who was as prudent in his generalship as he was careful in his conveyancing in his career at the courts in Granada, sent out two ranks of sentinels—one to watch the Panches, and the other to guard against treachery from Sagipá. As long as the Panches remained in the protection of their natural fortress in the rocks, Quesada was unable to attack them with his cavalry. This they appeared to understand, and his efforts failed to draw them out upon the plain. A deep ravine ran close to Quesada's camp. In it he posted Captains San Martin, Suarez, Lazaro Fonte, Zorro,[2] and his brother Hernan Perez, with all the horsemen he could spare.

He arranged that Sagipá with his Chibchas should make a violent attack, and then fall back, as if in confusion, towards the ambuscade. All happened as he had planned. Sagipá attacked, retreated hurriedly, and then from the ravine the horsemen dashed out, lancing the Indians and killing dozens of them. The Panches were completely routed, and in the morning sent an embassy to sue for peace. Much against their will, Quesada made them swear allegiance to Sagipá, their hereditary enemy. Quesada and his Indian allies retraced their steps through the dank forests to Bojacá, the first town on the plains. The journey took them from high summer into winter, or gave the effect of doing so; for as the tropic vegetation slowly disappears and grows more scanty each league upon the road, a greyness seems to fall upon the world, oppressive both to the body and the mind.

Quesada now was bound by gratitude to Sagipá, who had not only made a voluntary alliance with him, but had fought bravely by his side.

By this time many of the Spaniards had acquired a smattering of the Chibcha language. This was the occasion of their finding out that Sagipá had usurped his power at the expense of the Cacique of Chiá. It cannot be supposed

---

[1] By the actual cautery.
[2] Zorro = fox, a good name for the leader of an ambuscade.

that any of the Spaniards cared a single maravedi[1] for the rightful succession in an Indian dynasty. No doubt they saw a pretext to extort more gold, just as Pizarro did when he slew the Inca in Peru, or as Cortés in Mexico would certainly have done with Montezuma had not death freed him from his hands.

Quesada, either carried off his feet by the amount of gold he had already got together, or by the thirst for more, or threatened by his soldiers, as the letter he received from them seems to imply, or urged on by his brother, the unscrupulous Hernan Perez, ordered the arrest of Sagipá. The pretext was that, as he had usurped the throne, he could not claim the treasure of the late King Bogotá.

Nothing more futile or unjust could have been possibly contrived. The indignation of the Indians knew no bounds: but they were powerless to resist. They had, indeed, good reason for their indignation. Their king, with a noble generosity, had voluntarily placed himself in Quesada's power, and had been accepted as a vassal of the King of Spain. All this availed him nothing, and Quesada, who must have known the vileness of his act, charged Sagipá with being not only a usurper of his own king's authority, but, by having laid his hands upon the treasure of his predecessor, a rebel against Spain.

The unlucky Sagipá listened attentively to the revolting charge, and showed no little prudence[2] in his answer to it. He said it would take him at least forty days to gather up the treasure of his predecessor, as it was concealed in different hiding-places deep in the recesses of the hills. He urged Quesada to allow him to have the gold brought in by night, for fear of robbers by the way. After a day or two, some Indians brought a sack of gold just about nightfall, and this the soldiers saw.

Sagipá offered to keep the gold in his own apartment, and the Spaniards set a guard outside the house. When the

---

[1] The maravedi was worth less than a farthing.

[2] El Cacique no mostró poca prudencia en la respuesta á esa platica.

guard, following the usual custom of a watch, had gone to sleep, the Indians silently carried it all off, and on the next night they returned bringing the same gold. At length the trick was found out, and Quesada, in his rage at having been outwitted, had the cacique flogged. The wretched man, thinking to gain time, threw the blame of the trick on the inferior chiefs. These were arrested, put to the torture, and ultimately hanged. As the poor creatures were ignorant of the details of the plot they died without a word.

As a last resource, the Sagipá offered to lead the Spaniards to the place where the gold was concealed. They started off into the mountains, carrying with them the miserable man with a rope round his neck, and its ends in the hands of soldiers. After a long and arduous march, he led them to a path beside a precipice. In the middle of it he jumped into the void, thinking to drag the soldiers after him, and end his misery. Fate was unkind. The rope held fast, and the soldiers dragged him back on to the path.

So that there should be nothing wanting to complete the infamy, on his return Quesada had him tried for rebellion, appointing his own brother Hernan Perez to be his advocate. With a devil's advocate of such a kind his condemnation was assured. The court condemned him, finding him a rebellious vassal of the emperor, and the penalty was death. This suited nobody but Sagipá himself, for a quick death was not a thing that any Indian feared. To brand his memory with an indelible black stain, and place him on an equality of infamy with his two prototypes Pizarro and Cortés, Quesada yielded to the solicitation of his soldiers, and Sagipá was so severely tortured that he died. Under the torture he never spoke a word, wrapping himself up in the stoicism of the Indian race, a stoicism that no torment ever broke through in all the annals of the conquest of the New World.

The gold was never found. The stain remains upon the name of one who, but for this one lapse into the cruel ways of his compeers, would have gone down to history as the best of all the conquerors. It is but just to say that Herrera,[1] no mean authority, says that Quesada acted under compulsion of his followers. If this was true, he showed a lamentable weakness, hard to be believed of a man who in such desperate perils had made proof of so much resolution, and whose authority and prestige with his men had ever stood so high.

[1] Los soldados insolentes y codiciosos por la fama de los grandes tesoros del Bogotá, hicieron requerimiento á Gonzalo Ximenes (de Quesada) para que pusiere en hierros á Sagipá y le diese tormento y porque no lo hacia, entendiendo ser injusto, las murmuraciones y quejas de los soldados eran grandes, diciendo que se entendia con Sagipá, y de nuevo volvieron á los requerimientos y protestas y dieron poder a Geronimo de Ansa para que pusiere demanda en juicio y Gonzalo Ximenes, nombró por defensor de Sagipá á su hermano Hernan Perez de Quesada, con juramento de que haria bien su oficio, y oidas las partes se llegó al tormento, y alli barbaremente le mataron sin que descubriese nada.

CHAPTER XII

THE conquest of the Chibcha nation now was an accomplished fact. The last Zipa had been cruelly and unjustly done to death. The King of Tunja (El Zaque) had died, in freedom it is true, but none the less of the effects of the invasion of his territory. The third chief of the nation, he who held the spiritual power and was represented at Quesada's coming by the Cacique of Suamos,[1] had little military power, and from the first was not unfriendly to the Spaniards. Thus Quesada found himself absolute master of the Sabána of Bogotá. The Chibcha territory had been bounded on all sides by wild tribes, such as the Panches and Pijaos. For the present the Panche power was broken.

Being, as he was, a man of judgment, and having had his judgment fortified by experience, Quesada clearly saw his forces were not strong enough to undertake any further conquests, till he had reinforcements sent from Spain. He also saw it was of first importance, as did Pizarro and Cortés when they had found themselves in positions almost identical with his, to procure recognition of his *de facto* governorship from the Emperor Charles V. The title of marquess accorded to the conquerors of Mexico and Peru gave them great prestige with their followers, and this Quesada knew.

Even more important to him was to keep his popularity with his soldiers, so once again Quesada made a division of the spoil. He found he had about twenty thousand dollars' worth of gold and a considerable quantity of emeralds to distribute. Each man received his share. The chaplains seem to have been specially favoured[2] in the distribution. After it was over Padre Fray Domingo de las Casas, a

[1] Now called Sogamoso.
[2] No siendo de los menores la (porcion) que se dio á los capellanes, el Padre Juan de Lescames y el Padre Fray Domingo de las Casas.

Dominican, preached powerfully to the soldiers on the necessity of founding an oratory, with money for masses for the conquerors' souls, to be said in perpetuity. This he did, knowing that the gold and emeralds would soon be lost at cards.[1] This was the second time that the good friar had preached to the soldiers to give him money for an oratory. Either they were really moved by the preacher's eloquence, or else they thought their souls would require perpetual prayer to save them, for they once again contributed liberally. The sum they gave was three thousand dollars—no mean contribution. Quesada evidently was impressed by it, for he refers to it in his will, executed at Mariquita just before he died.[2] The oratory[3] was founded, but not until long after the conquest was achieved. There were so many difficulties about the money that in his will Quesada left specific directions as to this same oratory. A mass was to be sung on every Saturday for the repose of all the conquerors, either alive or dead,[4] throughout the period of Lent. At it there was to be a sermon[5] and a responsory, also a mass of requiem on the day when any conqueror died. In addition to all this, there were to be masses for the soul of every Indian chief who died during the conquest. Quesada would, without doubt, have given many masses to undo his cruelty or weakness in the matter of the death of Sagipá, for Piedrahita, quoting from the now lost writings of Quesada, says he regretted bitterly[6] what he

[1] "Antes que el oro y las esmeraldas que les habian tocado á los soldados, fuesen á sujetarse á la suerte del dado y naipe ": Fray Simon.

[2] February, 1579.   [3] Capellania.   [4] Vivos y difuntos.

[5] "Con sermon y responso." Quesada wrote a book of sermons for the chapel.

[6] "Entonces los Españoles le pedian ahincadamente que le tornasen de nuevo á reiterar los tormentos pedido con tanta porfia que el Licenciado (Quesada) se les entrego . . . y quien leyere este suceso en el Compendio Historial que escribió el mismo Adelantado [by that time Quesada had been made Adelantado of New Granada] tendra bien que lastimarse del sentimiento y dolor con que confiesa haber cooperado en la injusticia con el fin de complacer á su gente." " El Compendio Historial " was a history of the conquest written by Quesada. It is now lost, but existed in Piedrahita's time.

had done. It appears that Fray Domingo de las Casas, although a moving preacher, was not an exemplary character. Quesada says of him in his will that it was rumoured that El Padre de las Casas had kept[1] the money for himself. He goes on to say that the said friar had gone to Italy in an indecent[2] habit. Whether he took the money or no, it clearly was not forthcoming at the time Quesada made his will, for he devotes a portion of his own estate to found the oratory.

Before he returned to Spain, Quesada was determined to found a city on the Sabána of Bogotá.

He did not know that the Adelantado Lugo of Santa Marta was dead, therefore he determined to say nothing of his projected voyage to Spain. He intended, according to excerpts from his lost " Compendio Historial," quoted by Herrera and Piedrahita, to take all the gold and emeralds he had collected with him, knowing that at court no suitor thrives without a bag of gold to back his claims. By all the rules of fairness, he ought to have informed the Adelantado, his superior, seeing that he it was who fitted out the expedition. Still, he only followed the example of Cortés, who returned home to Spain to ask the Emperor Charles V. to confirm him in his generalship of Mexico, without informing Velazquez, the Governor of Cuba, who had sent him to explore.

In the case of Cortés there was more excuse for his behaviour, for Velazquez repented of his choice, and tried to thwart Cortés throughout the conquest. The Adelantado Lugo, on the contrary, treated Quesada most loyally, and it is little to his credit that he should have thought of slipping off to Spain upon the sly. Fate was upon his side on this occasion, and the mean action remained without completion, for in the year that had elapsed since Quesada parted from Lugo he had died, leaving his son Alonso to become Quesada's evil genius when he arrived in Spain.

[1] Habia quedado con el oro.
[2] "En habito indecente." Clearly Fray Domingo seems to have been " un abate danzante."

Above all things it was expedient for Quesada to lose no time in founding a city, so that upon arrival at the Spanish court he should be able to point out, that besides conquering the country, he had done something tangible towards settling it.

At once he set about to choose a site, and after hesitating for a little as to whether he should build at Tunja, he determined on the site of the old Indian town of Muequetá that to-day bears the name of Bogotá. Many things influenced him in his choice. In the first place it had been the capital of the Zipas (kings) of the Chibchas, and thus enjoyed a prestige with the Indians that a new city would have lacked. Then the situation was incomparable. Backed by its mountains that rise up behind it from the plain much in the same shape that Gibraltar rises from the sea, crossed by a river, that rushes from the hills, giving to some of the side streets a strangely rustic look, the city looks out over the Sabána, bounded, but in the far distance, by the sierras above Facatativá.

At sunrise, or on fine evenings, the distant peaks of El Ruiz and El Nevado de Tolima, running up to seventeen or eighteen thousand feet in height, are tinged with rose colour, when the rising or the setting sun falls on their eternal snowfields; during the day, they stand like sentinels. The actual place where he determined to erect his capital was at the village called Teusaquilla, that, in the Indian kingdom, had been a summer residence not far from Muequetá. A council was assembled at which all the captains gave their opinions upon the site. Their decision was unanimous, to build the city on the site it occupies to-day.

Stone was abundant in the hills for building, the air was good, the water excellent. Thus, there were all the requisites but one, that Spaniards of those days most looked for in their towns. Good bells[1] were lacking. They came in season, and no one can deny but that the inhabitants of Bogotá still make good use of them.

---

[1] The Spanish adage runs: "Buen aire, buenas aguas y buenas campanas."

There was another aspect of the situation that may have weighed both with Quesada and his captains. It was easily defensible—in fact, before artillery developed, practically impregnable.

Having come to a decision, Quesada mustered all his captains and his soldiers, and getting off his horse tore up a tuft of grass. Then, placing his right foot on the bare ground, he said, " I take possession of the land, in the name of the most serene Emperor Charles V." Then he remounted, and, drawing his sword, challenged anyone to deny his right, offering to uphold it, either on horseback or on foot. He then sheathed his sword, and told the notary of the army[1] to draw him up a deed of confirmation before witnesses. This done, he marked out the sites for twelve straw huts, for it was his intention at that time to leave only a detachment in his new-founded city, and take the bulk of his men with him as a bodyguard to Cartagena, where he proposed to find a ship for Spain.

The huts were built of canes by the Indians of the place, for by the virtue of their conquest all the soldiers had become gentlemen, and none cared overmuch to work. The roofs were thatched either with straw or palm-leaves, or with reeds cut on the river bank.

Tradition has it that Quesada built twelve huts to typify the twelve apostles. He did not forget to leave a space in the middle of the huts to build a church upon. On the site of the humble church they subsequently built, of the same materials as the huts, stands the cathedral of Bogotá.

Fray Simon makes the date of the foundation the month of August, 1538, but Castellanos, Piedrahita, and some others of the chroniclers fix it at 1539.

Thus Bogotá, like Rome, rose from a cluster of mere huts to be a city. There the resemblance ended, for Bogotá did not become the Rome of South America, but its Athens, a title for just pride.

It was now five months since Quesada had entered the Sabána of Bogotá: five most eventful months, during

---

[1] El Escribano del Ejercito.

whose course he had made his name for ever, and un-luckily for his fair fame had left an indelible blot upon his memory.

Being a native of Granada, or at least having passed his youth and early manhood in that city, he gave the name of New Granada to the country he had discovered and had subjugated. There is a certain look of Granada about Bogotá; not very strong, but perhaps sufficient for a conqueror upon foundation day.

The city does not stand upon a rocky height overhanging a deep river bed as does Granada; but it looks out over a fertile plain, and El Ruiz may well be set against Mulhacen. Both mountains are snow-capped, and both are features in the view. The hill of Suba is not unlike Monte Elvira behind Granada, and the city of Santa Fé, built by the Catholic kings during the siege, has an identical position with the town of Fontibón.

Colonel Acosta[1] sees an exact resemblance between the hill of Suacha and the hill known at Granada as the " Last Sigh of the Moor." Both cities enjoy incomparable panoramas, over the Vega in one case, and the Sabána in the other. Bogotá, like Granada, has a temperate climate, and in both places roses and pinks, carnations, jasmines, and all the flowers of Northern and of Southern Europe bloom extravagantly. The natural vegetation is not much dis-similar, for in both climates, oaks, elms, and ashes flourish, and blackberries, mint, thyme, sage, and pennyroyal all grow wild, or at the least in Bogotá have become wild, after having been introduced from Spain.

The day of foundation was " El Dia de la Transfiguracion,"[2] called by the vulgar the Feast of Christ.

The Spaniards of those days, who to the time of Charles V. had had perhaps the freest constitution of all Europe, enjoying privileges under their laws unknown in any other country, still held tenaciously to legal forms.

[1] P. 242.
[2] " El Dia de la Transfiguracion, que el vulgo llaman la Fiesta de San Salvador ": Fray Simon.

The very soldiers who had submitted to the authority of Quesada without a murmur, were now the first to demand a municipality for the new-founded town. For all that, Quesada did not at once establish any legal administration. He named no magistrates, with power of "knife[1] and gallows," and the rest of the matters that are important for the ruling of a state. Neither did he appoint a parish priest, leaving all these matters to be settled till his return from Spain, not thinking he would be twelve years absent from his new-founded town.

The first mass was celebrated in Bogotá upon the 6th of August, 1538; it is not known with accuracy by which of the two friars who had shared all the dangers and the hardships of the adventurous year. Quesada's first house is supposed to have occupied the site of the little Plaza de las Nieves in the modern Bogotá.

The conquest was now over, and the seal of the Spanish possession set upon the land by the foundation of the town. For the present nothing further was done towards the evangelization of the Indians, and their souls apparently were left in jeopardy. No voluntary conversion seems to have taken place after that of the Cacique of Subá.

All appears to have been quiet, when suddenly an incident occurred that touched Quesada on his weakest side, but in the end turned out most fortunately for him. All through his military career he had shown himself extremely jealous of the least encroachment on his authority. News was brought to him that in the country of the Laches[2] there was a temple, known as La Casa del Sol, richer by far than either that of Sogamoso or of Tunja.

The soldiers, always ready to believe all stories of the kind, besought Quesada earnestly to stay, and before undertaking his journey back to Spain, lead them to plunder it. They said they had heard the temple was so full of gold, that the

---

[1] "No nombró sin embargo el General Quesada justicia ni regidores, ni estableció horca ni cuchillo ni las demas cosas importantes al gobierno de una ciudad ": Fray Simon.

[2] This tribe had its territory on the right bank of the Magdalena, in La Tierra Caliente.

riches either of Crassus or of Crœsus[1] were as nothing to it. Either there was some tincture of the humanities amongst his men, or else it was the voice of the Italian soldier who had thought the conquering donkey Marobaré was an Olympian bird. Quesada did not want much urging upon such a quest. At once he determined to attempt the capture of the place. Had he but reflected, he might have known that to look for a golden temple on the Magdalena was a fool's errand, for any riches he had found were on the plains of Bogotá. He was preparing for a start; but fate had other things in store for him.

At the very moment of his departure, rumours reached him that Captain Lazaro Fonte had declared that on his arrival at Cartagena he would denounce Quesada for having concealed valuable emeralds that should have gone into the royal fifth.

Nothing was better calculated to lash Quesada into fury, for as regards the royal fifth he had been, and was, during the whole course of his life, most scrupulously exact. So much he prided himself on his exactitude in this respect, knowing that many of the conquerors had acted differently, that in his will he put a clause to testify that the king had never lost a dollar of his dues by any fault of his. This statement is the more credible by the general uprightness of his character, and his high standing with those who knew him best. When the rumour reached his ears, Quesada instantly put off his journey home, for in all things that touched his honour he was most ticklish. All might have passed off smoothly, for Captain Fonte was the soul of loyalty towards Quesada, as events very shortly showed; but most unluckily an Indian, either from spite or from some other cause, appeared and made a countercharge. He accused Captain Fonte of having bought emeralds from him and kept them for himself. Quesada instantly had Fonte brought before him, and after charging him with conspiring to defraud the king, he sentenced him to death. It was hard

---

[1] " Mientras se quedaban las riquezas de Crasso y de Creso ": Fray Simon.

justice, even supposing that the charge was true, for Fonte all through the expedition had been the first in any peril, and exposed his life to countless dangers in the service of the king.   Great was the amazement and the indignation of the soldiers, for all loved Fonte for his frank character and for his bravery.   It may be, too, that his great prowess as a horseman endeared him to them, for to the horsemen (after God) they owed the riches they had won.

The soldiers, headed by the other captains, besought Quesada earnestly to revoke the penalty and to spare Captain Fonte's life.   Although alone, and without force to carry out his sentence, he was inexorable.   No one except a priest can be so much unmoved by mere humanity, as is a lawyer, when the majesty of law is touched.   Captain Gonzalo Suarez then took up his parable, appealing to their general's generosity and sense of justice, that, as he said, had never been at fault.[1]   Then he recounted all Fonte's services, and said both officers and soldiers loved and respected him.   " Let not," he said, " your sense of justice be overclouded by a feeling of resentment at the false tales of lying[2] Indians.   We know they have said he has attacked your honour.   This our comrade denies, and we believe his word.   Even supposing he has sinned, the circumstances are exceptional.   We are far from Spain and cannot get recruits; and Captain Fonte is one of the best soldiers that you have; why sacrifice so good a soldier for a mere trumped-up tale ?   General, spare him, we all implore you on our knees."

Quesada would have been more than human, situated as he was, to disregard so moving and so well-reasoned an appeal.   He yielded none too willingly nor too generously,

---

[1] Captain Suarez seems to have forgotten the case of Sagipá, but then he was a " native."

[2] That the Spaniards thought the Indians great liars is evident from an extract from a MS. in " El Archivo Historico Nacional," Madrid (Papeles de Indias): " Es gente muy perdida por cantar y bailar á su modo . . . es gente muy mentirosa como toda la otra gente de Indias que nunca saben decir verdad "—a common fault in a conquered race.

showing more of the lawyer than of the soldier, in his reply to the appeal. Quesada had, like other men, the defects of his good qualities. His resolution was adamant, for none but a man sure of himself and certain of his authority could have ventured to proceed so far, against a man loved and respected as was Fonte, without even the formality of trial. This time his indomitable will betrayed him into a serious error, and showed his character in an unenviable light. It was the moment to have yielded gracefully and taken Fonte into favour—an act that would have endeared him to his followers. Instead of that, he spared his life, but banished him to Pasca, an Indian town that was not properly subdued.

The decision was not pleasing to his captains, for they saw that to send a man unarmed into a hostile town was to condemn him almost certainly to death. The captains did not actively protest, so great was the ascendancy Quesada wielded over them. However, they made a strong moral protest that Quesada evidently had no power to prevent.

Next morning, when poor Fonte was preparing, quite unarmed—for by a refinement of harshness he was not allowed to take arms with him—to set out on his exile, twenty-four horsemen[1] mounted and escorted him. It must have been bitter for Quesada to see the flower of his followers all mounted and well-armed turned out to escort the man he had sent into banishment.

Besides the horsemen, he had one admirer, an Indian girl, who bravely offered to accompany him. To this girl Lazaro Fonte owed his life, as Piedrahita says, most justly in this case, under God's providence. Who the girl was is quite uncertain, though writers in Colombia have given her the name of Zoratama, and built up quite a legend round her, giving her children by the man she saved. Perhaps she had been taken by his skill in horsemanship, as he was the best of all the Spanish riders in Quesada's host, or, what is still more probable, by his youth and gallantry.

[1] Veinte cuatro de á caballo.

When the band of horsemen, bearing Fonte in their midst, came to the town of Pasca, the Indians fled into the woods. In the deserted town Fonte was left alone, unarmed, but with the Indian girl to keep him company. The twenty-four[1] departed weeping,[2] thinking him as good as buried, as Piedrahita says. He passed the night in prayer, consoled but by his faith in the Blessed Virgin, and by the broken phrases[3] of the poor Indian girl.

At last, let the plan have come from one or other of them, the Indian it was who saved her master, and in the following way.[4]

As soon as it was light the Indian girl dressed herself up in her best finery to look as if she had been a Chibcha princess, with necklace, bracelets of beads, and feather diadem. Thus attired, and with the natural grace and air that she possessed,[5] she was prepared to meet the Chief of Pasca when he returned. The simple Churchman[6] who chronicles the episode would not have been astonished at the plan, " had not the Indian girl been an infidel,[7] for after all it was the same stratagem that occurred to Esther, to placate the wrath of King Ahasuerus in the Scriptures." Fidelity, or infidelity, except in regard to Captain Fonte, does not seem to have been what actuated the Indian heroine.

At the first streaks of dawn the Indians by twos and threes began to straggle back into the town. With what interior tremors the strangely assorted pair, the sole inhabitants of the deserted place, regarded them, can be imagined easily enough. The Indians on their side, seeing a princess (cacica) from Bogotá, stood still, not daring to advance.

The Indian Esther instantly addressed them, saying, " Come into your town, my friends, we are not enemies. This Spaniard is a good man, so good that he detests all

---

[1] Los veinte cuatro.   [2] Con lagrimas.
[3] Las mal contadas razones que le dió la India.
[4] " A fin saliese la traza de lo uno ó de lo otro, la India la tuvó para librar á su amo de esta manera ": Fray Simon.
[5] Que con esto y el buen cuerpo y buen natural que tenia.
[6] Fray Simon.
[7] Si esta India no fuese infiel.

war.[1] On this account his chief wanted to kill him. He has been exiled to this town, and now asks me to say that he trusts to your generosity."   The girl's words made a great impression on the Indians. She was of a good figure and well-graced person, qualities that quite as often carry conviction with them, as do mere arguments. The chief, through the medium of the girl, who knew a little Spanish,[2] said, " Captain, Son of the Sun, be of good cheer. We know the reason of your coming. Therefore, consider this your home, and ask for anything that is in our power to give."

The story reflects credit on all concerned. The simple love and ready wit of the Indian girl[3] were only matched by the generosity of the Chief of Pasca, who, having got one of his enemies into his hands, treated him as a son.

Whilst Fonte and his Indian " Esther " lived out their involuntary idyll in the town of Pasca, a meeting, stranger than anything of the same kind that history records, was to take place by a concatenation of hardly possible events, upon the plains of Bogotá.

[1] It seems a little difficult to look at Lazaro Fonte as a pacifist.

[2] Era algo ladina de nuestra lengua.

[3] There are many instances of Spaniards having been saved and assisted by Indian women, preserved in the annals of the conquest. Bernal Diaz del Castillo has told the loves of Cortés and La Malinche, the Indian princess who acted as his interpreter, and to whom he owed so much (" Historia Verdadera de la Conquista de la Nueva España," por el Capitan Bernal Diaz del Castillo). There is also a moving story in the " Comentarios Reales " of Garcilasso de la Vega (p. 210), of the fidelity of an Indian girl at the battle of Huarina, in the war of the Pizarros: " Entre los cuales â poco mas de un quarto de legua del Real alcanço un Español herido que iba sobre un Rocinejo de poca cuenta, y entre otras heridas, llevava una encima del Riñon derecho, iba cavallero echado sobre el percuezo del Rocin, porque no podia ir enhiesto. Una India de su servicio iba con el à pie, llevava la mano izquierda en la herida de su Señor, y en la derecha un palillo, con que iba aguijando el Rocin, y decia á su amo, ' Esfuercate Señor á huir destos traidores y no temas que yo te deje hasta verte sano.' "

CHAPTER XIII

AT the time of Quesada's expedition[1] Sebastian de Belalcazar was governor for Pizarro at Quito, a city that he himself had founded in 1534.[2]

Belalcazar was one of the most remarkable of all the conquerors. His life was like a fairy-tale. It is not known with certainty what his original surname was; but his Christian name was Sebastian. All that is known of his early life is that he was born at the little town of Belalcazar in Estremadura, that nursery of the conquerors. His father was a woodman, and the young Sebastian used to be sent to sell wood, that was loaded on a donkey, about the little town. One day the ass stuck in a mud hole, and Sebastian struck him on the head with a stick and killed him instantly. Being afraid to return home, he went to Cadiz, arriving there in the year 1514, and shipped abroad the fleet that the celebrated Pedrarias Davila was fitting out to take him to his government of Panama. Sebastian, who must have been about fourteen at the time, for he was not quite seventy when he died in 1550, refused to give his name or had forgotten it. His comrades, therefore, called him Sebastian de Belalcazar,[3] and by that name he became famous, both in New Granada and Peru. Almost as soon as he arrived in Panama he had the opportunity to show his worth.

Being upon an expedition with Pedrarias Davila, they lost their way in one of the great, virgin forests in which

[1] 1538–9.

[2] It had been, of course, an Inca capital, but Belalcazar had founded a Spanish city there.

[3] The Inca Garcilasso de la Vega says of him: " Sebastian de Belalcazar de su alcuña se llamaba Moyana, tomó el nombre de la Patria, por ser mas famoso " (" Comentarios Reales del Peru," Madrid, 1722).

the isthmus still abounds. Provisions were exhausted, and though Pedrarias set several soldiers to climb high trees to see if they could find a landmark by which to steer themselves out of the labyrinth, they could see nothing. Despair was settling on them, when the young Sebastian from a treetop saw a thin smoke in the far distance, invisible to any eyes but his. He led the expedition towards it, and it proved to have been the camp fire of some Indians, who showed them the way home. As in the Indians' camp there was some gold, Pedrarias adjudged this to Sebastian for his services. He refused it, saying he had but done his duty, and as all had suffered equally, all should share in the gold. From that day he began to make his mark. He became a friend both of Pizarro and Almagro; was sent to Nicaragua by Pedrarias Davila, and helped to found the city of Leon, and was its first Alcalde for a year or two. Tiring of a quiet life, he went with some companions to Peru. There he rose high in the service of Francisco Pizarro, who sent him as his lieutenant to Quito to found a capital. When there he seems to have made himself quite independent of Pizarro, conquering new territories, and much loved and respected by his soldiers, for he was courteous with everyone and, above all, disinterested in money matters, a rare thing in those times. Of middle stature, but well proportioned, Belalcazar had an expressive face, small eyes, and kindly aspect, though on occasions[1] he could show severity if it was required.

To this notable captain in his government of Quito, where he lived in considerable state and splendour, one day an Indian presented himself with the kind of tale no conquistador ever could resist. It was the story of El Dorado (The Golden Man), but mixed up with another of a golden city, the Indian who brought it having seen the ceremony of the gold-anointed chief plunging into the Lake of Guata-

---

[1] " Fué Belalcazar mediano de cuerpo pero bien proporciando, de ojos pequeños, rostro expresivo pero mostrando en ocasiones la severidad que era menester ": " Descubrimiento de la Nueva Granada," Colonel Joaquin Acosta, p. 373.

vita in his youth. In the years he had been wandering from tribe to tribe, he had added to and adorned his tale.

Belalcazar, although he was well established in Peru, the richest country in those days, of the Americas, at once sent out Captain Ampudia to prepare the way. Ampudia started from Quito, marched to Pasto, and from there to Popayán.[1] From Popayán he went to Cali, where Belalcazar overtook him with a well-appointed expedition, well mounted and well armed.

Belalcazar did not approve the site Captain Ampudia had selected for a new town, and ordered it to be abandoned, and pushed on rapidly towards the land of the gold temples and the Golden Chief. He found the difficulties in front of him so great that he determined to return to Quito and render an account of all that he had seen to Francisco Pizarro, his superior in command. Before he started, he founded Popayán and Cali, choosing a better site for the latter than that Ampudia had marked out. Pizarro confirmed him in his office of Governor of Quito; but Belalcazar made up his mind to return secretly to Spain, and get himself made Governor of Popayán. After a year or two he again set out for the land of El Dorado, and in due course arrived at Neiva. There he marched down the Magdalena to a place called Fortabecillas,[2] and learned from the Indians that other Spaniards had been there before him, but had now gone away.

News was soon brought to Quesada in his new town of Bogotá, by a friendly Indian, of the arrival of his countrymen. The Indian told him that the newcomers were far better dressed and armed than he was and far more numerous. What Quesada thought can be imagined easily. His troops were few, his powder had run out, his crossbowmen were short of bolts, his men without defensive armour, and his

[1] Pasto and Popayán are two old towns in Colombia, very clerical in their aspect. The latter has given rise to the Colombian proverb, " Todo el mundo es Popayán," meaning the world is much the same everywhere.

[2] The name is so curious that it may very likely be a mistake or a misprint.

position insecure. Of one thing he was sure, of the fidelity of all his followers. They all were men accustomed to face odds, immune to every climate, and had made friends amongst the Indians on whom they could rely.

Honour demanded that he should return to Santa Marta. Interest summoned him to Spain to secure a grant of all the country he had conquered and explored. Belalcazar's coming disarranged his plans. He was not long in making up his mind, but sent his brother Hernan Perez, with Captains Cespedes and Colmenares, to see how the land lay. As they marched onwards to Neiva, their Indian guide picked up some arrows by the way, and, showing them to Hernan Perez, said, " These are Peruvian arrows, and quite unlike to those we use." This made the captains cautious, and just outside the camp they hid themselves in a thick cane-brake beside a river's bank. As they lay hidden in the canes, one of the scouts of Belalcazar's army rode up carelessly. His horse saw better than himself, or perhaps smelt the other horses hidden amongst the reeds. He snorted violently, reared, and set off towards the camp, his rider shouting as he rode, " To arms, the enemy is here !" Captains Cespedes and Colmenares, seeing they were discovered, rode boldly towards the Peruvian camp. Belalcazar sent out a band of horsemen to meet the band of twenty that he saw advancing, as it were, from the clouds. Not having any warning of their coming, he not unnaturally took them for enemies.

The opposing horsemen drew up some twenty paces from each other and exchanged salutes. Then, after explanations, the leader of the Peruvian cavalry rode out, and, taking Captain Colmenares by the hand, welcomed him cordially. They all saluted, and with great courtesies[1] rode hand in hand up to the general. He received them cautiously[2] and assigned them tents.

Belalcazar had just come from Peru, and under the Pizarros' rule, faction ran high, and the various parties often fought furiously, giving scant quarter on either side. There-

---

[1] Hubo grandes cortesias.   [2] Con gusto sagaz.

fore, it is not to be wondered at that, in spite of his frank character, he was upon his guard. Quesada's captains were equally inspired with caution, and the first night there was but little sleep throughout the camp.

It was, indeed, a strange and fateful meeting in the wilds. The war-worn veterans of Quesada must have been at least as astonished at the fat horses, plumed helmets, shining arms, and retinue of servants, as were Belalcazar's followers at the lean, sunburnt mummies on their unkempt horses, with ropes for bridles and saddles made of skins.

Hernan Perez de Quesada and Belalcazar soon made friends with one another, for they were of the same adventurous breed. Both were fine soldiers, both respected by their men, and both of them sanguinary in their dealings with the Indians, though neither was a religious bigot, as were so many of the conquerors. Belalcazar, always open-handed and generous, as all the chroniclers confess of him, offered his new-made friend horses, arms, and money, and promised to furnish a contingent to assist him in his conquests. Hernan Perez on his side had nothing of equal value in his power; but he gave all that he had—that is, some plates of gold and Indian cloths. He invited Belalcazar to go on to Bogotá to meet his brother there. Both chiefs were naturally a little cautious as to their future movements, for neither knew that he might not fall into some ambuscade upon the road; but outwardly, between them, all was harmony.

Some of the soldiers upon either side were not so cautious, but talked openly of a resort to arms to settle which party should possess the land, as each were conquerors. Neither band of adventurers seems to have considered that the Indians came into the scheme of the creation, or, if they had come, were, as it might be, stowaways who had no business on the ship. These murmurs reached the ears of Captain Juan de Cespedes, who said in a loud voice: " Gentlemen, into these lands that we have conquered, no one shall enter, but at the lance's point." Luckily for the future peace of the two conquering bands, the man who replied to him was one Captain Juan Cabrera, who, for a wonder, for he was a man who had fought all through the wars of the Pizarros in Peru, answered him peacefully.

" I hope," he said, " this matter will not go to the decision of the sword, for well I know how much it costs to conquer even a small territory. Therefore, it is not well that we, who have endured such dangers, should turn our swords against each other's breasts." Then, taking his hat in hand, he advanced towards Cespedes, saying, " May I ask your worship's name ?"

Spaniards of those days, who had such long and frequent dealings with the Moors, had imbibed, most likely unknown to themselves, many of the peculiarities of the Arabs, who, if once brought to parley, but rarely come to blows. So it was in this case. The rival captains braved·one another, quite in the Homeric style, and afterwards made friends.

" I am called Juan de Cespedes," said Quesada's captain, " better known than rue.[1] My name is known throughout the Indies, both by land and sea."

Cabrera, not to be outdone, rejoined: " The smell of rue has never reached my nostrils, for I am but a poor captain known as Cabrera, son of neglect and of my works."[2]

Having thus braved each other, quite in Pistol's vein, these two valiant ancients saluted one another and fell back into the ranks. The soldiers laughed, and no doubt said they were a pair of Andalucians, and once more friendship reigned.

For his part Belalcazar had no desire to fight, for he had conquered the enormous territory between Quito and Popayán, almost without a blow. He knew he had enemies behind him in the shape of the Pizarros, who must by this time be aware of his desertion of them, and it was no part of his plan to make new enemies who might bar his way to Spain. Still, he could not make up his mind to march to

---

[1] " Mas conocido que la ruda." An old Spanish saying that has never been satisfactorily explained, except that rue is a common plant in the Castiles. The Scotch say " as fusionless as a docken " with apparently as little reason.

[2] Hijo del olvido y de mis obras.

Bogotá. Perhaps he feared to be attacked upon the way, or perhaps thought that Quesada would make terms with him if he hung back a little.

Hernan Perez returned to Bogotá to report all that had occurred, and to take counsel with his brother as to their next move.

It is not to be wondered at that these two conquerors were very cautious of their dealings with one another. Spain was so far removed by time and distance that the central authority was very slack, and in most cases could only exercise a moral influence, for the kings of Spain had not resources to fit out expeditions to reduce revolting governors. In the case of the Licentiate La Gasca in Peru, he arrived without a single soldier, and raised an army solely by his own force of character[1] under the ægis of the king.

All the time this curious and unexpected meeting of Belalcazar and Hernan Perez de Quesada was taking place, poor Captain Lazaro Fonte still was in exile, with the Indian girl who had preserved his life for sole companion. As he lived quietly, and gave himself no airs of being a

[1] La Gasca was a priest who belonged to the Inquisition. Charles V. chose him to go to Peru and raise an army against Gonzalo Pizarro, who had rebelled against his authority and wished to separate Peru from Spain. La Gasca left Spain almost alone, and without much previous knowledge of affairs, except what he had gained when employed in negotiation in the affair of the rebellion of the Moriscos in Granada. The emperor gave him letters to all his governors to furnish him with horses, ships, and men. He was a man of superior abilities, though of extraordinary appearance. Fray Francisco de Gómara, in his " Historia General de las Indias," says: " He was a man of better understanding than he appeared. He was very small of body, and of a strange build. From the waist down, he had as much body as a tall man, and from the waist to the shoulder not the third part of an ordinary man. On horseback he appeared smaller than he was, for he was all legs. His face was very ugly, but Nature, that had denied him gifts of body, doubled them in his mind." The Inca Garcilasso de la Vega says of him (" Comentarios Reales," lib. v. de la ii. parte, p. 269): " . . . sus haçañas que aunque no fueron de lança y espada, fueron de prudencia y consejo." With these gifts of prudence and counsel he utterly defeated Gonzalo Pizarro, who was a brave soldier and accomplished leader, and saved Peru for the emperor.

"conquistador," and possibly because of the presence of the Indian girl with him, the Indians trusted him, and by degrees began to look on him as one of their own tribe.

News travels quickly amongst the Indians, as it does amongst the Arab tribes, and even to-day in districts inhabited by a purely Indian population, news seems to be carried on as if by magic, passing from tribe to tribe. One day an Indian arrived at the village where Captain Fonte lived to report to his chief that, whilst out hunting, he had come upon a band of Spaniards with dogs and horses, such as those owned by Quesada and his men. The Indian reported that the Spaniards were all dressed in skins of animals, and that they were lean and travel-worn. He said they were encamped only six leagues away.

Lazaro Fonte's first thought was for Quesada's safety, for he was one of those who bear no malice in their soul. He took a piece of polished deerskin, and with red ochre and the juice of bija[1] wrote to Quesada in the following terms: "My Lord, I have had certain news that a band of Spaniards is at hand. They are coming from the Llanos.[2] They are close by and will arrive here to-morrow. Let your worship determine quickly what measures to take."[3]

It was an honourable and 'a generous letter, for, situated as he was, Fonte could have given infinite trouble to Quesada had he been so inclined. Certainly he had been most unjustly treated, and that he was alive to write and warn his chief was a mere accident, due to the devotion of the Indian girl.

An Indian gave the letter to Quesada just six days after his brother's meeting with Belalcazar in the Neiva valley.

Quesada had need of all his diplomatic talent, and, luckily for him, his popularity with his soldiers now stood him in good stead. However, none knew better than himself how few they were, and how much the privations

[1] "Vija y almagre."
[2] "Los Llanos"—*i.e.*, the plains on the Meta and Orinoco.
[3] "Mi señor nueva cierta he tenido que viene gente española, por los Llanos; que esta cerca y que llegaran de aquí a mañana. Vea vuestra merced lo que se debe hacer": Fray Simon.

of the past year had worn them out. Moreover, he was out of powder, and his arms in bad condition; but his supply of horses still was excellent. He had no knowledge of the numbers of either of the advancing bands, for Belalcazar had taken care that Hernan Perez and the two captains who accompanied him should have no real access to his camp. Of the band that Captain Fonte warned him was advancing from an opposite direction he had less knowledge still. One thing was certain, that, if the two converging armies joined to attack him, he would have no chance.

As was habitual with him, throughout his life he rose at once to the occasion when a difficulty appeared. Without delay he had his best horse saddled, and ordered every horseman that he had to mount and ride with him and make a formidable show. Then he set forth upon one of the most memorable of all his rides, accompanied by Captains Juan de Junco, Gonzalo Jimenez Rondón, Pedro Fernandez Valenzuela, and one may suppose by Captains San Martin and Cespedes, for he chose only those in whom his confidence was sure.

As they passed Pasca he sent a soldier with a horse and arms to Lazaro Fonte, who no doubt was waiting anxiously. Unluckily none of the chroniclers tells us how, once more armed and mounted, Fonte galloped to meet Quesada, pulling his horse up on its haunches and saluting with his lance before he fell into the ranks. He must have done so, as he was the finest horseman in the expedition, and through those war-worn, thinly peopled ranks a murmur of welcome must have run, as their old comrade reappeared. What happened to the Indian girl the chroniclers, often so full of detail on less interesting points, have left untold, perhaps, as Churchmen, not thinking such an episode, now that the girl had played her part, worthy the chronicling. What they have said is that in the future Quesada treated Fonte generously, keeping him always in attendance on his person and furthering his advance.

Hardly had Quesada and his band of horsemen been joined at Pasca by Lazaro Fonte, once more equipped as a Spanish gentleman and restored to favour, than up rode a strange skinclad figure on a thin, way-worn horse. The rider's hair was long, his beard unkempt, and he was roughly dressed in ill-cured deerskins. He said his name was Pedro Limpias, an old conqueror of Venezuela.[1]

As Quesada and his men were looking at him in amazement he announced himself as an advance rider of the expedition of Captain Don Nicolas Federman, of German nationality, and the lieutenant-general of Don Jorge Aspira,[2] Governor in Venezuela for the Emperor Charles V.

Neither Quesada nor the skinclad Captain Limpias had heard of the other's expedition, and Belalcazar had not heard of either of them, so that the meeting of the three generals—Quesada, Federman, and Belalcazar—in the middle of a continent, starting as they had done from points so far from one another, reads like a fairy-tale.

Quesada had set out from Santa Marta on the Caribbean Sea, and Belalcazar from the town of Quito in Peru. Federman, starting from Coro in Venezuela, had traversed all the Llanos, crossed the Andes at the pass of Suma Paz, and after three years' wandering in the wilds had reached the plains of Bogotá.

Nothing so strange as was the meeting of the three fateled generals could have been imagined, and certainly no expeditions had endured more hardships than those that Federman and Quesada led in the whole conquest of America.

How Federman, a German, came to be leading Spanish soldiers is a strange episode. The Emperor Charles V., himself a Fleming, had granted lands in Venezuela to the great banking house of the Weltzers, known to the Spaniards as " Los Belzeres," sometimes " Los Velzeres."

The Weltzers[3] sent out a German colony, and in command

---

[1] Un antiguo conquistador de Venezuela.

[2] " Jorge de Aspira "—that is, George of Spires.

[3] Fray Francisco de Gómara, in his " Historia General de las Indias," p. 60, is very indignant about this action of Charles V. He says: " La Reina Isabel no consentió pasar á Indias hombre que no fué su vasallo. . . . El emperador (Carlos V.) abrió la puerta á los Alemanes y estrangeros en el comercio que hizo con los Belçares."

of it a certain general, one George of Spires. The Spaniards called him Jorge de Espira,[1] and by that transformation of his name he is universally known to all the chroniclers. This George of Spires, himself a prudent governor and a man of great humanity, had for a general one Alfinger, a brave man, but more bloodthirsty than the most cruel of the Spaniards. When he saw that Alfinger was disgracing him,[2] he appointed Nicholas Federman to lead the next expedition that he fitted out. Federman was very popular with the soldiers, although a foreigner. No commander showed himself more humane in his treatment of the Indians, and few, except Quesada and Cortés, were called upon to face more perils or more hardships.

He is described as of medium stature, red-bearded, and very active and enduring,[3] very valiant and adventurous. Starting from Coro, he went to the Cabo de la Vela to try his luck at pearl fishing, but without success. He then set out to discover and to conquer territory, apparently with no fixed plan,[4] or the least idea where he was going to.

Following the shores of the Lake of Maracaibo, and passing marshes so treacherous that men and horses disappeared in them, keeping the cordillera of the Andes always in sight, to guide himself by, he struggled on for a whole year. Finding game scarce, and hearing it was more

[1] Sometimes "Aspira." The Spaniards of those days altered proper names to suit their own pronunciation, making of Cavendish, Candish; Hawkins, Aquino; and Frobisher, Ofrisba. We ourselves did the same with their names, and turned La Coruña into The Groyne, Bilbao into Bilboa, and sometimes Bilbo.

[2] Herrera says of George of Spires that he was "hombre honrado y cristiano, templado y de buena condicion." This is confirmed by the fact that when Judge Navarro was sent from Spain to examine into his affairs (in Spanish this was called "tomarle la residencia") he found nothing at all against him, a most unusual thing, in those days, to happen to a Spanish governor in the Indies. Jorge de Espira remained Governor of Venezuela till his death in 1545.

[3] "Descubrimiento de la Nueva Granada," Colonel Joaquin Acosta, p. 162.

[4] He may have followed "where the Holy Ghost did lead," after the fashion of the good missionary to the Californias, Fray Marcos de Niza.

abundant in the plains, he left the foothills of the Andes and plunged into the vast and grassy Llanos of the Casanáre, that stretch out like a sea. Rivers innumerable that have no name on any map cut them in all directions, and marshes intersect them, whose paths are known but to the wandering Indians and the rude herdsmen of the plains. Great cane-brakes, so tall that a man on horseback disappears completely in them, spring up on the rivers' banks, and clumps of the Moriche palm, slender and feathery as ostrich plumes, are scattered here and there. Even to-day the traveller who loses his direction perishes. He wanders up and down until his horse is either eaten by a tiger, escapes at night, or falls down dead from sunstroke and fatigue. Then the doomed man wanders round in a circle, till at last he sits down with his back against a palm-tree, and is found months afterwards a skeleton, his flesh devoured by the wild beasts, or a dry mummy shrivelled by the sun.

How Federman kept his direction in such a labyrinth of streams and marshes seems a miracle. Even Quesada had the River Magdalena as a guide; but Federman, when he had lost the Andes from his view, was like a shipwrecked sailor set afloat upon the sea, without a compass or a chart. The Indians whom he met were far more warlike than those Quesada met upon the Magdalena, and attacked perpetually, killing his horses and his men.

Three years of travel and of wandering to and fro reduced his force, from the four hundred who had set out with him from Coro, to but a hundred men. These were ill-fed and fever-stricken. Their clothes had long dropped off in rags, rotted by the perpetual rain and the hot sun, and to replace them they had contrived rough hose and doublets from the skins of animals. Most of them were bareheaded, pro-tected from the sun by their long shaggy hair, that they wore loose upon their shoulders after the Indian style. Their horses all were lean and went unshod, for their shoes long ago had dropped off in the mud. Burs filled their manes and tails, and ticks stuck on their skins, looking like gooseberries. Still, neither Federman nor any of his men lost heart, but struggled onward, always pushing towards the south. Wonderful to relate, in all their sufferings, and pushed by hunger as they were, they saved some cocks and hens they carried with them, and these lived to be the ancestors of the domestic fowls of Bogotá.

Whether Federman went by design back to the Andes, tired of his wanderings in the plains of Casanáre, or whether after striking the Rio Meta he followed it, hoping that it would lead to somewhere out of the interminable plains, none of the writers on the conquest seem to know. At last he reached the Indian town of Pasacote, between which and Pasca lies the pass called Suma Paz. Over the awful precipices of that trail, never used since his passage, by horsemen, or by mules, he hauled his horses up with ropes. Then, camping to rest his followers and find out where he was, he sent out Captain Limpias with a few men, who to his astonishment met Quesada, who had had notice of his coming by Fonte's messenger.

Quesada's men had been abashed before the splendour of the Peruvians, all dressed in silks and in well-woven cloth from Perpignan.[1] When they saw Federman's skin-covered starvelings, they felt like kings, dressed in their Indian cloths.

Many of Quesada's captains were moved to tears when they beheld the miserable state of the newcomers, and learned that of four hundred men who had set out from Coro only a hundred had survived. They asked about their friends, for in the ranks of Federman were many who had served with them in other conquests, and to their inquiries always received the answer, " Killed by the Indians, or perished of hunger and of thirst."

News was sent off at once to Quesada of their arrival, and he, who did not fear them as he feared the well-equipped Peruvians, set off at once, met and received them hospitably. He gave them Indian cotton cloths to hide their nakedness, and baskets full of food. Then, being a sagacious man, and knowing how much appearances influence mankind, he sent for all the tributary Indian chiefs to come at

[1] Perpiñanes.

once to him, bringing their best-dressed followers with music and with flags. Quesada then formed them into squadrons with his own infantry upon their flank. He himself on horseback led the way, with martial music—that is, a soldier beat upon their solitary drum, and Indians blew their war whistles and sounded blasts on conches brought from the sea-coast.

Federman and his ragged regiment stood to their miserable arms, thinking they were about to be attacked by the imposing army that was advancing on them. Seeing he was mistaken, he rode out on a half-starved horse, seated upon a deerskin saddle, and met Quesada, who advanced before his men to welcome him. Then both got off their horses and embraced with courtesies and compliments such as gentlemen[1] use on such occasions, and taking one another by the hand rode back to Bogotá.

The next two or three days were passed in feasting, and in running at the ring and other sports on horseback,[2] such as the " game of canes."

Quesada soon found out that in Federman he had a man, perfectly honest, and of a noble, open nature, and made a friend of him.

Moreover, he had no need to stand in any fear of him, for he had but a hundred followers, half starved and ill equipped. Yet, as he still was doubtful of the Peruvians,[3] though without reason, for Belalcazar was the soul of generosity, he drew up an agreement with Federman in which he undertook to share all future conquests with him, and assist him with his arms.

After the days of feasting and of sports were over, news

[1] Con palabras hidalgas.

[2] " Juegos de á caballo." La Sortija (running at the ring) was much practised by the Spaniards of those days, and also El Juego de Cañas (the game of canes). This was a sport they had inherited from the Moors, and was always played with the Moorish saddle with short stirrups, known in Spain as " La silla á la gineta." It consisted in an imitation of a battle with javelins, and the players threw canes at one another, to simulate the javelins used by the Moors.

[3] " Los Peruleros," as the Spaniards of those days called Peruvians. The proper word is " Peruanos."

was brought in to Bogotá that Belalcazar and his Peruvians were a short league away.

They came on gallantly riding their fine Peruvian horses, their bright, steel corslets glittering in the sun, their helmets with their plumes all fluttering in the wind, their silks and " perpiñanes " making a brave show.

Both Quesada's and Federman's soldiers were so badly clothed, their arms so rusted, and their half-bare skins so tanned by sunburn and so rough with mosquito bites, that the Peruvians looked on them with amazement, hardly recognizing them for their own countrymen.

Belalcazar and Federman became friends at once, and Quesada's singular[1] aptitude for diplomacy no doubt contributed to the peaceful attitude that their relations immediately assumed.

There was, indeed, almost a certainty that three[2] such men, accustomed to command, who had been for so long a time a law unto themselves, would quarrel, situated as they were.

It is possible that Belalcazar was the most brilliant commander, as he had experience in the Pizarro's wars of fighting on a greater scale than any that had fallen to the lot either of Quesada or of Federman. The latter was a man, easy to agree with, open-handed, large-hearted, and without malice in his composition, brave and upright as his sword.

Quesada evidently had the keenest judgment and the most diplomatic brain.

Curiously enough, all three of them were in the same position in respect to their superiors. Quesada had intended to deceive the Adelantado Don Pedro de Lugo, and slip off to Spain without his knowledge to get the emperor to confirm him in his government. Belalcazar was actually upon the road to Spain, without Pizarro's knowledge or

---

[1] " La prudencia del General Jimenez de Quesada, que la tenia singular para negocios arduos ": Fray Simon.

[2] The old Spanish saying ran: " Dos gorriones en una espiga hacen mala liga." Fray Simon says: " Three sparrows would make a worse job of it."

consent. Federman also had gone away from Coro during the absence of his superior, Jorge de Espira, but, as it appears, had no idea of slipping off to Spain.

This memorable meeting took place in February, 1539, according to Fray Simon, and in 1540, if we accept the date given by other chroniclers.[1]

The three conquistadores remained in Bogotá until the month of May of the same year, resting from their hardships, employed in sports, in feasting and the chase. They chiefly hunted deer, and these they chased on horseback, killing them with their spears. The sport must have required good horses, and the deer must have been both tame and plentiful. This lancing of the deer on horseback was a favourite diversion of the conquistadores. Cortés, upon his journey to Honduras, engaged in it, and also Alvar Nuñez on his journey up the Paraguay. The latter even landed his horses from the ships to engage in hunting, passed a day or two in sport, then re-embarked the horses and went on up the stream.

All their time was not spent in hunting, for they held frequent councils, and at one of them Belalcazar, who was the most experienced of the three in American affairs, advised Quesada to found more towns in his new government. He pointed out that the neglect to found towns in Venezuela had caused that colony's want of progress, and had allowed the Indian tribes to become powerful again.

He dwelt upon the difficulty there would always be in navigating the great River Magdalena to the sea, without more towns upon its banks. Ships could refit if these were ports, he said, and get provisions, whilst the garrisons patrolled the river in their boats to keep the passage clear.

Let but towns once be built, and people soon will flock to them, as it has happened in Peru.

I have, he said, no intention of staying here, but intend to return to Spain to ask the " unconquered Cæsar "[2]

---

[1] Piedrahita, Castellanos, etc.

[2] El invictísimo César.

(Charles V.) to make me Governor of Popayán, the land that I have won.

Quesada saw the force of his advice, and acted on it, having been spurred on to greater energy by news that Belalcazar had received of the death of the Adelantado Don Pedro de Lugo, an event that seemed to better his position with the authorities in Spain. His first act was to improve his capital, for nothing further had been done since the twelve miserable huts were built, and the whole place looked like an Indian " rancheria," squalid and miserable.

Streets, squares, and public buildings all were planned, and the whole town laid out, just where it stands to-day on the same plan of the first conquerors.

This done, in the month of April (1539–40 ?) Quesada named the first Alcaldes, who were Jeronimo de la Inza and Juan de Arrévalo. The Regidores[1] were his chief captains, Juan de San Martin, Cespedes, Antonio Diaz Cardoso, and Captain Lazaro Fonte, now restored to grace. Baltazar Maldonado he named Alguacil Mayor[2] of Bogotá. Hernan Perez de Quesada was appointed Alguacil Mayor of the whole conquered territory, and lieutenant-general to the governor. The notary public was one Juan Rodriguez de Benavides, who now exchanged the sword and crossbow for the pen, as a more lethal instrument.

Then came the consecration of the church, under the title of La Concepcion de Nuestra Señora, that it still bears to-day. The first priest of the new-made parish was one Juan Rellejo, a bachelor of arts. For an assistant he had Fray Vicente Requesada; both came with Federman.

Little by little the miserable huts gave place to houses built of bricks; but bricks[3] dried in the sun. The first tiled house was built by Captain Colmenares, and it may possibly still stand in some forgotton quarter of the town.

---

[1] Roughly speaking, Alcaldes and Regidores correspond to Justices of the Peace and Aldermen.

[2] High Constable.

[3] " Adobe y tapia." Adobes are bricks dried in the sun. Tapia is a wall built of " pisé." The word is a corruption of the Arabic " tabieh."

Whilst the new town was slowly rising from the ground, at the port of Tocaima on the Magdalena, a ship was being built, to take the generals down to Cartagena on their return to Spain.

When all was ready for the start, Quesada named his brother his lieutenant-general during his absence, giving him, like a prudent lawyer as he was, two titles to the office: one from himself as the discoverer and conqueror of the land, and one as lieutenant-general of Don Pedro de Lugo, in case he still should be alive.

Lastly, in order to make his own position sure, he got himself elected governor by the town council of the newly founded city, till his return from Spain.

He left instructions to Captains Gonzalo Suarez de Rondon to found a town in Tunja, the scene of his first exploit, and Captain Galiano had his command to found in Velez;[1] these orders, they both executed.

The last scene that took place before the three generals were ready to depart was the sale of their horses, arms, and slaves, guns, crossbows, "perpignans," and silks by Belalcazar's men. Poor Federman had nothing to dispose of but his horses, and these sold well, a reasonable horse[2] fetching a thousand dollars and the best two thousand, whilst even those in poor condition, that had come all the way from Coro, commanded a good price.

All was now ready, and Quesada, after having gathered everyone together, addressed them movingly. He spoke of all the dangers they had shared together; of all the hardships they had undergone, the hunger, thirst, the battles with the Indians, and how at last fortune had brought them safely into the promised land.

Lastly, he took farewell of everybody, enjoining peace,

---

[1] Tunja is now a curious, old-fashioned town, full of churches. Velez is the capital of the department of Santander, and is a thriving and important place. Herrera says of it (Decada V., p. 45: Madrid, 1601): "Es tierra adonde caian infinitos cayos . . . y no caen tantos despues que en ella assiste el Santísimo Sacramento del Altar: tiene un ' bolcon ' que echa muchas piedras."

[2] Razonable caballo.

goodwill, and fellowship upon them, promising to advance their interests at home, and speedily return.[1] Then, for the last time he mounted, and slowly rode out of the city he had founded, that he was destined not to see again for twelve long years, with the whole population crowding round his horse.

Accompanied by Federman and Belalcazar, whose soldiers nearly all insisted upon going with them to the port, Quesada set his face towards Tocaima,[2] where the new ship was waiting for them.

At Tocaima they embarked, and at their shoving off from shore, the sound of weeping mingled with the " Vivas " that the soldiers shouted to their departing friend and general.

Slowly the new-built vessel felt the current, and as the Indian " bogas " strained upon their oars, she drifted out of sight.

[1] There is a Spanish saying, " Uno pienso el bayo, y otro el que le ensilla "—that is, The bay horse thinks one way, and the man who saddles him another.   This was the case with Quesada, for twelve years were destined to elapse before he saw Bogotá again.

[2] Herrera (Decada V.) says: " Tocaymo no tiene oro, y es lindisima y de noche no cae sereno en ella."   It is certainly a very pretty place.   The lack of gold seems to have been little remedied since Herrera's time, and it appears to me he was mistaken about the dew (sereno).

CHAPTER XIV

A CHAPTER of Quesada's life closed, when he, with Belalcazar and with Federman, pushed off into the stream.

Although he was reserved for the most strange adventures up to extreme old age, the acme of his fortune had been reached, and he was fated never to attain the honours that the Emperor Charles V. so freely meted out, both to Pizarro and Cortés.

The voyage that he found himself engaged in on the Magdalena was new ground to him, for in the past no vessel had gone farther up the stream than to the mouth of the Opón. As they with due precaution felt their way down the swift current of the Alto Magdalena, the sound of rapids fell upon their ears most disagreeably. They were close to the well-known rapids of the town of Honda,[1] that still stop navigation on the river except to little craft. When he arrived above the rapids, as they were quite unknown and appeared dangerous, Quesada was obliged to make a portage, carrying all his effects by land through the thick forests on the bank, and lowering down the empty vessel by the help of ropes.

During this portage Quesada learned that there was gold

[1] Simon Perez de Torres, in his " Viage del Mundo," says: " De Onda, no encuentro nada que decir." That is not complimentary, for I remember that the last time I passed through it, a man on horseback was taking a bullock through the chief street, lassoed round the horns.

Simon Perez de Torres goes on to say, as if he had repented of his want of courtesy: " Cerca de Onda hay una venta, La Villeta, y pasa un rio. La mitad negra y la otra clara, como los ojos de la cara." As the eyes of the face (los ojos de la cara) are not commonly black and light-coloured, it would appear that Torres had spoken without due reflection about Onda.

found in the neighbourhood.   Of this he wrote to his brother,
Hernan Perez, when he arrived at Cartagena, and many years
afterwards the town of Mariquita was founded not far from
the spot where he had made the portage, and heard about
the gold.

On re-embarking, as they dropped down the river through
the interminable walls of vegetation, fleets of canoes attacked
them constantly.   Luckily Belalcazar's men were well
supplied with guns and powder, and easily repelled attacks.

For the first five or six days downstream the country was
unknown to them, for hitherto no Spaniards from the coasts
had reached the rapids that Quesada recently had passed.
When they came to the territory of the Cacique of Malambo,
they met some Spaniards, who were amazed to see a boat-
load of their countrymen, many dressed only in Indian
cloths, who had appeared from out of the unknown.

They left the vessel that they had built in Tocaima, at
Malambo, and marched through trails just opened in the
woods to Cartagena, not without difficulty and frequent
skirmishes.

When they arrived at Cartagena the excitement was
intense, for nobody had ever heard of Bogotá.   Fabulous
legends of its richness soon were circulated, and both Peru
and Mexico were now declared to be mere dustheaps in
comparison with the new colony.

When the three generals appeared upon the streets crowds
followed them about, eagerly asking to be allowed to enlist
in their next expedition to the interior.

The phrase of " El Dorado " naturally contributed to
the astounding stories as to the wealth of the new conquest.
From the first it seems the Spanish settlers applied the
expression to a city, not knowing, or not understanding,
that it was used in relation to a man.   These rumours soon
would be circulated and exaggerated, and by degrees give
rise to the legend that was so widely believed in at the
time.

Everyone wished to hear the details, and Quesada was
besieged by people eager to interview him, as naturally he

was the man who had most information about the golden town.[1]

For the first time Quesada learned with certainty of the Adelantado's death, and that another governor, one Jeronimo Lebron, was reigning in his stead. Certainly, Santa Marta was the last place Quesada wished to visit at the time, for there the people knew the terms that he had made with the late Adelantado when embarking on his quest.

Two years had now elapsed since he set out from Santa Marta, and as he had sent back no letters to the coast, partly no doubt from lack of vessels to convey them, and partly from the not unnatural feeling that he wished nobody should share the profit and the fame that he had earned with so much suffering. Thus both in Santa Marta and in Cartagena, everyone believed him dead. When he appeared upon the coast, accompanied by Federman and Belalcazar, and the news of their strange meeting got about, excitement knew no bounds.

News of Quesada's unexpected return was not long reaching Santa Marta. The governor, Jeronimo Lebron, sent at once charging Quesada, as the successor of his former chief, to come to Santa Marta and report to him all that had taken place. This Quesada not unnaturally refused to do, saying that, as Don Pedro was no more, he would not give account to anyone except the emperor.[2]

Jeronimo Lebron was obliged to content himself with Quesada's answer; but he at once set about to fit out an expedition to the interior, alleging that the newly conquered lands fell under his government, according to the capitulation made by Quesada with his predecessor.

Quesada sent him a strongly worded protest, charging him upon his peril not to set out upon his expedition, till

[1] "Como quien mas de raiz sabia la sustancia de la cosa": Fray Simon.

[2] Most unfortunately, owing to this dispute, Quesada, whilst he was in Cartagena, melted down all his gold into ingots. Thus many interesting idols, cups, and Chibcha ornaments, that he most certainly would have presented to the emperor, were destroyed.

he had laid his claims to the new governorship before the emperor. The protest did not stop Jeronimo Lebron from starting up the Magdalena, for the account of the great wealth of Bogotá had been so talked about, that all the Spaniards on the coast were itching to set out. Lebron soon found himself involved in difficulties of much the same kind as Quesada had to encounter, and as he neither had the courage nor the abilities of the man he was endeavouring to supplant, it proved disastrous to his reputation. On his return to Santa Marta, with only twenty-five of those with whom he had set out, he resigned his governorship, and retired to his estates in the West Indies.

Quesada, Federman, and Belalcazar then embarked in a light galeas. On the 28th of August, 1539, they reached Cuba[1] after touching at Jamaica, and then, after a favourable voyage, safely arrived in Spain.

In Spain the three adventurers who had been so strangely drawn together, for a brief interval, for ever separated.

Both Federman and Belalcazar went at once to court, and received confirmation of their governments. Quesada, who had greater cause than had the others to see the emperor at once, by some strange circumstance never properly explained, allowed his enemy, Alonso de Lugo, the Adelantado Don Pedro's son, he who had so basely left his father in the lurch, to steal a march upon him.

Federman solicited and obtained a government in Venezuela; returned there, and history makes no further mention of him. He left the reputation of a humane and an enlightened man in all his dealings with the Indians. His soldiers loved and respected him, although he was a German, a circumstance that in itself speaks volumes to his character to anyone who knows how jealous is the Spanish attitude towards all foreigners.

[1] On the 28th of August, 1539, the Governor of Cuba, Gonzalo de Guzman, wrote to the emperor " El 24 de este mes llegó aquí un navio que venia de Jamaica . . . con gente de Cartagena, é hizo allí escala . . . venian el Licenciado Ximenez, Belalcazar y Federman ": Piedrahita, p. 181. Quesada sailed from Cartagena on the 8th of July, 1539.

Sebastian de Belalcazar, who was already well known at court as the conqueror of Quito, was favourably received by Charles V., and at once appointed Adelantado and Governor of Popayán. The rest of his career was as adventurous as that of any conqueror of the Americas. In the year 1541 he returned to Popayán, and his first action was to send out his lieutenant, Jorge de Robledo, to explore the valley of the Cauca, that was reputed rich in gold.

About this time the Marquess Francisco Pizarro had been assassinated, and the civil war between his brothers and the Almagros was raging furiously. An official, Vaca de Castro, had been sent out with plenary authority from Spain to reduce affairs to order in Peru. His first act was to call upon all those who were loyal to the crown to help with arms and men.

Belalcazar marched at once to his assistance, and after a short campaign with Castro, who in the interim had been named viceroy, was dispatched back to Popayán.

It is supposed the newly appointed viceroy felt himself overshadowed by the fame that Belalcazar justly enjoyed for his military skill and as a conqueror. This jealousy, natural no doubt in the case of Castro, who was a newcomer, was complicated by the fact that Belalcazar had granted a safe-conduct to his government of Popayán to one Pedroso,[1] who had been a principal in the assassination of Pizarro, and whose life was forfeit to the king.

As Belalcazar was a well-known royalist throughout his whole career, he probably merely protected Captain Pedroso out of kindness and not from policy.

[1] Fray Pedro de Aguado says in his " Historia de Santa Marta y Nuevo Reino de Granada," p. 659 (it was first published 1906 in Madrid, though long known in MS.; Piedrahita uses it): " Pedroso era hombre que avia andado y estado en Peru muchos dias, provincia donde por la influencia y virtud de los astros y planetas que allí reinan, cobran los hombres que en ella estan . . . una eloquencia en el hablar tan acompañada de eficacísimas palabras y razones, que con ellas atrahen á sí los animos de gentes estrañas, y que nunca vieron, á que hagan lo que ellos queren y pretenden." These " astros y planetas " still appear to exert their influence, not only in Peru, but all over South America.

Belalcazar retired disgusted to his government, where he found other troubles waiting for him. For long he had received no news of Jorge Robledo, whom he had sent into the Cauca valley to explore. He marched there with a considerable force, and learned upon arriving at the newly founded town of Cartago that Robledo had slipped off secretly to Spain, to get himself declared the governor of the new territory.

The fact that he himself had done the same thing when as a lieutenant of Pizarro he conquered Popayán, naturally did not weigh with him, and he swore vengeance on his lieutenant if he should ever fall into his hands.

Belalcazar went on to the town of Cali, then nothing but an Indian rancheria; now an important place. There he received the visit of the Licenciado Armendariz, who handed to him in the emperor's name copies of the new code of laws for the Indies, which had been promulgated through the exertions of Fray Domingo de las Casas,[1] the greatest advocate the Indians ever had in the New World. This code, excellent and humane in its provisions and setting out in distinct terms that the Indians were, as subjects of the emperor, not to be enslaved,[2] was yet difficult to carry out at such a distance from Madrid. Naturally it was received with disgust by the older conquerors. They had not come so far, and undergone such perils, to look too closely into the rights of man. Most of them had set out from Spain under the rule of Ferdinand and Isabel, when manners had not undergone the change in Spain that they soon underwent under their grandson Charles V. Charles, though he had

[1] Bishop of Chiapas in Mexico, and known as the Apostle to the Indians.

[2] One of its provisions ran: " Que ninguna persona se pueda servir de los Indios por via de naboria, no de otro modo alguno, contra su voluntad." Naboria was, as it may be remembered, an Indian who was not a slave, but had to work whether he liked or not. A still stronger clause declared that, " Que por ninguna causa, de guerra, rebelion, ni otra, ni rescate, ni do otra manera, no se pueda hacer esclavo Indio alguno, sino que sean tratados como personas libres y como vasallos Reales, que son, de la corona de Castilla."

not the least idea of any liberty beneath his rule, and though he stamped out with an iron heel all the free institutions[1] that his grandfathers, the Catholic kings, respected, and were obliged both to respect and ratify, still found himself insensibly influenced by the tendencies of a new century.

The contempt that the new legislation evoked throughout the Indies gave rise to the phrase so often quoted, " I obey, but I do not comply."[2]

This fatal phrase, that saved the legal conscience, was the shield under which every cruelty was still committed, years after the protective laws were passed.

Belalcazar, who throughout his life had been a law unto himself, wrote at once to the emperor a letter (dated 1544) impugning most of the provisions of the new code in good set terms, and at the same time complaining of the treatment that he had received from the new viceroy of Peru.   Seldom, indeed, the emperor can have received a letter, couched in such terms; but Belalcazar was too useful in his sphere for him to quarrel with.   Hardly was the letter written and dispatched before news came to Cali of a fresh rebellion in Peru.   To Castro had succeeded a new viceroy, Blasco Nuñez Vela, an elderly and not particularly able man, who at once came into collision with the Pizarro faction over the new laws.   Fortune declared itself against him from the first, and he was forced for refuge into Belalcazar's government of Popayán.   Belalcazar at once went to his assistance, and pushed the rebels back to Quito, where he obtained a partial victory over them.   Had it been followed up at once, as Belalcazar urged, all would have been well for Blasco Nuñez Vela; but the right moment passed, and the Pizarros rallying inflicted a defeat upon the royalists, and after having taken the viceroy prisoner, at once beheaded him.   Belalcazar was made prisoner, covered with wounds and fighting bravely.   He would have been beheaded on the

---

[1] At the battle of Villalar, in 1521, the last free institutions so long prevalent in Spain were finally destroyed.   Captains Padilla and Juan Bravo, the leaders of the Commons (Los Comuneros), were taken and beheaded.

[2] Obedezco pero no cumplo.

spot had not one Captain Alvarado[1] protected him and begged hard for his life. Gonzalo Pizarro, who very likely did not care to push the matter to extremity with his old comrade in arms, spared Belalcazar's life, on the condition that he returned at once to his own government. On his return to Cali he learned that Jorge Robledo, the lieutenant whom he had sent to explore the Cauca valley and who had slipped away to Spain, had been named governor of Antioquia and created marshal. By a forced march across the mountain paths that lead from Urabá to Antioquia, paths that to-day are hardly traversable and at that time had only been attempted by the hardiest conquerors, he surprised the new-made marshal, and in a night attack made him a prisoner. Marshal Robledo, who might have got away, relying on the fame of Belalcazar's generosity, gave himself up without resistance, not thinking that his life could be in danger at the hands of his old friend.

This time he counted quite without his host, for Belalcazar, after reproaching him both as a traitor and deserter of his friend, and as a base usurper of his rule, instantly had him hanged. This cruel action, the only crime of a like nature that Belalcazar is ever known to have committed, remains a blot upon his fame that nothing can wipe out. Without it history might have numbered him amongst the best of all the conquerors, as he was certainly one of the bravest in the field.

After a month or two he once again got orders from Peru to raise an army for the royal cause to help the President La Gasca, who had arrived from Spain.

Always a staunch adherent of the royal cause, Belalcazar, for the third time, marched into Peru with a well-ordered force. He was present at the final struggle of the Pizarro faction, against the royalists at the great battle of Xaquizaguana, where he was general of La Gasca's cavalry. After the battle he was publicly thanked for his great services, and returned home in triumph to his own government.

[1] This Alvarado was a brother of Pedro de Alvarado, the chief captain of Cortés, in Mexico.

There he found the Oidor[1] Briceño waiting for him, armed with a mission to take his residence[2]—that is, to inquire into all matters of his government.

This man Briceño was about to marry Jorge Robledo's widow, Doña Maria Carbajal, a lady who, since her husband had been hanged, had never ceased to clamour for revenge upon his murderer. Though there was no doubt of Belalcazar's guilt in regard to Robledo's death, in the affairs of his own government he was above reproach, always having been the soul of honour in all money matters. Still, in the circumstances of the marriage with Doña Maria Carbajal, Briceño naturally was biased, and he condemned Belalcazar to the death penalty, solely upon the count of the execution of Robledo.

To condemn and carry out the sentence in the town of Popayán, where the inhabitants adored their governor, and most of them had been his soldiers in his many expeditions to Peru, were very different things. Instantly Belalcazar wrote to the emperor, getting his friends to become surety for him, and sadly set out on his return to Spain. So much did the disgrace of having to appear before the emperor as a criminal weigh upon his mind, that on arriving at the port of Cartagena, he fell seriously ill.

Don Pedro de Heredia, who at the time was governor of the town, a man who had himself experienced every vicissitude of fortune, strove hard to comfort him, taking him as a guest into his house, and treating him with the consideration that his great services deserved. All was in vain, and Belalcazar, after a short illness, died, and was buried in the cathedral. Grief, more than any actual illness, hastened his decease, for the proud spirit that had stood up so bravely against the vicissitudes of his strange, adventurous career was broken by disgrace.

His life was like a page in a romance of chivalry. From his first exploit in the muddy lane hard by the little town

---

[1] Oidor—literally, a hearer. These were judges specially appointed for cases of the kind.

[2] Tomarle la residencia.

from which he took his name adventure dogged his path. A conqueror of Peru, and an explorer of the wilderness, governor, general, and statesman, he filled many offices, and saw much world,[1] as say his countrymen; but nothing in his whole career was more romantic or more strange than his first meeting with his two rivals on the plains of Bogotá.

All the inhabitants of Cartagena honoured his funeral and lamented him, and Don Pedro de Heredia buried[2] him splendidly. Thus died Belalcazar, disgraced and broken-hearted, a man who, but for one blot on his name, stands in the first rank of the conquerors.

[1] Vió mucho mundo.

[2] El Don Pedro de Heredia puso luto
Con los demas vecinos principales
Haciendole sepulcho bien instruto
Honrosos y cumplidos funerales
Y encima de la tumba do yacia
Pusieron una letra que decia.

Ista Belalcazar potuit concludere tumba
Ipsius ad famam claudere non valuit
Succubit fatis qua passim candida turbunt
Gesta tamen calamo sunt celebranda pio.

" Elegias de Varones Ilustres de Indias," part 3,
Juan de Castellanos. (Madrid, 1589.)

CHAPTER XV

QUESADA landed in Lisbon late in the year 1539, and whilst Federman and Belalcazar posted at once straight to Madrid to see the emperor, unfortunately for himself he stayed in Lisbon, where he seems to have acted most imprudently. There he fell in with Don Hernando Pizarro, one of the brothers of the conqueror of Peru. The two seem to have had a spell of gambling and feast-making, a course of conduct singularly unlike any Quesada had pursued whilst in America, and the more imprudent on account of the presence of his greatest enemy, Don Alonso de Lugo, at the court.

How it occurred is wrapped in mystery, or rather in that fog of history as dense as that of war, that frequently descends upon most interesting events, blotting them out completely from our view. The fact remains that both Quesada and Pizarro were sent to prison for gambling after hours.

Whilst there, an incident occurred that showed him rather in the light of a swaggering soldier than as the prudent gentleman he was. It is said that, when she brought a stoup of wine to him as he sat playing cards in prison, the gaoler's daughter asked him for half a dollar,[1] and he, sweeping his winnings from the board into her apron, poured a hundred dollars in her lap.

Another time the same wench,[2] happening to pass close to the card-table where Quesada sat with Hernando Pizarro, Pedro Almanes, and various Peruvians,[3] one of them gave the girl a dollar, for what is called " baraio," so as to bring him luck. Each gave her something, according to his means;

---

[1] ". . . le pidió la carcelera un real de á cuatro ": Fray Simon.
[2] La misma mozuela.   [3] Y otros Peruleros.

but once again Quesada overtopped them all, with a hundred ducats, making all marvel at his prodigality.

The similarity of the sum recorded. in both the stories, and the fact that the "same wench" was the recipient, seems to point to the fact that the tale has been repeated twice, or that the gaoler's daughter was a good-looking girl.

The story was first set about by Rodriguez Fresle,[1] a man who lived nearly all his life in Bogotá, and could have had it only by report.

Quesada's enemies naturally made capital of it against him, and Piedrahita, who was unfavourable to nearly all Quesada did, repeats it in his own Chronicle, and makes the most of it. The fact remains that, for sitting late at cards, Quesada and Hernando Pizarro were sent to prison, most likely for a day or two, and the whole story of the gaoler's daughter and her apron full of gold may be apocryphal. One thing is certain, that Quesada wasted precious time in Lisbon, instead of posting off to court.

Early in 1540 Quesada seems to have been in Seville, as Piedrahita, in the Chronicle, speaks of a note in the registers of the Casa de Contratacion de Sevilla, mentioning Quesada, and saying that he had been there, stating he was upon his journey to Madrid to give the emperor a full account of all his conquests and of the riches of the new kingdom of Granada. He had a box with him containing eleven thousand dollars' worth of gold and five hundred and seventy-two emeralds, that constituted the royal fifth.[2]

Quesada's pulse must have beat high when he once more found himself in Spain, not now an unknown lawyer, but a

---

[1] "El Carnero Bogotano."

[2] "Y por los apuntes y registros de la Casa de Contratacion de Sevilla consta, El Licenciado Ximenez hizó relacion como venia á dar cuenta de la conquista y riqueza del Nuevo Reino, de donde traia una cajita con 572 esmeraldas y hasta 11,000 pesos de oro de quintos de su S.M. y descubra presentarlo en la Corte como venia y asi le mando á los officiales de Sevilla se lo entreguen sin abrir por cedula de Madrid de 17 de Noviembre de 1539": Piedrahita, "Historia General de las Conquistas del Nuevo Reino de Granada," p. 181. (Madrid, 1688.)

conqueror. He certainly had the right to hope he would be rewarded on the same scale as were the conquerors of Mexico and of Peru.

What he had achieved was not inferior to the deeds that they had done, though on a smaller scale. It is true he had set out from Santa Marta under a capitulation with the Adelantado Don Pedro de Lugo as his lieutenant, and at the time it was well understood that he was a subordinate, and all the conquests were in the Adelantado's name. Undoubtedly the Adelantado had pledged all his resources to fit Quesada's expedition out, and had he been alive, it would have been Quesada's bounden duty to report to him. However, death had removed him, and a new governor reigned in his stead, to whom Quesada was not bound by ties of duty, or by sentiment.

Still, Don Alonso de Lugo was a dangerous enemy. Nothing weighed more in the court of Charles V. than family connections, and Don Luis Alonso de Lugo, by his marriage with Doña Beatriz Noroña de Mendoza, had secured himself against all competitors. His wife's sister, Doña Maria de Mendoza, was the wife of Don Francisco de los Cobos, the secretary of Charles V. These two ladies were the protectresses of Don Alonso against Quesada's claims. However, Don Alonso had another advocate. When he arrived in Spain, after having stolen his father's money and his ship,[1] he brought with him some fifteen thousand gold castellanos,[2] and made good use of them, in order to make friends. By their aid he secured his high-born wife, and by a lavish use of bribery blocked all Quesada's claims.

Unluckily for Quesada, the governorship of Santa Marta had been granted to the Lugos for two lives. Thus, legally, Don Alonso's claim was strong. His conduct does not seem to have outweighed his legal claim, for on his arrival with the ship and money he had stolen, he was arrested and imprisoned; but it appears only for the sake of form. He

---

[1] See Chapter I.

[2] The castellano was the fiftieth part of the gold mark, and may perhaps be taken therefore as worth about eleven dollars.

was soon released, most probably the fifteen thousand castellanos forming an efficient key, and in a month or two married
into the Mendoza family.

At once he claimed his father's governorship of Santa
Marta, and alleged that the new territory of Bogotá, towards
whose conquest he had not moved a finger, fell within his
rule.   Nothing could well have been less just, or less within
the bounds of common sense.   A thousand miles lay between
Santa Marta and Bogotá.   No two countries of the world
were more entirely different from one another.   One situated
in the hottest tropics on the coast; the other in a high
plateau with a temperate climate in the hills.

Although Quesada certainly had entered into a capitulation with Don Pedro de Lugo before he set out on his
expedition, the capitulation contained no word about the
son, for after his desertion his father had renounced his
utterly.   The honour of the conquest was Quesada's
certainly, and Charles V. owed a debt not easy to repay.
Unluckily for Spain, neither the Emperor Charles V. nor his
son Philip ever rewarded faithful services, or, in most cases,
did so grudgingly.

The great Cortés died poor and broken-hearted, and the
great Captain Gonzalo de Cordoba was thwarted all his life,
and his plans often rendered nugatory by the king's jealousy.
He died in enforced retirement on his estates.

The Duke of Alba, one of the first commanders of the age,
a man who had not hesitated to bathe the Spanish name in
blood in the Low Countries to serve his monarch, was several
times disgraced; but in his case Philip was obliged to call
him from his retirement in his old age to conquer Portugal.

Charles, in regard to Quesada, surpassed himself in dull
tenacity of purpose, and disregard of his own interests.

As soon as Quesada had got over his little bout of gambling
in Lisbon, the only excess of the kind ever recorded of him,
he went post-haste to court.   It was unfortunate that
he did not associate himself with Belalcazar, for the latter
was *persona grata* with Charles V., as, in fact, were all the
conquerors of Peru.   However, Belalcazar quickly dis-

patched his business and returned back to the Indies, and thus the chance was lost.

Upon arriving at Madrid, Quesada put in his claim to be appointed governor of the country he had discovered and subdued. Charles V. owed him the acquisition of a territory, larger perhaps than Spain even in those days, before the whole of what is now Colombia had been occupied.

Pizarro and Cortés and Belalcazar all three had been appointed governors of the respective kingdoms that they had added to the dominion of the emperor. Most likely, for no record has come down to us of his first attempts, Quesada came to court with too much confidence, relying on his merit, a dangerous attitude to adopt with emperors.

Though he lacked interest, Quesada did not want for backing of another kind, for he had all that was most respectable in Spain upon his side.

A statement was presented to the emperor, signed by the Bishop of Lugo, the Cardinal Archbishop of Seville, the Count of Osorno, of the great Manrique family, and others of the nobility and clergy, in Quesada's favour. It set forth that he had made his conquest of El Nuevo Reino de Granada at the peril of his life. It dwelt upon the hardships he had undergone and the many battles in which he had been engaged.

The document declared Quesada was a godfearing Christian, who had made the conquest with little injury, either to the natives or to the soldiers he had led. The petitioners reminded Charles of the great territories Quesada had brought under his rule, contrasting all that he had done, with the one exploit of Alonso de Lugo, which was to rob his father and desert. Lastly, it declared Quesada the most fit and proper man to rule the country that he had subdued.[1] In a postscript the emperor was reminded that

[1] " En todo el tiempo que estuvo en las Indias y anduvo en la dicha conquista, usó muy bien y como buen Cristiano temeroso de Dios, sin hacer mal ni daño ni crueldad á los Indios ni Españoles, y demas desto es habil y tiene experencia grande en aquella conquista, y por tal le escogio el Adelantado Don Pedro Hernandez de Lugo entre mill hombres que llevó consigo en que habia gran numero

the inhabitants of Bogotá had all petitioned for Quesada to be their governor.

Lastly, the great Las Casas, the Apostle to the Indians, raised his voice against the appointment of Alonso de Lugo to the post. He called him " one of the most cruel tyrants and the most irrational, . . . and with less conscience than Barbarossa. He has robbed God's honour, and has also robbed your Majesty, and has skinned[1] both Indians and Christians."

Las Casas goes on to say that both the Council of the Indies and the Comendador Cobos knew well what sort of man Alonso de Lugo really was; still, he says they have given the sword of justice to a man so hard as he is. We shall see who will give the strict account that God will ask of him.

A curious feature of the whole proceedings is that whilst the memorial was before the emperor, and the claims and counter-claims were being agitated, Quesada never seems to have gone to court. He may have been in Madrid, for certainly he started out from Seville with the intention of proceeding there; but he apparently never had speech with Charles V. Extraordinary as this may seem, Herrera,[2] the official historian of the Indies, has the following:

" The Licentiate Gonzalo Jimenez, knowing that the governorship was given to the Adelantado Don Alonso Luis de Lugo, through the influence of petticoats, did not go to court, either because the king had gone away, or because he feared the great favour that the Adelantado enjoyed."[3]

---

de caballeros é hijos dalgo, y le nombró su lugar Teniente y Capitan General del dicho descubrimiento y confió mas del, que de su proprio hijo, por las muchas y buenas cualidades que habia en su persona ": " El Carnero Bogotano," Rodriguez Fresle.

[1] Archivos Nacionales, September 15th, 1544. Printed by Jimenez de la Espada, in his edition of the Chronicle of Castellanos.

[2] " Historia General de los Hechos de los Castellanos en la Islas y Tierra Firme del Mar Oceano," Antonio de Herrera, Madrid, en la Emprenta Real, 1601.

[3] " El Licenciado Gonzalo Jimenez sabiendo que la Governacion estaba dada al Adelantado Don Alonso Luis de Lugo (por influencia de faldas) no fué á la Corte, asi por ser el rey partido, como porque temió los grandes favores del Adelantado ": Herrera.

No historian of the New World carries more weight than does Herrera. If he was sometimes partial in his judgments, he was invariably accurate in regard to facts. Thus we may take this passage as destructive of the foolish legend, first set about by Rodriguez Fresle in his " Carnero Bogotano," and copied afterwards by Bishop Piedrahita, that Quesada lost his appointment owing to having appeared at court wrapped in a red cloak. If he did not frequent the court, as Herrera definitely states, this could not have been the reason. It appears, as Herrera himself says, to have been an affair of petticoats, not cloaks, that lost Quesada his well-earned governorship. Quesada was, above all things, a perfect gentleman, and a judicious man. The court of Charles was at that time in mourning for the death of the Empress Isabel. All the world knew that Charles had been deeply attached to her, and, mourning or no mourning, Charles always dressed in black.

Having been brought up a gentleman, and with the inherited caution he was likely to have acquired during his long years of practice of the law, Quesada was not likely to have committed such an indecency. The report reposes only on a rumour Piedrahita copies from Rodriguez Fresle, which he says was current in Bogotá,[1] that, " Quesada went to court all dressed in scarlet, with a scarlet cloak." We may dismiss it as an action totally unlike any other action of Quesada's life, and, so, incredible.

Neither Quesada's services nor the memorial, signed as it was by people of great weight in Spain, nor the adverse criticisms of Las Casas upon Lugo's character, were of the least avail.

Don Alonso was confirmed in the appointment that his father had enjoyed, and Bogotá and the New Kingdom of Granada adjudged to fall within his government. No more sinister decision could have been taken, both as regards the Indians or the Spanish colonists. The dictum of Las Casas, that Lugo had less conscience than the pirate Barbarossa, was amply justified.

[1] " Segun se dijo en Santafé " (Bogotá): Piedrahita.

Charles had not the least excuse for his decision, for he says himself, writing from Brussels on the 13th of September, 1540: " As regards the government of Santa Marta,[1] I have heard what both sides have to say." That is, after having heard the wondrous tale of Quesada's strange adventure, his perils, hardships, battles, and all the difficulties he had to meet, he chose the robber of his father's gold and base deserter of his duty to fill the hero's place.

After the perpetration of this injustice on him, Quesada went to France and Flanders, where he remained a year, and not improbably wrote one or more of his lost books. During his absence he was tried before the Court of the Council of the Indies for his participation in the torture and the death of the last Zipa of Bogotá. He was condemned to five years' exile from Granada, to which place, it appears, he had returned, and to a fine of a thousand ducats. The fine it is uncertain if he ever paid, as it was impossible to condemn Manlius in the sight of the Capitol.

The exile does not seem to have much troubled him, for, for the next ten years, he travelled over most of the countries of Europe, quite contentedly,[2] coming back now and then to Spain. What he did all the time has never been revealed; but as the list of his known works is quite an ample[3] one, most likely literary work engrossed a good part of his life.

Captain Don Gonzalo Fernandez de Oviedo, the writer on the natural history of the Indies, met Quesada in Valladolid and in Madrid in 1547 and 1548, and refers to him as an " honourable man, of a good understanding, and very able."[4]

It is supposed that Oviedo got many of the details of his adventures in New Granada from him. Oviedo says he

[1] Cuanto á la gobernacion de Santa Marta, he visto lo que unos y otros decis.

[2] " Piso muy a lo verde las provincias de Europa ": Fray Simon.

[3] See Appendix I.

[4] " Hombre honrado de gentil entendimiento y muy habil ": " Historia Natural y General de las Indias," Gonzalo Fernandez de Oviedo.

had a large notebook[1] of Quesada's in his possession for many days.

Oviedo's four and twenty chapters on the conquest of New Granada constitute one of the most authentic records of that conquest that we possess. The closest scrutiny has not hitherto revealed much of Quesada's life in Spain and Flanders, Germany, Italy, and the other " provincias de Europa "[2] that he visited during the twelve years he passed away from Bogotá. It may be that an examination of the archives in Bogotá, or some other of the old cities of Colombia, may contain documents that will prove valuable to future writers on his life.

However, it was not in Europe that the adventures fate still had in store for him were destined to be passed.

[1] Un gran cuaderno.   [2] Fray Simon.

CHAPTER XVI

HAD Alonso de Lugo wished to discredit the judgment of the Emperor Charles V., he hardly could have imagined any more successful course than that which he adopted in his new government. As he was in favour both at court and with the Council of the Indies, he had no difficulty in getting together his expedition, for adventurers, attracted by the fame of the new conquest, flocked to him readily. He sailed from Spain with a well-appointed fleet, taking on board with him horses and cattle for his new government of Santa Marta and of Bogotá.

In the year 1542 he was off El Cabo de la Vela, where in these days there was an important pearl fishery. As this place fell within the territory of Santa Marta, he called upon the government officials to give him the twelfth part of all the pearls they had in store. They not unnaturally refused. Don Alonso had the coffers in which they kept the pearls ready to send to Spain violently broken open, and appropriated the greater part of their contents.

It was not very far from the Cabo de la Vela that he stole the ship and left his father in the lurch. Thus, for the second time, and nearly in the same place, he showed that love of money was the mainspring of his actions, and to obtain it no baseness or no violence seems to have frightened him.

From the Cabo de la Vela he sent on some of his officers to Santa Marta to prepare ships of lighter burden for the voyage up the Magdalena, for he determined to make his capital in Bogotá. It may have been that shame deterred him from appearing in Santa Marta, where the inhabitants all knew about his base desertion of his father, a man they all had loved. To avoid the city, he determined to disembark upon the coast, traverse the Valle de Upar, and strike the Magdalena at a point agreed upon, some distance up the stream, where he had given orders that the ships should wait for him.

The journey, even to-day, would be a serious undertaking, for the country lying between the coast and the Valle de Upar is wild and mountainous. Still wandering tribes of Indians dwell in the forests and attack isolated travellers. As soon as he advanced into the interminable woods, the Aruaco and the Guanebacan Indians fell upon his troops.

Though the Indians were miserably armed, and Don Alonso's men were all equipped in the best outfit to be procured in Spain, their ignorance of colonial warfare exposed them readily to Indian attacks. The flights of poisoned arrows launched upon them from the woods did them considerable damage, for they were not provided with the quilted armour worn by Quesada's men.[1]

Don Alonso's expedition crossed La Sierra de la Herrera, and emerged upon the Magdalena at Tamalameque, that by this time had grown into a town. Passing the Sierra some of the cattle he had disembarked got lost, and becoming wild, there grew up herds of wild cattle that were still in existence during the Independence wars against the Spaniards.

Once on the river all should have been plain sailing, for the way that at the time of Quesada's expedition was an unblazed trail was now well known, and pretty frequent communication was established between the coast and Bogotá. Although he followed almost exactly in Quesada's tracks, his difficulties were immense. The Indians with fleets of canoes attacked him as they had attacked the Conqueror, but with more system, as they were led by a youth called Francisquillo, brought up and educated in Santa Marta by the missionaries. This youth had returned back to heathendom, and had become the greatest danger to the Spaniards on their transit up and down the river from the coast. All the way up from Tamalameque to the

[1] See Chapter II.

entrance of the valley of Opón he harassed Don Alonso's fleet, taking considerable toll of boats and men by his guerrilla attacks.

The expedition disembarked at the mouth of the Opón, following Quesada's trail. Hunger and sickness and constant Indian attacks so decimated them that three times they were on the point of turning back to Santa Marta, and would have done so had not the colonists of the town of Velez heard of their plight and sent guides and provisions to encourage them. With their assistance the expedition gained the plains, with a considerable loss of prestige, for all allowed that Don Alonso, in following a well-known road, had suffered more losses than had Quesada marching through the primeval woods. So greatly was the prestige of the Spaniards diminished by Don Alonso's expedition that the route to the plains by the valley of Opón had to be given up. The settlers chose another by the River Craré that runs very nearly parallel to the Opón, and on its banks they set up stores and blockhouses. The change was for the better, for the road to Velez was shortened by it; but the poor Indians were the sufferers. The Spaniards, having at that time no beasts of burden, made the Indians carry their supplies and merchandise, not caring how they overloaded them or how many of them died. This cruel treatment and the continual outbreaks that it occasioned, with a great epidemic of the smallpox, reduced the population of those valleys from more than two hundred thousand, as had been estimated at the conquest, to about one thousand six hundred souls, in the short space of eighty years.[1]

As soon as Don Alonso actually arrived in Bogotá, he set about a system of peculation of an ingenious kind.

All over South America, when the conquest was achieved, the conquerors shared out the Indians by systems known

[1] Fray Simon's " Noticias Historiales de las Conquistas de Tierra Firme en las Indias Occidentales " was printed at Cuenca in 1627. He gives the above figures of the decrease of the Indians.

variously as Encomiendas[1] and Repartimientos. As nearly all the original conquerors held these Encomiendas from the Crown, they were exempt from the exactions of the governors; Don Alonso, either by force or by cajolery, persuaded most of these Encomienda holders to renounce their rights to him, alleging that they wanted certain formalities to put them straight in law. Those who were foolish enough to fall in with his plan were stripped of all that they possessed, for Don Alonso, on one pretext or another, always deferred the legitimizing of the title, and in the meantime drew the rents himself, treating the unlucky Indians who went with the land with every cruelty.

By degrees he got into his hands almost the entire revenues of the kingdom, and became immoderately rich. Captain Gonzalo Suarez Rondon was at the time one of the most influential men in Bogotá. One of Quesada's captains, his old general, had left him orders before he sailed for Spain to found a town at Tocaima, and he was just about to start to do so when Don Alonso entered upon his governorship. As Captain Suarez Rondon was much respected by the colonists, he made himself their spokesman to the governor and complained of his injustice. For answer Don Alonso seized him and his son, threw them into prison, and confiscated all their property.

Had he displayed the same activity in pacifying the outlying tribes that he put forth in persecuting his own countrymen, he would have made a stirring governor; for his audacity was great, his will was iron, and he recoiled before no difficulty in carrying out his plans. His one achieve-

---

[1] An Encomienda was in its first origin a military fief that carried certain duties and privileges with it. In America, it was a fief held from the Crown granting to its holder the labour of the Indians and the duty of teaching them the Christian religion, doctrine, and precepts. The system became much abused and the Indians practically slaves. The code known as the Laws of the Indies dealt severely with the abuses of the Encomiendas and Repartimientos. There was also another system known as La Mita, that was originally a choosing by lot in the Indian villages of men suitable to be employed in public works. It became chiefly applicable to mines, and was turned into the most cruel slavery.

ment was to found Tocaima and subdue the Panche Indians. Even this he did not execute in person; but sent out Captain Hernan Vanegas with a small expedition to do it in his name. This Captain Vanegas accomplished, after some fighting with the Panches, and in the year 1544 founded Tocaima and took possession of the surrounding territory in the name of Charles V.

Quesada, just before he had returned to Spain, had delegated his authority to his brother Hernan Perez de Quesada, leaving him as his deputy, with full power to govern in his name. Unluckily for him, Hernan Perez, seduced as were so many others by the false vision of the Golden City of the plains, had set out several months before the new governor arrived, had encountered many hardships[1] and had been forced to return, after the loss of nearly all his men. On his return to Bogotá, thin, miserable, and ill, an object of compassion to the inhabitants, with whom he was extremely popular, Don Alonso seized him with a younger brother who had just come from Peru, and after keeping him in prison for a considerable time banished them from the land.

This was the finishing stroke to Don Alonso's popularity, and in spite of his court favour and the numerous expedition that had accompanied him, he saw that his banishment of the brothers of the discoverer and founder of the country would bring about a rising of the inhabitants against him that might deprive him of his power, and possibly of life. From that time he devoted himself to amassing wealth by confiscation of estates, fines, and by appropriating all the emeralds from the mines. The unfortunate royal commissioners who had charge of the mines having protested to him of his conduct, he had them arrested and imprisoned; but luckily for them they managed to escape, and finding a ship in Cartagena just about to sail, they went

---

[1] On this unfortunate expedition, the " conquering " donkey Marubaré was killed and eaten. Fray Requesada rode him to the last, and pleaded hard for his life; but the starving soldiery, pushed by the extremity of hunger, killed and devoured him.

to Santo Domingo in her, and lodged a protest in the court, known as La Real Audiencia, against the governor. Alonso de Lugo was furious at their escape, and in revenge he hung an unlucky notary who had championed their cause.

The Quesadas were beyond his vengeance. At the first notice of the decree of banishment, Hernan Perez de Quesada and his brother Francisco at once went down the river, and by so doing probably saved their lives. In Cartagena they took ship for Cuba, and on the passage Hernan Perez was struck by lightning and died instantly.

In Bogotá, though he was very much beloved, the people held it was on account of his share in the death of the last Zipa that divine vengeance had overtaken him. This may have been so, for into the ways of Providence we have no means of penetrating; but it seems curious that the same lightning flash that killed Hernan should at the same time have killed Francisco, who was standing at his side, and who was far away in Cuzco when the last Zipa was condemned to death.

The death of Hernan Perez de Quesada removed one of the most energetic of the first conquerors. Hernan had been his brother's right-hand man from the first moment that Quesada's expedition sailed from Santa Marta at the discovery. In all the perils and the hardships of the first tremendous year of wandering in the dank forests of the Magdalena, Hernan had never failed. First in the fight, and ever last to retire from combat, he never spared himself. His brother owed him much, and reposed his confidence in him more than in any of his other captains, appointing him his lieutenant-general when he sailed for Spain. It is most probable that, had Hernan Perez known about the coming of Don Alonso, he would not have gone away upon his expedition to the Llanos to lose his credit and his men.

On his return to Bogotá Quesada must have often missed his energetic brother, who had always stood to him in evil and in good repute, and all the citizens of Bogotá mourned and regretted him.

Hernan Perez was a man of a good presence, robust and

powerful, and, above all things, most agreeable to all he had to do with; temperate[1] in good fortune, he suffered reverses patiently. Of pleasant manners, he had the gift of governing men, and he was notable for his skill in horsemanship. In fact, a conqueror, with all the virtues and the vices of the age he lived in. His death was such as he himself might well have desired, could he have seen his fate. He must have been a year or two past forty. His name was made, and is still unforgotten in the country that he did so much to discover and to subjugate. No Indian arrow, shot from a clump of guaduas, found some weak spot in his armour, causing him an agonizing death. He did not die upon the scaffold, as did so many of the conquerors. The assassin's dagger did not make away with him, as in the case of the great conqueror of Peru. Fevers and hardships, perils by land and sea, had left him all unscathed. He was reserved for fire direct from heaven. It may be that it struck him standing on the high poop of the galleon, talking with his brother of more conquests. Perhaps his last glance saw the tall, white peaks that tower above the town of Santa Marta in the far distance, illumined for a moment in the flash that struck him dead. At any rate, age had not touched him, and the hand so apt upon the bridle, had not grown feeble, or the legs lost their grip. He died as he had lived, suddenly and without warning: the death that every man who knows well how to govern men and horses would choose, if such things were in the choice of men. He sleeps at sea, the fittest burial-place for conquerors, and his place in the annals of the conquest of the New World is beside Belalcazar, Gonzalo de Sylvestre, Nuflo de Chaves, and the rest of the bold riders who crowd the ranks of the conquistadores, a pace or two behind Cortés,

---

[1] " Era hombre de robusta y buena presencia, agradable sobre encarecimiento á quantos le trataban, templado en las cosas prosperas, y sufrido en las adversas, de costumbres populares para governar hombres y de notable destreza en regir un caballo ": " Historia General de las Conquistas del Nuevo Reino de Granada," Piedrahita, p. 433.

Pizarro, Soto, and his own brother, Gonzalo de Quesada, whom he served so faithfully.

By this time Alonso de Lugo found his position untenable in Bogotá, and hearing that an official was coming out from Spain to inquire into the abuses of his government, about the end of the year 1544 he set out down the Magdalena for the coast. He took with him three hundred thousand ducats' worth of gold and emeralds, and Captains Suarez Rondon and Galiano as prisoners.   In Santa Marta he bought a ship and embarked for Spain; but having touched at the Cabo de la Vela, the government authorities, whom he had robbed upon his way to Bogotá, placed an embargo on his ship. He was forced to repay the value of the pearls that he had stolen, and the authorities released his prisoners, fearing he would murder them when he had got to sea.

In the Habana, where he touched, he was again arrested, but escaped by bribery and soon arrived in Spain.   There he was forced to restore the property of Captain Suarez Rondon that he had stolen in Bogotá.

He had been absent just three years from Spain, and in that time become so rich that, with the protection of his wife and of his sister, he was well received at court.

This rogue and tyrant, who had robbed his father and deserted him; had plundered both the royal treasury and the inhabitants of New Granada; and had oppressed both the Indians and the Spanish colonists, by rights should have been tried and forced to disgorge his ill-gained fortune, and to make restitution to the people he had robbed.   Nothing of this occurred, but, on the contrary, honours were showered upon him by the court.   Appointed colonel of a regiment of infantry, he went to Italy and served with some distinction there, especially at Milan.   Then he held influential posts at Siena and Naples, and died at Ghent, possibly in the odour of sanctity, but certainly in the enjoyment of a high command.   He left two children: a son, Luis Fernandez de Lugo, known as the " handsome," and a daughter, Doña Luisa, who was married to the Duke of Terra Nova and left a numerous family.

All his dishonourable life he seems to have been successful, and it may be that much of his success was due to his good manners and his amiable address.[1] This may have been the case, for amiable manners and a good address go a considerable way at courts.

Good Bishop Piedrahita sums up his character in an apt phrase: " He attacked all of the vices boldly, excepting avarice."[2] It is a pity that his character was not quite complete; but Don Alonso's one redeeming virtue, except good manners, one of the greatest that mankind is heir to, seems to have been that of generosity.

Quesada still continued absent, and although history has preserved few of his movements, it is most probable that he kept in touch with Bogotá.

It appears that in January, 1544, Quesada was in the town of Valladolid,[3] for he is known to have been a party in a lawsuit, at that date, with Don Juan Castellanos, who had been treasurer in San Juan de Puerto Rico in the year 1539.

However, in his absence, Bogotá was slowly growing, and towns were being founded in various parts of the new territory. Many of the wild tribes were brought into subjection, and by degrees the little city of the twelve straw huts Quesada had founded was becoming the capital of a great viceroyalty .

Lugo had left his cousin, Captain Montalvo de Lugo, as interim governor; but in a month or two there arrived from Spain Don Miguel Diaz de Armendariz, charged to take the residences of the governors of Cartagena, Popayán,

---

[1] " La suavidad y discrecion de sus palabras fueron gran parte para que muchas veces no parecieren tiranias sus acciones ": Piedrahita, p. 433.

[2] " Atropello todos los vicios con entereza, menos la codicia ": Piedrahita.

[3] " En Valladolid 21 de Enero 1544 se emprendio cierto pleito entre Juan de Castellanos y el Licenciado Gonzalo Jimenez de Quesada sobre ciertas cantidades que el dicho Tesorero le pedia ": Jimenez de la Espada, edicion de Castellanos.

and Santa Marta, who caused him at once to be replaced by Pedro de Ursua, the nephew of the new official.

Pedro de Ursua proved to be one of the best governors that Bogotá had had. He at once restored Suarez Rondon, Quesada's captain, who had been imprisoned and his possessions confiscated by Lugo, to a place of confidence, and returned his property.

Under Ursua, by a royal deed executed in Valladolid in 1549, the seal of the Real Audiencia that was to be set up was dispatched to Bogotá. The deed provided that the official seal[1] was to be met with the same ceremony as if the emperor in person was going to be received. When it arrived the chief inhabitants, mounted on their best horses, richly caparisoned, took it in procession to the house of the governor Thus whilst, as some of the chroniclers aver, Quesada was wasting his time in Spain, or as is more reasonable to suppose, in view of all the books he wrote in his twelve years of absence, engaged in literature, his Rome was growing, both in importance and in size.

[1] " Este sello de la Real Audiencia que es de plata y de grandes dimensiones, existia en el Museo Nacional de Bogotá, como una curiosidad ": " Descubrimiento de la Nueva Granada," Colonel Joaquin Acosta, p. 331. It seems to have disappeared, for Colonel Acosta adds: " Ojalá se conserve con otros objetos antiguos á que el tiempo añade cada dia mayor precio."

CHAPTER XVII

TWELVE years had now elapsed since Quesada, Federman, and Belalcazar bade good-bye to their followers at the little port of Guataqui upon the Magdalena, close to Tocaima, and in their home-made vessel, probably the first built on the river, set out upon their return to Spain.

Many of those who watched the vessel out of sight as she swung down the stream and disappeared between the walls of vegetation of the primeval woods, that still come down to the water's edge upon the Magdalena's banks, must have been dead, either killed in Indian fights or worn out by the hardships they had undergone.

Federman was in his governorship at Coro in Venezuela, and Belalcazar had died at Cartagena, broken-hearted, on his way to Spain to lay his cause before the king.

The Emperor Charles V. had abdicated, and in the monastery at Yuste was riding his one-eyed chestnut pony about La Vera de Plasencia, still keeping watch upon the politics of the whole world. Philip the Prudent was on the throne, a strange and complex character, even more averse from rewarding faithful servants generously than was his father Charles V.

Most of the greater countries of Spanish America, as Mexico, Peru, Chile, and Venezuela, were, if not all explored, at least reduced to order, within more or less the same limits as to-day.

Communications with the Peninsula had become easier and quicker, for the average passage lasted some five and forty days, although ships had been known to acoomplish it in thirty-five.

From Bogotá to Cartagena or to Santa Marta the way was

clear. The trail from Facatativá, by Gúaduas, coming out
on to the Magdalena close by Honda, was established, and
possibly some of the rough cobble stones over which mules
still stumble had been laid down. Another route by Velez
followed the Cararé River, avoiding the more dangerous
valley of Opón.

Quesada, Federman, and Belalcazar, when they embarked
twelve years before at Guataqui, had taken twelve days to
reach Cartagena. This journey could not have been much
shortened,[1] as twelve days was a quick passage, considering
that they were perpetually attacked.

In all the states of South America, at that time, and even
to-day to some extent, there were great tracts of territory
unexplored. Especially this was the case in New Granada,
where all the country on the other side the Andes was
practically unknown. Still, in the past twelve years, great
strides had been accomplished, and anyone who, like
Quesada, had been long absent, returned to a new world.

By this time he had spent his money, and his emeralds
and gold were all exhausted, so he quite naturally turned
his eyes once more towards the country that he had conquered for his fatherland. Why he remained so long without
apparently taking any steps in order to secure employment
is a mystery. All through his life he had been ambitious
of renown. Throughout his whole career he had wished to
emulate Pizarro and Cortés, and it is known he thought his
merits equal at least to theirs. Besides all that, he always
thought he was entitled to be made Marquess of the Valley
of the Palaces,[2] as in good truth he was.

Perhaps pride held him back, or perhaps he knew that
the influence of the two ladies of the great Mendoza family,
who had protected and advanced before him the worthless
Lugo, was still all-powerful at court.

[1] It takes a week to-day, and, if there happens to be " novedad "
upon the voyage, quite easily may last ten days.   " Novedad "—
literally, novelty, or news—may comprehend in this case, a low river,
with the chance of sticking on a sandbank; perhaps a flood, with an
equal chance of sticking on a snag.

[2] Marques del Valle de los Alcazares.

In 1549, being without resources, or means of livelihood, he sent in a petition to the king, asking to be employed in New Granada, and Philip, who not once in his career seems to have been moved by generosity, appointed him Marshal[1] and Alderman of Bogotá with a small grant of two thousand ducats annually, and a repartimiento of Indians at Honda.

It was not much; but no doubt Quesada was glad to return to Bogotá on almost any terms.

About the end of 1549 he set sail for Cartagena with the three judges of the Audiencia Real and some Dominican and Franciscan friars.

As the three judges were to govern New Granada, it is likely that on the voyage they profited by the advice Quesada had in store as to the affairs of the New World.

The eldest of the three legal functionaries, one Mercado, died in Mompox, a town upon the Magdalena; but the other two, Gongora and Galarza, both young men, governed most wisely, having profited perhaps by the old conqueror's advice.

No details are preserved of Quesada's voyage up the Magdalena; but it is easy to imagine all he must have felt. Standing upon the vessel's deck as she forged slowly up the stream, gaining each yard by the hard labour of the " bogas,"[2] straining upon their poles, when the toucans and tunagers shot across the woods, and flocks of multi-coloured macaws sailed past like hawks, and parrots chattered in the trees, Quesada must have felt that he was coming home again.

He was now fifty years of age, but time had touched him lightly and preserved his strength for more adventures, perils, and hardships that might have broken down a younger man.

At early morning, when the white mist enshrouds the

[1] Mariscal y Regidor.
[2] " Boga " is a word used in Colombia to designate the men who row, but more usually punt, the great barges on the Magdalena. " Bogar " is to row.

Magdalena, blotting the forests out, except the tops of a tall palm-tree here and there, leaving the stream confined between two banks of vapour, that make it seem like an immense but turbulent canal, Quesada, wrapped in his cloak, shivering in the dank air that penetrates right to the marrow of the bones, must have looked anxiously about for hostile Indians waiting to attack. At midday, as the sun poured down its rays like molten brass upon the stream, stretched underneath the palm-thatched toldo, in the middle of the boat, the alligators lying motionless like logs awash upon the edges of the sandbanks, must have seemed as familiar to him as does a seal to northern navigators.

At evening, when the day's battle with the sun is over, and the night's skirmishing with every kind of insect is begun, taking the cool,[1] how often he must have started up to point out well-remembered spots and say, " There is the place the Indians attacked us, and so and so was slain—may God have pardoned him."

Then night would fall, and in their camp, sitting around the fire, or to the lee of it, to let the smoke drive the mosquitoes off a little, what recollections must have risen to his mind, when the long howling of the monkeys, or the snarling of the tigers, fell upon his ear. The dark, high walls of vegetation, that seem so hostile to mankind, especially to those but newly come from Europe, with the mysterious noises of the night, made by wild animals parting the brushwood with a soft swishing sound, all unfamiliar to his companions—these could have held no terrors for the conquistador.

Gazing out on the river in the moonlight, listening to the great fish leap and fall back with a resounding crash, watching the wake the tapir leaves behind him, in his noiseless swimming, his head erected like a horse, his back scarcely visible above the water, Quesada may have pointed out the animal invisible to eyes less trained to peer into the darkness of the night. Which route he followed is not known; but not unlikely it was up the Cararé to Velez,

---

[1] Tomando el fresco.

for it was more secure from Indian attack. No matter which way that he went, whether stumbling up the steep trail from Honda to Gúaduas, or on the path from Tocaima to Juntos de Apulo,[1] or if he set off straight from Velez across the plains to Bogotá, his impressions must have been the same. Each feature of the landscape would have been familiar to him on either of the roads. Each hill and wood and stream must have recalled some strange adventure of the conquest to him, when he and his two hundred Spaniards, with their sixty horses, were the first Europeans who had ever seen the sunset glowing red upon the white cone of the Nevado de Tolima, or the tall peak of El Ruiz.

When at last Bogotá broke upon his view, how eagerly he must have gazed at it, for though it cannot be supposed that in twelve years the city had assumed its present aspect, the changes must have been immense since he last looked on it.

His old companions, when they heard he was expected, mounted their horses and escorted him to make his entry to the town. The inhabitants welcomed him respectfully, and after a few days of feasting and rejoicing, Quesada settled down to take stock of the new city that he found so marvellously[2] changed.

Stone houses had sprung up where he had left huts thatched with straw. Roads had been made in several directions through La Sabána de Bogotá, and gardens had been planted outside the town, and plants and flowers from Europe had been sown.[3]

Though poor in fortune, he was rich in prestige, and though he lived in honourable poverty, he was much respected by his fellow-citizens, and on occasions when difficulties arose, with the home government or with the Indians, they all consulted him.

Especially in cases of complaints against unjust

[1] The railway follows this old road.

[2] " Halló todas las cosas trocadas ": Fray Simon.

[3] All European flowers grow well in Bogotá, and usually attain a much greater size than in Europe.

magistrates, or corrupt judges, the colonists looked on Quesada as their natural champion. Nor did he ever fail them, his legal training proving invaluable in cases of the kind. In the year 1556 the government sent out as " oidor "[1] a lawyer called Montaño, a man of a most severe and violent character, to inquire into the administration of Don Miguel Dias de Armendariz, who always had been popular with the colonists. Not only did Montaño proceed with rigour against Armendariz, but he soon got all the citizens of Bogotá almost in a state of revolt by his severity.

Bishop Piedrahita, who generally was an unfavourable critic of Quesada, confesses in this instance that " one cannot deny the diplomacy[2] and thoroughness with which Marshal Quesada examined into this difficult affair."

A saying of Quesada's is preserved in reference to Montaño, " that even if Montaño[3] were to cut off all the heads in the kingdom, and his own the first, . . . that he would not consent that a judge should arrest anyone except with an express order from the king, giving him power for it." His meaning seems to have been that Montaño had been sent out for a special purpose, to take the residence of Armendariz; but that he had no power to arrest the citizens.

Quesada stood up so stoutly against Montaño that he was forced to confine himself to the affairs of his mission and leave the colonists in peace.

During these years of peace and of retirement, Quesada seems to have had more opportunites of exercising his early legal training than his talents as a general.

For all that, his mind was always planning more ex-

---

[1] This official was a sort of Judge Ambulant, sent out from Spain to inquire into (or create) abuses.

[2] " No puede negarle al Mariscal Quesada, la politica profundidad con que discurrió tan zelosa materia :" Piedrahita.

[3] " Aunque Montaño cortase todas las cabeças del Reyno y la primera la suya . . . jamas consentiria á que Juez Supremo se prendiere, sin orden expreso del rey, persona, á quien diese facultad para ella ": Piedrahita.

peditions and further conquests; for once a conqueror, always a conqueror, and there was still a world of territory to explore and subjugate.

All through those quiet years of Quesada's poverty, Bogotá was growing and putting on airs of a capital. Convents and churches were springing up on every side, although there was no lime to build with, and the stones were set in mud,[1] which in that climate proved a substitute.

Quesada by degrees returned to his old position—the actual, if not the titular, head of the whole colony.

In 1553 he was sent at the request of the Real Audiencia to Cartagena, to take the residence of the Licenciado Juan Maldonado, an interim governor, who had been sent from Spain. The details of his proceedings in Cartagena are not preserved; but in 1557 he returned to Bogotá, as his health was suffering in the hot, damp climate of the coast.

About that time he began to petition Philip II. for permission to set out into the Llanos upon the Rio Meta, and seek the city of the El Dorado, an ignis fatuus that haunted him, in common with all the conquerors of the New World. Things in the palace at Madrid went slowly, as slowly as in the Spanish proverb,[2] and the correspondence between Quesada, Philip, and the Real Audiencia occupied several years. The Real Audiencia of Bogotá accorded him permission for his expedition, but on one pretext or another Philip delayed, perhaps because Quesada was insistent on being made a marquess, for his ambition to be equal with Pizarro and Cortés pursued him all his days. Whilst he was waiting for the pleasure of the dilatory king, he still kept on consolidating his position in Bogotá, and by degrees became a sort of unofficial court of appeal on

---

[1] " Por el modo con que se fabricaban estos edificios . . . se infiere que en aquella epoca, no se habia descubierto todavia la cal en las inmediaciones de dicha ciudad ": Colonel Joaquin Acosta, p. 339. He goes on to say that in repairing his father's house (in 1840–49) he found all the stones were merely laid in mud, and that the house was very old, being the same as the ancient convent of Santo Domingo.

[2] Cosas de palacio, van despacio.

every kind of cause. No doubt his fellow-citizens knew he was a sound lawyer as well as a born man of arms.

An Indian girl, by name Luisa, described in the petition that the injured husband had addressed to Quesada, as a jade,[1] had left her Lares and Penates and run off with one Cetina, and all her husband's prayers to her to come back to him had proved of no avail. The jade alleged that the Real Audiencia had given her liberty to choose[2] the master that she liked, and it appears Cetino was the master of her choice.

Quesada instantly swooped like an eagle on the weakness of the plea. The girl Luisa came from one of his own repartimientos, thus giving rise to a nice point of law that he at once perceived. He answered, saying, that this "liberty" was null and void, because Luisa was attached to the repartimiento, and not in service[3] or a slave. A fine kind of "liberty" it would be, he said, that though the husband was doing all he could to please his wife, that she should be allowed to choose another man to live with, merely as his concubine.[4] He therefore begged the Real Audiencia to send a magistrate to send his "pieza" back to his repartimiento, and give the husband back his wife.[5] It is not known how the affair concluded, or if the fickle jade Luisa was restored to her own lawful husband or went on living in her sin.

The duties that Quesada's fellow-townsmen laid upon

[1] La picara.

[2] "Una de esas Indias llamada Luisa se marchó con un tal Antonio Cetina quien la llevó á Anserma. La picara que no deseaba volver al lado de su esposo, decia que tenia una permision de la Audiencia Real, que le daba libertad para escoger, al amo con quien quisiera estar." This curious incident is preserved in a History of Bogotá by Dr. Ibañez (Pedro M.), Bogota, 1892.

[3] Era pieza de repartimiento y no de servicio.

[4] Y buena libertad seria, que esta el pobre marido haciendo los extremos que hace cada dia por la mujer, y que ella escogiere de vivir con el que la tenia por manceba.

[5] "Pido y suplico á Usia, mande enviar á mi costa un juez de comision que me vuelva mis piezas á mis repartimientos, que aunque sea á costa mia, no es justo que el pobre marido este sin su mujer": Dr. Ibañez.

him were not, however, of this semi-humorous nature, for at times the newly conquered kingdom of New Granada ran serious perils from attacks, either of Indians or by free-booting bands of Spaniards who had rebelled against their governors.

At that time a celebrated bandit, Lope de Aguirre, after a career of crime almost incredible,[1] had established himself near the mouth of the Amazon, and report said was about to sail up the Magdalena to the attack of Bogotá. The judges of the Real Audiencia who were governing the country were both young lawyers, without military ex-perience; but they were men of sense. They listened to the unanimous wishes of the colonists, that they would have no leader but Quesada, whom they had seen a hundred times at work in that capacity. Enthusiasm ran high in Bogotá. The Real Audiencia made him captain-general of the army, and the inhabitants swarmed round his house begging to be enrolled beneath his banner. From distant places the old conquerors who had accompanied Quesada during the fateful year upon the Magdalena, when they and he had suffered thirst and hunger, and all the terrors of the unknown, converged on Bogotá. They left their farms and wives, and, mounted on their best horses, bringing their friends

[1] Lope de Aguirre was a soldier who accompanied Don Pedro de Ursua from Quito on a voyage down the Amazon. Don Pedro was beloved by everyone for his good character. The Inca Garcilasso de la Vega says of him: " Un cavallero llamado Pedro de Ursua, que yo conoci en el Peru, hombre de todo hondad, y virtud, gentil hombre de su persona, y agradable á la vista de todos " (" Co-mentarios Reales," vol. ii., p. 495, Madrid, 1722). Lope de Aguirre rose against him, murdered him and all those of the expedition who would not join in the revolt. He then attacked and plundered several settlements, murdering all the inhabitants, and established himself in the island of Margarita. At last he was hunted down and slain; but before his death he killed his daughter, not that he feared ill-treatment for her, but because he did not wish after his death people should say she was a traitor's child. " Mató una hija suya que consigo llevara, no por otra causa mas de porque despues de el muerto no la llamaren Hija de el Traidor. . . . Aguirre era de ruin talle y de perversa condicion ": " Comentarios Reales," El Inca Garcilasso de la Vega.

and neighbours, with parties of armed Indians, they gathered round their old and trusted general.

As he stood in the plaza and watched the bands arrive, and recognized and greeted many a captain who had fought by his side, and soldiers not a few that he might have forgotten, or at least disremembered till he saw them once again, Quesada's heart must have beat high with pride. As they arrived from the hot country by Tocaima, from Anolaima, Honda, Guataqui, and Velez, from Ubaté and Facatativá, Zipaquirá and Gúaduas nestling in its thickets of bamboos, from Tunja, Sogamoso, and from the little towns on the Sabána de Bogotá, he must have felt he had not lived in vain.

Kings might neglect, and envious rivals rise above his head, pushed on by petticoats;[1] but the old friends who knew him best had rallied to his flag when the new colony was in danger of attack.   It was his glorious hour, and all that he had suffered and endured, his disappointments, the long delay to recognize his claims (the claims of merit), all would disappear, and when he got upon his horse to ride along the ranks of his embattled friends, he must have felt himself a twofold conqueror.   As things turned out, Lope de Aguirre was killed before he could carry his raid into effect, and the warlike preparations never were required.

Naturally Quesada rose still more in the estimation of the citizens of Bogotá, and seems to have enjoyed that rare and enviable position of wielding power without the onus of responsibility.

Quesada must have been accumulating property by degrees, for it appears that as administrator in lands that he possessed in Tierra Fria, he had one Señor Alonso George, a Portuguese, a magnificent gentleman.[2] The Portuguese showed himself both generous and most magnificent in an Indian adventure that happened to him.

A soldier, whose name Fray Simon withholds to save his

[1] Falditas.

[2] " El magnifico señor Alonso George, caballero portugues ": Fray Simon.

honour,[1] pursued an Indian on his horse. Having caught him up, he attacked him with his lance. The Indian, however, caught the horse's bridle, stopped him, threw the rider to the ground, and would have killed him had not several other horsemen galloped up to his aid. The Indian gallantly faced them all, until one horseman lanced him through the stomach, so that his entrails came out. The Indian, nothing daunted, held them in with his left hand, and faced his enemies with a club he wielded in his right. Luckily for him, as he was engaged with the three Spaniards, Captain Alonso George galloped up, and seeing the bravery with which the Gandul[2] fought, drew up his horse beside him, and with his lance kept the three soldiers off, saying so brave a man should not be slain. Then, this magnificent but humane Portuguese gentleman mounted the Indian on his horse, took him to his home and cared for him, and in a week or two his wounds were healed.

The Indian, it is said, was grateful, as well he might have been. The name of the gallant Portuguese cavalier has been commemorated by Fray Simon in his veracious chronicle, and it deserves to be preserved. Those who come after him, perhaps, may be allowed, in the retelling of the tale, to brush the dust off from the monument that Fray Simon has raised, as Old Mortality cleared away the moss from the lone graves in Galloway kirkyards.

If Quesada had to double the functions of judge of appeal and captain, he also now and then was called upon to keep the peace amongst the citizens.

Fresle[3] relates a curious instance, showing the enormous personal respect paid to Quesada, and how all bowed to his authority.

A tactless but well-meaning governor, Dr. Don Andres

---

[1] Por su honor.

[2] " Gandul " was used in New Granada, and I think in Peru and Venezuela, at that time, to designate an adult Indian. In Spanish, " gandul " means vagabond, and it may be that the word has been brought from the Indies and become incorporated into the language, as have " maiz," " hamaca," and several other words.

[3] " El Carnero Bogotano."

Diaz de Leiva, a man full of good impulses; but who, as runs the Spanish phrase, seems to have heard bells,[1] but was uncertain where. His legitimate wife,[2] who is described as a valorous woman, was of great help to him, though he may possibly not always have followed[3] her advice.

Being a great protector of the Indians, he issued a proclamation, that anyone who ill-treated them should receive two hundred lashes and be fined. Those who have lived in colonies in any quarter of the world can judge how such a proclamation would be received to-day amongst the ruling race. In the days of Quesada it was flat blasphemy, and certain to offend.

It happened that the day the edict was stuck up in the chief street of Bogotá, many of Quesada's ancient captains had come into the town; all of them conquerors. They gathered round the notice-board and read it silently. No doubt their hands felt for their swords, and oaths were muttered; but no one spoke a word. At last Captain Zorro, throwing the corner[4] of his cloak over his left shoulder, exclaimed, " God aamn me; gentlemen captains, are we to be flogged ? Was it this paltry rogue of a governor who conquered Bogotá ? Follow me, gentlemen, I intend to cut him into shreds."

They all rushed off towards the palace of the governor, with their cloaks wrapped about their arms, and their drawn swords in their hands.

Hearing the noise in the street, Quesada rushed up to the audience chamber, where he found a magistrate, Don Melchor Perez de Artiaga, at the stair head, armed with a partizan and with his wand of office on the ground. It

---

[1] Ha oido campanas, y no sabe donde.

[2] Su legitima mujer.

[3] The Moors in Morocco say, " Always ask your wife's advice, but never follow it." The Spaniards, on the contrary, have an adage, " The counsel of a woman is of little weight, but he who does not follow it is mad " (" El consejo de la mujer es poco, quien no lo toma es loco ").

[4] " Echando el canto de la capa sobre el hombro izquierdo, y diciendo Voto a Dios ": " Carnero Bogotano," Rodriguez Fresle.

would have fared but poorly with Don Melchor had he been there alone, for all the captains were crowding up the stairs. Finding Quesada standing by his side they halted. Doña Maria de Leiva, hearing the noise, came out of her apartments, and placing herself beside Quesada, took the partizan from Don Melchor, and picking up his wand of office she put it in his hand. The valorous and legitimate lady saved the situation, for the captains, pleased at her ready wit and her bold bearing, put up their swords, and, after listening to a harangue Quesada made, no novel experience for the most of them, they quickly went away.

With an occasional trial, or a dispute about the Indians whom the conquerors held in semi-slavery; with threats of war, as in the case of Lope de Aguirre; and no doubt with much material progress in the construction of the town, life wore away in Bogotá. Quesada still was without an answer from King Philip, and he was drawing near to seventy years of age.

CHAPTER XVIII

At last King Philip, who had muddled so much of the world's business, and in especial that of the Americas, from the seclusion of El Escorial, made up his mind as to the petition Quesada had addressed to him so many years ago.

By a Real Cedula, dated at El Escorial the 15th of November, 1568, Quesada was appointed Adelantado of El Nuevo Reino de Granada, but without jurisdiction or the usual powers the office carried with it. His salary was raised, and more Indians were given him in " Encomienda," at Tunja, Mariquita, and other places, whose very name King Philip only knew through the exertions of the man he now so grudgingly was obliged to recognize.

Thus did the Emperor Charles V. and his son Philip, but Philip far more than his father, so often fail to appreciate that an empire had been placed within their hands, as it were, from the skies.

With the long-withheld title of Adelantado, came permission to undertake the conquest of the Llanos, and the illusory concession of four hundred leagues of land between the Rivers Pauto and Papamene.[1]   He was to be the governor of these far-off territories, with power to leave the office to his son, or in default, to anyone he chose to name.   What Quesada probably valued more than all was the promise of the title of marquess, should he succeed in conquering and settling the lands.

Though, when the long-desired and oft-delayed permission at last arrived, Quesada was near seventy years of age, he set about his preparations for the expedition with the same energy that he had displayed when he first sailed from

[1] The Pauto and the Papamene might just as well have been rivers of Damascus, for they were situated in country, but little explored even to-day, on the Llanos of the Orinoco.

Santa Marta, up the Magdalena, in his youth. His old prosperity seemed to be going to take a new lease of life. His prestige and his popularity had never stood so high. It seemed to everyone that in his old age he was about to achieve new conquests, receive fresh honours, and that the conqueror of New Granada was at last to be placed on the same footing as the conquerors of Mexico and of Peru. No one seems to have doubted for a moment of his ultimate success. Against all reason, the inhabitants of Bogotá were perfectly convinced of the existence of a mysterious Golden City, in the great plains along the Orinoco and the Amazon. Stranger than that, they thought that these alluvial plains were rich in gold, although they must have known by their own experience that all the gold that they had found themselves came from mines situated in the hills.

All his old captains and his soldiers who were still alive once again flocked to Quesada, and begged to be enrolled under his standard, and colonists but just arrived from Spain caught the fever of adventure, and prayed to be allowed to march with him.

Quesada bound himself by his agreement with the Real Audiencia of Bogotá to take five hundred men all well equipped and armed. With them, for the welfare of their souls, and to spread the tidings of the Gospel amongst the infidel, he took eight priests and friars, two of whom were to prove the historians of the expedition, and were both men of letters and of intelligence.

One of the friars was Pedro de Aguado, whose History of Venezuela is one of the chief works upon the conquest of that country.[1] The other was Fray Antonio de Medrano,[2] who died of privation in the Llanos during the expedition. Little is known of him beyond the fact that he had resided fifteen years in the Indies,[3] consecrated to preaching the

[1] " Historia de Venezuela."

[2] He wrote " La Historia de Santa Marta y Nuevo Reino de Granada."

[3] Residió quince años en las Indias consagrado á la predicacion del Evangelio y conversion de los indigenas.

Gospel and to the conversion of the Indians. Fray Pedro de Aguado was far better known. In 1573 he was elected provincial of the Seraphic Order of Franciscans in Bogotá. In 1575 he returned to Spain, and probably died in Cordoba, in which city he is known to have lived for a considerable time.

After Medrano's death, Aguado continued the account of Quesada's expedition,[1] to which Fray Antonio de Medrano had been appointed chronicler.

Though the conditions of his capitulation with the Real Audiencia were onerous, Quesada never seems to have been more confident of ultimate success. Of course, he was quite ignorant of the intricate system of rivers, such as the Meta, the Casanáre, the Guaviare, and a thousand more of greater or of lesser size, that flow, some into the Orinoco, some into each other, and make the crossing of the Llanos a work of difficulty. The Llanos were not so utterly unknown as they had been thirty years before, when Federman crossed them from Venezuela on his adventurous march to Bogotá. There was by this time a half-way house between the plains of Bogotá and the great plains across the Andes, for in 1555 Captain Juan de Avellañeda had founded a town that he called San Juan de los Llanos, nearly five hundred miles away from Bogotá. This town was valuable chiefly on two accounts. In the first place, it was the point from which all expeditions to the Llanos had to jump off into the unknown.

[1] The joint work of the two friars is the only authentic account of the fantastic and most unfortunate expedition. It remained unpublished till 1906, when the first nine books were published in Bogotá. A complete edition appeared in Madrid in 1916, published by La Real Academia de la Historia. Both Fray Simon and Bishop Piedrahita are known to have used the original manuscript. The book is valuable, as Aguado declares in his prologue, dedicated " A la S. C. R. Majestad Don Philippe segundo deste nombre Rey de las Españas, Monarcha universal del Nuevo Mundo," that the writer was " testigo de vista, hallandome á todo, ó en la major parte." The dedication is signed " Vassallo y Capellan de V. C. R. Md. que sus Reales manos besa." He styles himself, " Frayle menor y el menor y mas humilde de sus criados," and concludes by wishing Don Philippe " salud y gloria inmortal."

Moreover, there were valuable mines upon the River Ariari not very far from it. These mines had much enriched a certain gentleman, Don Francisco Aguilar, who had exploited them, probably by the forced labour of the Indians.

The settlers in the town must have acquired a certain knowledge of the Indians living on the Rio Meta, and have learned from them, if only vaguely, something about the plains that lay beyond it and extended to the Orinoco, like an enormous sea of grass, with islands here and there of tall Moriché palms.

In addition to the five hundred[1] men and the eight friars he had to take upon his expedition, Quesada had obliged himself to take great quantities of stock to found a colony and to set up cattle farms. Upon arrival at his destination, he agreed to build forts to defend his territory from the Indians, and to found several towns.

Within four years he was to send out five hundred colonists, and to have houses ready for them when they should arrive. The colonists were to be married, if it was possible to find so many married men in Bogotá willing to risk so much, and to adventure with their families and wives into the wilderness.

He had to take five hundred mares, three hundred cows, four hundred horses, and a thousand pigs, and in addition to this troop of animals five hundred negro[2] slaves.

By a provision of the capitulation, he was specially debarred from taking with him any " chontal "[3] Indians— that is to say, Indians who had not lived amongst the whites. As regards Indians who had been baptized, and had received some little education, he might take as many as he chose.

Animals must have multiplied extraordinarily in the last five and twenty years in New Granada, for there does not

---

[1] At the last minute he was allowed to take four hundred as a minimum.

[2] Machos y hembras.

[3] " Chontal " was used at that time in New Granada and Central America, in the sense of " wild."

appear that he experienced any difficulty in providing those he was bound to take.

In order to establish good and fitting government,[1] he was to build mills on the rivers, where it was possible, and to plant sugar-canes. All this Quesada pledged himself to do out of his own resources.[2] He never was a man who for a moment allowed money to stand between him and anything he had at heart. So without hesitation he pledged his lands, his slaves, haciendas, and everything he had. For all that he would have been unable to equip his expedition properly had not Don Francisco Aguilar, the wealthy mineowner of the Ariari River, come to his assistance with a considerable sum.

All his old captains that were still alive joined him, and soldiers flocked into his camp. In addition to his soldiers and the herdsmen who he must have had to drive and care for so many animals, he took some fifteen hundred semi-civilized Indians to serve as baggage-carriers. With the whole force, and with the flocks and herds he had to take, Quesada's camp must have resembled an Arab tribe upon the march.

In addition to the four hundred horses that he was under obligation to take with him, counting the horses of the cavalry and the spare horses taken by the richer of his followers, more than a thousand horses started with him from Bogotá. No expedition of such magnitude had ever been assembled in the New Kingdom of Granada, or started out under such favourable auspices.

Quesada, although past his prime[3] in years, was still active and vigorous. He had the confidence of those he led to an incredible degree.

All knew his prowess as a captain, and many of the soldiers and the officers had served with him and knew his infinite resource, his power of suffering hardships, and his skill in dealing with the savage tribes. His superior educa-

---

[1] Para el buen gobierno.

[2] Todo á su costa y mision.

[3] He must have been between sixty-nine and seventy years of age.

tion, and the great personal magnetism he undoubtedly possessed, raised him to a height as a commander that, with the possible exception of Cortés, had been enjoyed by no one Spaniard in the New World.

When all was ready early in 1569, after, we may suppose, a solemn ceremony in the church, according to the fashion of those times, Quesada started on his momentous expedition, the horses, cows, and other animals having been driven on ahead. All the inhabitants of Bogotá turned out, and some escorted him for a few miles upon the road.

One Captain Diego Soleto was Quesada's guide, as he had been before upon an expedition to the Llanos. On his advice they marched towards the River Ariari, hoping from there to find a better route than that traversed by Hernan Perez de Quesada so many years ago.

From the first misfortune dogged the steps of the expedition, for, owing to the quantity of animals, they marched so slowly that it took twenty days to reach the River Guejar, where he encamped to rest. At that place, by a misadventure, his powder magazine blew up, killing a number of his men and burning down his tent. The loss of all the powder did not prove so disastrous to the expedition as might have been expected, for they had little fighting other than skirmishes with the wild Indians, and, as was usual in those days, the game they found was killed by the crossbowmen, or by the mounted soldiers with their spears. Quesada, nothing daunted by his first misfortune, pushed on until he reached San Juan de los Llanos, the farthest outpost of the Spanish power.

Whilst the animals were being slowly driven on ahead towards the Llanos, Quesada determined on a rest, as the expedition already had suffered a good deal of loss through hardships and disease. It seems impossible that there was nobody in San Juan de los Llanos to inform him that he was going on a wild-goose chase.

The guide, Captain Soleto, was perhaps the man who had the most experience, for he had been upon the River Meta. and must have known the nature of the country, the deadly climate, and the difficulties of the road. Still, he does not appear to have raised his voice against the folly of supposing that a Golden City could exist in the great plains, destined so soon to prove the ruin of the best-appointed expedition that had left Bogotá.

The mine-owner, Don Francisco Aguilar, who had lived long, or long enough to make a fortune, on the Ariari River, must have been well aware that the great plains about the River Meta were not fit places for a colony. Still, he did nothing to dissuade Quesada from rushing on his fate. So far from that, he seemed quite certain that the expedition would prove successful, for he advanced considerable sums towards its equipment and fitting out.

Whilst the expedition rested at San Juan de los Llanos, two soldiers, Pedro de Fuentes and Francisco Bravo, having quarrelled on some point or other, agreed to fight the question out alone and without seconds, and to fight to the death. Having repaired into the woods, they drew their swords and fell upon each other most determinedly. At the first pass or two Bravo ran Fuentes through the arm, and could have killed him; but knowing well Quesada was opposed to combats of the kind, and fearing punishment, he ran off towards the camp, leaving, as he thought, Fuentes dead upon the field. However, Fuentes bound up his injured arm, and, having drawn his dagger with his left hand, ran after Bravo, who did not look behind him, thinking his adversary dead. When Fuentes overtook him, he stabbed him rapidly three times between the shoulders, and left him lifeless on the ground. The story is preserved by Castellanos,[1] who in his youth had been a soldier and a conqueror, before he was a priest. Whether the old leaven still stirred in his mind or whether he expressed merely a truism, he remarks cavalierly, that " he who neglects precautions with his foes[2] will perish at their hands." The fact is obvious, although not many Anglo-Saxons

---

[1] " Elegias de Varones Ilustres de Indias," Juan de Castellanos, Canto 23, p. 223. (Madrid, 1589.)

[2] Quien que á los contrarios suyos papa, á manos suyas muere.

care to admit it in their writings, although they act upon it.

Quesada, who had the example of the sufferings endured by the expedition that his brother once had led towards the Llanos, present before his eyes, determined to avoid them, if it were possible, by following a new road. Hardly had he passed the mountains and emerged upon the plains, than the ill-fortune that had dogged him from the first, once more attacked him, but with redoubled force, for leagues in front of them stretched out an interminable waste of high, rough grass, so high as to rise above a man's head, so thick that when the Indian tribes were on the march,[1] they used to put their strongest men in front to break a way, and those who followed stepped in their tracks, like mountaineers opening a path through snow.

Above the grass, buzzed countless myriads of mosquitoes, horseflies, and sandflies, and if the passer-by by accident touched the branch of a tree, a swarm of ants or wasps was certain to descend upon him.

All the winged torments of the insect world were nothing in comparison to the green mosquitoes,[2] whose bite causes a swelling that gives intolerable pain and brings on fever in the sufferer.

Snakes were abundant and extremely venomous. Game was both scarce and shy, and the provisions soon got mouldy and uneatable. The constant rains rotted their clothes, and the old soldiers who had suffered all the horrors of the year upon the Magdalena with Quesada, declared that all that they had then endured was nothing in comparison with their present sufferings.

Exposure to the sun and rain, poor food and want of

---

[1] " Primero marchan los mocetones fuertes . . . la paja que brotan aquellos Llanos de ordinario excede la estatura de un hombre ": " El Orinoco Ilustrado," P. Joseph Gumilla, p. 189. (Madrid, 1741.)

[2] " Todo esta multitud de enemigos es despreciable y se hace llevadera en comparacion de unos mosquitos verdes que llaman de gusanos ": " El Orinoco Ilustrado," P. Joseph Gumilla, p. 475.

shelter, ravaged their ranks with fever, and they began to die like bugs, as goes the Spanish phrase.[1]

The troops of animals that the expedition was taking with them were preyed on nightly by the tigers; bitten by snakes; drowned in the passage of the frequent rivers; lost in the cane-brakes; and rendered desperate by the attacks of millions of flies. They died off fast, and a long trail of bones soon marked the passage of the doomed expedition, on its Calvary.

The dreams of pearls and precious stones, of cities full of golden temples and mines of incalculable wealth, must soon have vanished as league succeeded league, and not a soul appeared, but a few naked, wandering Indians. Even the stimulus of fighting was not there, as it had been upon the Magdalena, in the days of old. Each night there were desertions, for the unlucky soldiers, unable to bear their sufferings, straggled away on the back trail, only to die of hunger or of thirst or to be eaten by wild beasts. Seeing that the desertions were becoming serious, Quesada hung two soldiers as an example; but the misery that they were suffering made his men careless of their lives, and the desertions always became more frequent and more ominous.

From his camp on the River Guaigo, Quesada determined to send back to Bogotá his sick and wounded men, under Captain Juan Maldonado. This officer, after a journey of six months, and having suffered countless miseries, arrived with a small portion of the sick, at San Juan de los Llanos. The rest had perished on the road.

Only Quesada still bore up against the universal misery. He still pushed on towards Manoa,[2] the supposititious capital of the unattainable golden country, that had stirred all his dreams.

His captains died around him, unable to resist the climate, and the unlucky chronicler of the expedition, Father Medrano,

[1] Morian como chinches.

[2] " Manoa, nombre que dan los Mapas á la ciudad principal del Dorado ": " El Orinoco Ilustrado," P. Joseph Gumilla, p. 282.

worn out with fever, also breathed his last. His death[1] cut short his chronicle of the expedition in which he had endured so many perils and such hardships; but luckily Fray Pedro de Aguado, his companion, carried it on for him.

Months dragged on into years; but still the unlucky expedition struggled on, daily diminishing, for death took heavy toll both of the animals and men. The miserable soldiers were reduced to eating roots and herbs, the bark of trees, and such wild fruits as they could chance upon. Even Quesada had to live upon some herbs he knew by the experience of his old campaigns. He ate them, flavoured with a piece of rock-salt[2] that he carried with him. This after God, as the pious chronicler observes, was the best help he had.

Most likely the roots and herbs he ate were what are known as " guapos " in the Llanos of the Rio Meta, a kind of ground-nut well known to the Indians.

At last even the long-suffering Spanish soldiers had had enough of it, and broke out into mutiny, demanding to return. Notwithstanding the straits that he was in, his poverty, the misery that all of them had endured, and the hopeless nature of the quest they were engaged upon, Quesada's prestige with his men was still so great that, when he spoke to them, the wretched, but heroic men at once returned to duty, swearing to follow him unto the death. Few men have ever been in a more desperate position than he was, at that time, after the mutiny.

Of all his men, but forty-five remained alive, with only a few horses and fewer Indians. The cows, the mares, the pigs, and all the animals were either dead, or had been eaten by the soldiery. Of the five and forty heroes who remained, Quesada found himself obliged to allow some twenty to return. He himself, with the remaining twenty-five, camped on the River Guaviare, and, after some days'

---

[1] " La muerte cortó sus pasos, ó sacaria á luz muchas y muy buenas cosas ": Fray Simon.

[2] " Favorecióle Dios primeramente y luego un pedazo de sal, con que comia algunas yerbas que conocia ": " El Carnero Bogotano," Fresle.

rest, once more pushed on into the wilds. By this time, he must surely have been well aware that there was no Manoa, with its glittering towers, no Golden Country, and no mines of precious stones, and, above all things, no Indian kingdom comparable to Mexico or to Peru, in front of him. He struggled on, it is supposed, to somewhere near the junction of the Guaviare and the Orinoco. Then most reluctantly he gave up the quest, and returned back to Bogotá with five and twenty men, four Indians, and a few worn-out, half-starved horses, all that remained of the expedition that three years before had set out confident that they would find a golden country and a city built of gold.

Quesada now was either seventy-two or seventy-three years old. He had given one more proof of his indomitable will, and once again displayed a courage, proof against difficulties.

The expedition cost from first to last two hundred thousand dollars, a sum of which a large amount Quesada had himself furnished, or become pledged to pay. This left him poor and weighted down with debt to the last day of his life; but all his sufferings, his misfortunes and his debts, did but endear him to the inhabitants of Bogotá.

Though broken down in health, poor, and arrived at an age when he might well have sought repose, fate still reserved for him a last and stirring incident in his career.

CHAPTER XIX

THE expedition, although so unsuccessful, did not kill the hope of still finding out a way to the El Dorado, in spite of everything Quesada had undergone.

The citizens of Bogotá, although not blaming him, still said he must have taken the wrong road. Nothing seems eradicable in the human mind, but what is false. As to the truth, that is a plant that withers with the first breath of folly, and from that quarter there always is a breeze.

Of the great conquerors of America, Pizarro, and Pizarro only, never embarked upon a wild-goose expedition such as Quesada's proved. Cortés, already elderly, suffered the extremes of hardship on his unlucky voyage to California. Sir Walter Raleigh lost his head on account of his expedition to seek for El Dorado. All the bravest and the best of the discoverers and conquerors of those days seem to have believed in its existence, fervently. This, perhaps, was the reason why Quesada did not lose his popularity after his failure, for everybody thought that he had failed in a quite reasonable attempt. On his return he seems to have lived quietly, thinking, most likely, that he would never more be called upon to mount his horse and take the field again.

The city he had conquered now was growing fast, and taking on a little of the aspect of a capital.

When the first school was established in Bogotá, Quesada was delighted to see this evidence of progress in the city he had founded, and to show his appreciation of it he left his library to the Convent of St. Thomas,[1] as it was there the first school had been held.

---

[1] " Por manifestar el gozo de ver estudios en la Cabeza del Reyno que avia conquistado empezó desde este año á celebrar la fiesta de Santo Tomas, y despues dexó á este convento toda su libraria ": " Historia de la Provincia de San Antonino del Nuevo Reino de Granada," El P. M. Fray Alonso de Zamora, p. 73. (Barcelona, 1781.)

Between his town house at Bogotá and his country house at Suesca, Quesada must have passed his time not too unpleasantly. At Suesca he first seems to have had the idea of writing a complete history of the conquest. It was there he wrote his well-known " Ratos de Suesca," a book now lost,[1] but from which it is supposed many of the chroniclers and historians copied, when it was still to be obtained in manuscript.

No doubt the erstwhile gallant horseman used to ride out to Suesca on a pacing horse, as years and increasing broken health made him unequal to the fatigue[2] of a " trotón." At Suesca he occupied himself with the ordinary pursuits of a Spanish country gentleman of those days, filling in his leisure hours with literature.

Although Quesada had lost money, credit, and his army, had failed to find the El Dorado, had seen his long-coveted title of marquess vanish into the air, he seems not to have been discouraged, and to have resumed without an effort his old position of first citizen of the republic, respected and consulted in all difficulties. This was to appear in a marked degree when all the colonists appealed to their ancient leader, in his old age, once more to take the field against the Indians. Unfortunately no one of all the chroniclers has preserved for us those intimate traits of character, that show a man for what he is, far more than actions done in the public light. No one has set down how he dressed, as did the Inca Garcilasso, when he sums up Pizarro's character. The Inca tells us how the great Pizarro always dressed in black,[3] and in the antique style. We know that he was fond of

---

[1] See Appendix II.

[2] " Un caballo de paso "—*i.e.*, a pacing horse—is still much esteemed in Colombia, Peru, and Brazil, as it is throughout the East. " Troton " was the word used in Quesada's time for a horse that was not a pacer.

[3] " El Marques nunca se vistió de ordinario, sino un saio de paño negro hasta el tovillo . . . y unos zapatos de venado blancos, y un sombrero blanco y su espada y puñal al Antigua ": " Comen tarios Reales," El Inca Garcilasso de la Vega, lib. iii., p. 150,

playing bowls, and was a man of great simplicity of manners and affability of speech.

Bernal Diaz del Castillo has left so fine and so complete a picture of Cortés (whom he loved, on this side idolatry) that one can see him in his habit[1] as he lived.

Few details of Quesada's private life have been preserved. We know from Castellanos that he had some aspirations[2] towards poetry, and that he often talked with him about the " ancient Spanish metres[3] so fitting to our tongue." Whether these aspirations were towards active poetry is doubtful; but if they were, Quesada may be called the first of the great rhyming brood that has spread its wings, and soared so valiantly on the Parnassus of Bogotá.

As years went on, Quesada, in his retirement, busied himself with all affairs relating to the Indians, protecting them on all occasions from ill-treatment by the colonists.

He was naturally a kind-hearted man, and we know from the testimony of Piedrahita that his conscience pricked him sorely in the matter of the death of the last Zipa of Bogotá. A saying of Quesada's, that Piedrahita quotes, but without telling where he got it from, shows that Quesada always had his eye upon the conduct of the government officials from his retirement.

Speaking of the Oidor Briceño, an official of the Real Audiencia, he says, " There was no better minister[4] to make laws in favour of the Indians, nor a worse man to execute them."

Thus did Quesada pass his life, after his return from his disastrous expedition to the Llanos, striving to make amends

[1] " Historia de la Conquista de la Nueva España," Bernal Diaz del Castillo, cap. cciv., pp. 449–464. (Madrid, 1796.)

[2] Tenia infulas de poeta.

[3] " Y el porfió conmigo muchas veces sobre los metros antiguos Castellanos, los proprios y adaptados á su lengua ": " Elegias de Varones Ilustres de Indias," Castellanos.

[4] " No habia Ministro mejor para disponer leyes en favor de los Indios, ni peor para ejecutarlas ": " Historia General de las Conquistas del Nuevo Reyno de Granada," Piedrahita.

for his one great crime; perhaps pushed by his known humanitarian character, to which several of the chroniclers amply testify.

His early legal training must have stood him in good stead when it was necessary to explain the laws, for he most certainly was the most accomplished lawyer that the colony contained.

Especially was legal knowledge necessary in the interpretation of the laws of the Indies, a large and intricate code, whose liberal tendency all the Spanish colonists invariably endeavoured to evade. The code laid down that no Indian was to be enslaved on any pretext. True it was, certain of the provisions of the code went very near the line; but the main fact remains, to the credit of the Spanish kings. Much, in this case, depended on the attitude of the governors and the chief people of the colony. If they enslaved the Indians, the practice soon became general amongst the colonists.

This, to his everlasting credit, Quesada manfully withstood. Acosta, the historian of the conquests, perhaps the greatest of the Jesuits who went to the New World, says of Quesada that " he never would allow an Indian to be sold to slavery."[1]

Years slipped away, and it seemed probable that Quesada never would be called upon again to save the colony.

He was now seventy-seven years of age, and his health was broken, though his last fatal malady had not declared itself.

It was not fated that he should leave the scene without one more glorious exploit, and a piece of service that showed how high he stood in the estimation of the citizens of the kingdom that he had conquered for them.

Either in 1573 or 1575, for the chroniclers give the date differently, the warlike tribe of the Gualies under their chief Yuldama, a man of great ability, conceived the idea

---

[1] " Jamas permitió que se vendiese á ningun Indio como esclavo ": " Historia Natural y Moral de las Indias," El Padre José de Acosta. (Sevilla, 1596.)

of throwing off the Spanish yoke. Yuldama formed a confederacy of several tribes, and began to attack and burn the Spanish settlements about Tocaima, Mariquita, and in the hot country near the Magdalena's banks. For a short time it looked as if -the whole kingdom of New Granada would join in the revolt.

The Real Audiencia had put few troops at its command; but it thought that with the authority of Quesada's name sufficient forces could be raised amongst the colonists to restore order and reduce the rebel tribes.

Quesada instantly accepted the commission, and once more, in his old age, he found himself at the head of a sufficient force, that at the mention of his name appeared to rise out of the earth.

He knew his countrymen, and to enlist their aid put out a proclamation promising to found a new town on the frontiers, and to give grants of land to all who followed him and fought beneath his flag.

He himself, broken in health by all the hardships he had undergone, headed the expedition on his horse, although fatigue obliged him now and then to be carried in a hammock, borne by stout Indians. Age had not impaired his faculties for generalship, for he fell like a thunderbolt upon the Indians, burning their towns, and following them relentlessly until they sued for terms.

Their chief Yuldama fell in a skirmish, and at his death the confederacy dissolved. Once more, in his old age, Quesada entered Bogotá in triumph amongst the acclamations of the citizens.

His last achievement brought him amazing popularity. All knew that the old conquistador had never spared himself and that he was the first to mount his horse at daybreak, riding until exhaustion forced him to his litter, and dismounting last at night.

In all the skirmishes, despite the protests of his officers, he was the first to charge upon the foe, wielding his lance, as he had wielded it in the first battle of the conquest in his adventurous youth.

At the acme of his popularity, and that at an age when most men who have passed so hard a life as had Quesada, have done with public services, an enemy more insidious in its approaches than the most stealthy Indian of the Magdalenian everglades stole on him, and finished his career. Leprosy—then, as now, so common in Colombia—forced him to retire from Bogotá into a milder climate. He chose Tocaima, partly because of its amenity and beauty; partly because, not far away, there were some sulphur springs. These proved ineffectual, so he retired to Mariquita, where he built a solid[1] house of stone, whose ruins are still visible.

In his enforced retirement his mind remained as active and as clear as in his youth. His thoughts still ran on conquests,[2] and in especial on the conquest of the territories on Los Llanos that he had been granted by the king. He entered into various capitulations with several of his captains as regards the conquest of the lands between the Pauto and the Papamene, that had proved so disastrous to himself. His death cut all these projected conquests short, and they were never realized.

The only letter from his hand that is known to have survived, he wrote from Mariquita, just a year before he died.[3] It is dated 28th of May, 1578, and is signed " El Adelantado." It is the letter of a Spanish gentleman of those days living on his estate. He speaks of horses, cattle, goats, and of a jar of honey[4] that he wished sent to him.

[1] "Una casa solida de piedra": Dr. Ibañez, "Cronicas de Bogota," 1916. The ruins of this " solid stone house " are in lonely surroundings, on the edge of a great, stony plain that stretches nearly to the foot of the Andes, and is broken here and there with palm woods. Colombia, that has been so prodigal of statues to its great liberator, Bolivar, might do itself honour by erecting a monument on the ruins of the house of the discoverer and conqueror of the country.

[2] " No habiendose acabado los brios que tuvò siempre de conquistas ": Fray Simon.

[3] Mariquita á 28 de Mayo de 1578. It is quoted by Dr. Ibañez in his excellent " Life of Quesada," p. 68 (Bogotá, 1892). Dr. Ibañez says that it was in the possession of Dr. Don Nicolas Las Casas of Bogotá, who allowed him to copy it for his book.

[4] Una múcura de miel.

However, he was soon to leave those quiet occupations. Death, that he had sought so often in the field—for he had been of those who, like Cortés, " were the first in the fray, the last to leave it "—now sought him out, and, full of years and honours, still unconquered but by the Unseen Conqueror, he breathed his last at Mariquita on the 15th of February of 1579,[1] at eighty[2] years of age.

Like a true lawyer, Quesada always put off making his will. He actually drew it up on the day he died, before Andres Sanchez, the public notary of Mariquita. Little enough of this world's goods he had to leave, for he died poor in all but the respect and love of those who had best cause to know his worth.

His will states that he was in debt to the extent of sixty thousand ducats. This was most probably incurred for his disastrous expedition to the Llanos.

One touching item in the will is the provision of a small sum to sustain a jar of water for wayfarers upon the hill of Limba, for, as the will states, there is no water near at hand, and because the place is hot. Well did Quesada know what it was to go athirst, for heat and thirst had been his enemies throughout the three[3] and forty years that he had followed arms. This humble charity, the last provision of a man, before whose feet the golden spoil of Tunja had been

---

[1] " Murió en la ciudad de Mariquita en Febrero de 1579 con testamento cercado que otorgó el mismo dia, ante Andres Sanchez, escribano publico de allí ": " Genealogia del Nuevo Reino de Granada," Juan Flores de Ocariz. (Madrid, 1674.)

[2] Some of the chroniclers make him eighty-one years of age. He was the longest lived of the three great conquerors of the New World· Cortés died at the age of sixty-two. Pizarro, fighting with his last breath against his assassins, was nearly seventy.

[3] Quesada's brother, Melchor de Quesada, wrote and presented a memorial to the king, about the year 1577. In it he sets forth all his brother's services, and tells the king that he is old and poor. He reminds the king that for three and forty years his brother had been in his service, and that his services had had but scant reward. " Considere, vuestra alteza, que á 43 años continuos que mi hermano no ha dejado de servir en punto." Quesada had made his brother his " apoderado " in a document given at the Estancia de Rio Seco near Tocaima in 1577.

heaped, until it towered above his head, speaks volumes for the goodness of his heart. Few conquerors have thought of any but themselves, and there are fewer still who, in their last hours, have remembered travellers athirst upon the road. Those who have passed long hours upon the trail in the fell tropic sun, can understand the spirit that impelled Quesada, on his last day of life, to think of it, and many a traveller[1] must have been grateful to him.

Quesada, like so many of the conquistadores, was never married;[2] nor did he leave, as did so many of them, illegitimate descendants by Indian women. His life had been so full of adventure, that he appears to have had no time for love, nor does he seem to have had even a passing (known) attachment to any woman, Spanish or Indian. So the stamp was broken, and the old warrior, having lived his life alone, died as a barren stock.

It often, even usually, happens when a great man dies, there is an outburst of enthusiasm from those who might have helped him in his life, but kept their sympathy to pour out on his grave. In Quesada's case, the sympathy was not withheld in life, for all respected him, resorted to him for advice, and in all time of peril looked on him as their natural leader in the field.

His fellow-citizens left him in poverty, whilst adoring him; but it may well have been that the old general was not an easy man to help. At the news of his death, all Bogotá was draped in black. Everyone mourned him as if he had been their father, and in fact he was the father and the soul of the New Kingdom of Granada that he discovered, conquered, and gave its name.

The very fact of his great age, an age to which few men who have endured what he endured ever attain, gave to the

---

[1] It would be a graceful action of some patriotic Colombian to erect a memorial stone on La Cuesta de Limba, where the jar once stood.

[2] Colonel Acosta says Quesada had a sister, who was married and left descendants of the names Oruñas and Berrio, and that they are still represented in Bogotá : " Descubrimiento de la Nueva Granada," Colonel Joaquin Acosta, p. 372.

people a sense of loss, for they knew well that with him passed the race of the conquistadores. Even in his life he had become, as it were, legendary. The people knew that he was still alive; living retired and ill; but still available in times of national distress for counsel, and at the last resort for leadership.

Another generation had arisen both in the Indies and in Spain. Quesada's life stretched back to the Catholic kings, the glories of the Spanish race. In his youth, in Granada, he had seen the Moors. In childhood the discovery of the Indies; those Indies that he himself did so much to subdue, must have been as a household word, both in Granada and in Cordoba. He had lived right through the glorious reign of Charles V., when Spain attained the zenith of her power. Not bred to arms, he had achieved success in arms, and yet all knew that in his first profession of the law he was a man of note. If not, the Adelantado Lugo would not have chosen him, when he set out from Spain in the year 1535, as his chief magistrate.[1]

Thus all combined to make his death spectacular, and at the same time render it a loss to private citizens, who perhaps never beheld him in their lives.

Quesada was of middle height, of a grave countenance,[2] very attentive, and very courteous to everybody. This courtesy and affability was a common trait to all of the great conquerors of the New World. All three of them had had their periods of dissipation in their youth. All three[3]

[1] Justicia mayor.

[2] " Fué el Adelantado Quesada, de cuerpo y estatura regulares de rostro grave, muy atento y comedido con todos ": " Historia Natural y Moral de las Indias," por el Padre José de Acosta, p. 373. (Sevilla, 1596.)

[3] Oi decir que cuando mozo en la Isla Española fué algo travieso sobre mujeres," says Bernal Diaz of Cortés in his " Historia de la Nueva España," p. 456. He goes on to say in what is perhaps the finest description of a warrior in any literature: " Era buen ginete y diestro de todas armas, ansi á pie como á caballo, y sabia muy bien menearlas, y sobre todo, corazon y animo, qùe es lo que hace al caso." The same might be said both of Pizarro and Quesada.

of them, in middle age, became grave warriors and weighty counsellors.

The Spaniards of those days possibly placed courtesy as the first of all the virtues. Those who have lived with their descendants in the Americas, can understand why they set courtesy so high.

Without it, in Quesada's days, it was impossible to manage Spanish soldiers, for the most illiterate of them all esteemed himself a gentleman. Most probably the soldier was a gentleman according to his lights, and in his generals, as Quesada and Cortés, he saw what he admired and would have been himself had God so willed it. Hence, the love Quesada's soldiers bore him, and hence the reason that they never once rebelled against him.

He does not seem ever to have hesitated to execute those who he thought deserved to die, and never once was his decision challenged by his men.

His love of speeches probably was a recollection of his legal days, and if his soldiers did not always understand his somewhat high-flown words, they stood and listened, and, the speech over, set obediently to work.

Cortés, also a lawyer in his early life, had the same gift of words, and put it to the same use, and with the same effect. Pizarro, lacking education, yet was eloquent in his own way, as when he drew the line upon the sand at Tumbez, and invited those[1] who feared no hardships to cross over it and set out for Peru.

It is impossible for us to judge Quesada's character quite impartially. We read his actions, and condemn or praise them according to the standards of our world. Those standards ever shift, are always altering. Our vices and our virtues are not quite the vices and the virtues of the days of Prescott or of Robertson. To-morrow they will change again, are changing as we write, without our knowledge, as imperceptibly as day shades into night and night again gives place to day.

No living eye can mark the progress of the hands upon the clock of time. " Eppur si muovano."

---

[1] Thirteen crossed the sandy Rubicon.

So, summing up Quesada's character, it appears, firstly, that he was an honourable man, according to his lights.

Scrupulously exact he was undoubtedly about the royal fifth, so careful and so proud of his integrity in this, a matter that weighed lightly on the souls of almost all the conquerors, that he records it in his will.[1]

His was an open nature, quickly moved to jealousy, as in the case of Captain Fonte, but just as easily stirred again to generosity.   He bore no malice, never sought revenge, and through his long career set little store on wealth.

His views were large and liberal, as his delight at the first school set up in Bogotá so amply testifies.

Well did he know the difference between right and wrong; not by the touchstone of religion or of policy, but fundamentally.   That he failed always to square " his hirpling practice with his creed," is but to say he was a man.   Bitterly, in ashes and in sackcloth of the soul, did he repent his weakness in the matter of the torture and the death of the last Zipa of Bogotá, as we know from Herrera's[2] testimony. To a man of Quesada's temperament, the recollection of the treachery to the poor Zipa who had come to him for help, so trustfully, must have been like a poisoned arrow in his heart.

His attitude in regard to the enslavement of the Indians shows his better nature and his superiority to almost all the conquerors, who sold the Indians, just as they would have sold a mule, without a thought of the injustice of the act.

[1] The will is lost, but may yet be recovered in Honda, Gúaduas, Anolaima, Tocaima, or some other old-world town, in some forgotten chest.

[2] Even Piedrahita, a harsh critic of Quesada's, has the following: " Y quien leyese este succeso, en el Compendio Historial que escribió el mismo Adelantado tendrá bien que lastimarse del sentimiento y dolor con que confiesa haber cooperado á la injusticia con el fin de complacer á su gente."   Piedrahita is referring to a lost work of Quesada's that he consulted and used.

All who have written of Quesada, near to his age, held him for a humane and generous man. We who look at him, down the optic glass of time, reversed, can only judge him by his deeds, as they have been recorded for us, by men who lived in times so widely different from our own.

For a brief moment of almost unappreciable time, we are the men, our writ is absolute in our own court of piepowder. Still, just ahead of us (only a pace or two ahead), there lurks an enemy, the future, that will reverse our judgments, blow them to the winds, and not impossibly view us as cheaply, as from our Empyrean we regard the past. Therefore, in writing of Quesada, I have tried to dwell upon his generosity, his dauntless courage, and his contempt of hardships, of perils, and of death.

His faults, it seems to me, were matters for his contemporaries to pass their judgment on; for us, his strange, adventurous career, his struggles, sufferings, and the apocalyptic death, that took him still revolving conquests in his mind, are what most matter, when we read of him. No citizen of New Granada has equalled him, until Bolivar, who, though an actual son of Venezuela, is of the very entrails of Colombia, broke like a meteor on the scene.

Quesada, in his will, left a request that he was to be buried in the parish church of Mariquita. He rested there, in the quiet little church, till 1597. Then, his executor, Dean, Lope de Clavijo, had his remains removed to Bogotá.

All Bogotá turned out to escort to his last resting-place, the great commander, who once had been their captain general.

Clergy and laity, rich, poor, young, old, joined in procession to welcome home the illustrious dead, with chaunting and with flags. They dipped their banners over the bier on which the body of the Conquistador was laid. Then, in the Chapel of the Holy Cross, in the Square of San

Francisco, beneath the steps of the high altar, upon the side of the Epistle,[1] they lowered the coffin down into the vault.

Over his tomb, with the brief epitaph he wrote himself, " Expecto resurrectionem mortuorum," they hung the standard of the conquest, battered, but glorious.

[1] Al lado de la epistola.

APPENDIX I

RELACION DEL ADELANTADO DON GONZALO XIMENES DE QUESADA

SOBRE LOS CONQUISTADORES Y ENCOMENDEROS

MEMORIA DE LOS DESCUBRIDORES Y CONQUISTADORES QUE ENTRARON CONMIGO Á DESCUBRIR Y CONQUISTAR ESTE NUEVO REINO DE GRANADA.

UNOS son muertos y estos son los mas; otros están en España que con lo que acá úbieron se han ido á sus tierras donde viven; otros se han ido en tiempos pasados á otras partes de Indias; otros que se quedaron en este reino: de ellos son tambien muertos de treinta años á esta parte, de manera que, cuando esta relacion se escribe, hay solo vivos cincuenta y tres, cuyos nombres aquí irán puestos, y como van nombrados por su órden, así se ha de entender que llevan la misma órden en los méritos que tienen segun lo que trabajaron y sirvieron en el descubrimiento y conquesta de este reino, de los que agora hay vivos; y así mismo irá aquí puesto lo que cada uno tiene y se le ha dado en premio de sus servicios, y lo que mas se requiere para entender esta relacion y todo brevísimamente, de manera que, cuando alguno acudiere á España pidiendo gratificacion de sus servicios, no haya necesidad de mas que ver esta relacion, y ver por ella si es de los primeros, y si lo fuere ver pro ella si está pagado ó no y lo que merece.

El capitan Juan de Cespedes es, de los que hay agora vivos, uno de los que mas trabajaron y sirvieron en este descubrimiento y conquista, y entró conmigo por capitan de uno de ocho capitanes que metí con gente en este reino, y él tiene calidad; tiene tres repartimientos en esta ciudad de Santa Fe en que habrá mil y quinientos Indios poco mas ó menos llamados los repartimientos Ubaque, Caquenza, Ubatoque, tiene bien de comer para en este reino.

El capitan Antonio de Olalla vive y tiene de comer en esta ciudad de Santa Fe; no entró por capitan conmigo, pero fuélo despues y conmigo entró por alférez de infanteria: terná ochocientos ó mil Indios en un buen repartimiento llamado Bogotá, y así tiene bien de comer para en este reino y es hombre de calidad.

Juan Valenciano, aunque no entró en este reino por capitan sino por caporal, trabajó y sirvió mucho en este descubrimiento, ha tenido algunos repartimientos que unos por pleito y otros por otra manera se los han quitado los que han gobernado, y tambien por ausencias y peregrinaciones que ha hecho, entre las cuales ha sido una la de Hierusalen, y así no tiene repartimiento ni de comer, mereciéndolo muy bien, y tiene alguna calidad.

El capitan Gonzalo Suarez es hombre de calidad, entró conmigo por capitan en este reino y es uno de los ocho de este nombre, vive y tiene de comer en la ciudad de Tunja; tiene tres repartimientos y en ellos tres mil Indios llamados los repartimientos Icabuco, Tibaná, y Guaneca; tiene muy bien de comer.

El capitan Antonio Cardoso tiene calidad, aunque no entró por uno de los ocho capitanes que entraron conmigo, él antes de este descubrimiento habia sido capitan y vive en Santa Fe; tiene harto bien de comer en un repartimiento que tiene llamado Suba y Tuna en que habrá nuevecientos ó mil Indios.

El capitan Gonzalo Garcia Zorro tiene calidad, y aunque no entró conmigo por capitan, entró por alférez de á caballo; tiene razonablemente de comer en un repartimiento que tiene en la ciudad de Santa de llamado Fusagasugá en que habrá quinientos Indios poco mas ó menos.

El capitan Hernan Vanegas, aunque no entró conmigo por capitan sino solamente por hombre de á caballo, despues los que han gobernado lo han hecho capitan y es hombre de calidad, vive en Santa Fe, tiene muy bien de comer en un repartimiento principal que tiene llamado Guatabita en que habrá dos mil Indios poco mas ó menos.

Juan de Ortega y Francisco de Figueredo son dos hombres á quien con mi conciencia no me atreveré á dar ventaja mas al uno que al otro ni á ponello primero y así los pongo por iguales aunque vaya primero el uno: Juan de Ortega vive en esta ciudad de Santa Fe; es hombre rico y tiene alguna calidad, entró por de á caballo, tiene de comer en Indios menos que medianamente, llámase su repartimiento Cipaquirá, y otro mas adentro llamado Pacho, en que habrá poco mas ó menos trecientos ó cuatrocientos Indios.

Francisco de Figueredo tiene alguna calidad; entró por hombre de á caballo; tiene de comer en esta ciudad de Santa Fe donde vive, aunque no es el repartimiento grande,

sino menos que mediano; llámase Cipacón; terná docientos
ó trecientos Indios poco mas ó menos.

El capitan Salguero, que agora es capitan y no lo fué
en el descubrimiento sino hombre de á caballo, es hombre
que tiene alguna calidad; vive en Tunja y allí tiene de comer
medianamente, aunque los Indios son pocos, tiene dos ó tres
pueblezuelos, el uno Ura y los otros dos no me acuerdo;
paréceme que habrá en ellos docientos Indios poco mas
ó menos.

El capitan Juan Tafur, aunque no entró conmigo en
este descubrimiento por capitan, sino solamente por hombre
de á caballo, es persona de calidad, y está muy pobre porque
no tiene de comer á causa que el repartimiento de Pasca que
tenia se lo sacó por sentencia del Real Consejo de Indias
Montalvo de Lugo, que despues murió en España.

Gomez de Cifuentes y Domingo de Aguirre son otras
dos personas á quienes yo tengo por iguales en los servicios;
pongo no por ventaja primero al Cifuentes, es hombre de
mediana calidad, vive en Tunja y allí tiene de comer y
razonablemente, y aun mas que razonable, en un raparti-
miento llamado Paypa, que terná setecientos á ochocientos
Indios poco mas ó menos.

Domingo de Aguirre, así como en lo de los servicios así
en lo demás anda apareado con el pasado, porque en Tunja,
donde vive, tiene otro repartimiento en el valle de Sogamoso
que tendrá los Indios que el otro ó algunos menos y así
mismo tiene razonablemente de comer.

Bartolomé Camacho vive en Tunja y allí tiene de comer
en un repartimiento de Indios no bueno en el provecho.

Andrés de Molina vive en Santa Fe, tiene calidad y muy
bien de comer, así en riqueza como en Indios, porque tiene
un muy buen repartimiento llamado Chocontá.

Diego Romero vive en Santa Fe y tiene de comer bien,
porque tiene dos repartimientos, uno, llamado Une, que
es buena cosa, y otro; el primero terná cuatrocientos Indios,
y el segundo ciento cincuenta.

Paredes Calderon vive en Tunja y es hombre que tiene
alguna calidad y tiene bien de comer, porque es rico y el
repartimiento que tiene, llamado Somondoco, que terná
hasta trecientos Indios es de provecho harto.

Juan de Quincoces es persona de calidad, que es rico en
hacienda y en Indios, pues tiene tres pueblos que aunque
pequeños son de harto provecho; vive en Tunja.

Miguel Sanchez es hombre de alguna calidad y tiene
en hacienda muy largo de comer y en Indios dos reparti-

mientos el uno razonable y el otro muy bueno llamado Gonzaga; vive en Tunja.

Pedro Rodriguez de Carrion es persona que tiene calidad y es rico, y demás desto tiene un mediano repartimiento de Indios en Tunja, donde vive; terná trecientos Indios poco mas ó menos.

Diego Montañez es hombre que tiene alguna calidad y tiene de comer muy largamente en un repartimiento que terná quinientos Indios, pero de gran provecho y contratacion; vive en Tunja y llamase el repartimiento. . . .

Francisco de Mestanza vive en Santa Fe, no tiene de comer ni Indios ningunos de repartimiento; ha perdido por via de despojo en la Audiencia Real un repartimiento que tuvo llamado Cajicá, que está en la corona real; determinóse contra él y halláronle haber hecho en dicho repartimiento algunos malos tratamientos de Indios.

Francisco Gomez vive en Santa Fe, tiene alguna calidad y tiene bien de comer en dos repartimientos, el uno y el principal llamado Tibacuy y el otro Cueca, que habrá en ambos cuatrocientos Indios poco mas á menos, pero buenos y de provecho.

Anton Rodriguez Cazalla vive en Tunja y tiene pocos Indios y así mal de comer.

Juan del Olmo vive en Santa Fe, y tiene mediana calidad y la misma medianía tiene en el repartimiento, porque aunque tiene dos, el uno llamado Nemocon y Tasgata y el otro Tivitó, en que en todos habrá cuatrocientos Indios, no son muy buenos ni tampoco malos en el provecho.

Pero Ruiz Herrezuelo vive en Tunja y tiene mediana calidad y allende de ser hombre bien rico, tiene dos repartimientos cada uno bien razonable; en el uno habrá docientos Indios, y en el otro, llamado Panqueba, otros tantos.

Alonso Gomez Sequillo vive en Velez; tiene muy mal de comer porque tiene muy pocos Indios, aunque han sido hartos mas en tiempos pasados.

Roa vive en Tunja y tiene bien de comer y él tiene alguna calidad; es hombre que tiene un buen repartimiento llamado Tensa que terná setecientos Indios poco mas ó menos.

Pero Gomez vive en Pamplona; tiene para en aquel pueblo bien de comer; aunque los Indios no son muchos tiénelos en dos repartimientos; este vendió Indios de otro repartimiento que tuvo en Velez, donde primero vivia.

Juan Sanchez de Toledo es medianamente rico en Santa Fe, donde reside; no tiene repartimiento, porque el que tenia, llamado Gachancipá, lo vendió y se deshizo dél, con el cual dinero y con el que él mas tenia fué á emplear á España y volvió.

Juan de Montalvo vive en Santa Fe, tienen alguna calidad, no tiene Indios de repartimientos porque unos poblezuelos que tenia, se deshizo de ellos y los vendió.

Ramirez vive en Tocayma, tiene allí poco de comer porque el repartimiento es de pocos Indios que no serán ciento cincuenta, pero son de algun provecho.

Francisco Rodriguez vive en Tunja, y tiene alguna calidad, tiene menos que medianamente de comer porque tiene un solo pueblo llamado Sora que terná entre docientos y trecientos Indios.

Monrroy vive en los Remedios, no tenia de comer ni Indios de repartimiento; dióselos agora en aquel pueblo nuevo, el Presidente de este reino; creo que le dió cien casas de Indios poco mas á menos.

Macias, vive en Tunja; tenia mejor de comer que tiene agora, porque ha dado algunos pueblos de los que tenia en repartimiento á sus hijas como á manera de dote y en casamiento, y así agora quedanle pocos Indios.

Antonio de Castro vive en Tunja y tiene alguna calidad, y tiene bien de comer en dos repartimientos, el uno llamado Tinjacá, el otro Cerinza; terná este poco mas ó menos setecientos Indios y el otro docientos; compró el de Cerinza á otro conquistador.

Juan Rodriguez Parra vive en Tunja y tiene mediana calidad y muy bien de comer en un repartimiento suyo llamado Chicamocha y Tequia que habrá en ambas partes mas de quinientos Indios.

Salazar vive en Velez, tiene pocos Indios y por esta razon no tiene bien de comer; fueron estos Indios mucho mas antes, que despues que él los tiene.

Antonio Bermudez vive en Santa Fe, tiene mediana calidad y no bien de comer porque teniéndolo se deshizo de ello, y vendió el repartimiento de Ubaté que tenia de mucho provecho y el de Suta y Tausa tambien, en que en ambos habria mil Indios, y gastado el dinero compró otro de pocos Indios llamado Chivachi; terná docientos Indios poco mas ó menos.

Juan Rodriguez Gil vive en Tunja y es hombre rico de hacienda, y el repartimiento de Indios que tiene es así razonable, no sé los Indios que habiá en él.

Castil Blanco vive en Velez; creo que ya no tiene Indios porque los ha vendido.

Juan Alonso tiene Indios en Velez, donde vive; son pocos

agora y fueron antes muchos mas que despues que él los tiene.

Ledesma vive en Velez; creo que ya no tiene Indios porque los ha vendido.

Juan Lopez vive en Tunja, tiene bien de comer y él alguna calidad; llámase su repartimiento Sachica, en que habrá quinientos Indios; es repartimiento de harto provecho.

Juan Gomez tiene en Santa Fe, donde vive, menos que medianamente de comer, porque tiene un repartimiento que le llaman Usme que terná trecientos Indios ó docientos.

Monteagudo vive en Tunja, es persona rica medianamente y tiene dos repartimientos bien razonables en que habrá en ambos cuatrocientos Indios y mas.

Pero Rodriguez de Leon vive en Tunja, tiene bien de comer en un buen repartimiento de Indios de harto provecho.

Pedro Sotelo no tiene Indios ni repartimiento alguno; vendió uno que se le dió en Mariquita.

Manchado vive en Tunja; no tiene Indios ningunos y así no tiene de comer; antes está pobre y enfermo, llagado y de las llagas ciego.

Diego de Torres vive en Pamplona, tiene pocos Indios porque es pequeño su repartimiento, que no tiene cien Indios y así tiene muy mal de comer.

Pedro de Madrid vive en Tunja, tiene muy buen repartimiento de Indios y muy provechoso; terná el repartimiento seiscientos Indios poco mas á menos.

Juan de Salamanca vive en Tunja, tiene un pueblo de repartimiento pequeño en que habrá ciento cincuenta Indios poco mas ó menos, y otro pueblo que tenia, llamado Sutatasco, lo vendió.

Sin estos descubridores, y conquistadores, y pobladores de este reino, hay otros que fueron segundos, y otros terceros, y cuartos, y otros quintos, y sextos, que se hallaron en pacificaciones de alzamiento de rebeliones de naturales y que son bien antiguos, y que seria proceder en infinito; y por eso no hay que tratar de ellos—el Mariscal Ximenes—Vistos.[1]

---

[1] This curious " Relacion " was known to the historian Muñoz (Don Juan Bautista Muñoz, "Historia del Nuevo Mundo": Madrid, 1793), who quotes it, without a date. Colonel Joaquin Acosta (p. 404, " Descubrimiento de la Nueva Granada ": Paris, 1848) visited the Archivo de Indias at Seville in 1845, and discovered the original, dated 5th of July, 1576, in a bundle of papers marked 526–591.

APPENDIX II

THE LOST WRITINGS OF QUESADA

HERRERA says of Quesada that he was of keen[1] intellect, and no less apt for arms than letters. By a strange fatality, we cannot judge his aptitude in letters, as all his writings, except the list of the fifty-three conquistadores (given in Appendix I.), have perished or are lost.

It is possible that they yet may be recovered, for it appears that some of them were in existence within comparatively recent days.

It is known with certainty that Quesada wrote a report of his expedition, and is supposed to have taken it to Spain, to present it personally to Charles V. Many of the conquistadores—Cortés, Robledo, Andagoya, and others—wrote similar reports. They were styled " Cartas Relaciones." That of Quesada must have been presented about 1539 on his return to Spain. It has disappeared, whilst reports of Cortés, Alvarado, Andagoya, Robledo, and the rest, have all been carefully preserved. Quesada's report may have been either destroyed or hidden through the agency of Don Luis de Lugo, Quesada's enemy at court, and rival for the governorship of Bogotá. Luis de Lugo was a man who stuck at nothing, if it came between him and his own advancement.

The Spanish scholar, Jimenez de la Espada, so well known for his acute and careful study of all things American, found amongst the papers of the cosmographer Santa Cruz,[2] a curious manuscript. It was entitled, " Epitome de la Conquista del Nuevo Reino de Granada." As it contains an account of the conquest, with descriptions of the Indians, the birds, animals, fishes, and vegetation of the country, it seemed not unlikely that it was a report to the emperor, of the conquest, by Quesada. Jimenez de la Espada says the manuscript appeared to have been touched up a little,

[1] " . . . de agudo ingenio y no menos apto para las armas que para las letras ": " Decadas," Herrera.
[2] Alonso de Santa Cruz was born in Seville about the year 1512. He held the posts of Royal Astronomer and Cosmographer to Charles V.

but only very slightly, by Santa Cruz. " In various passages, Santa Cruz lets the conqueror and discoverer speak in the first person, sometimes in the singular, only for himself, and sometimes in the plural as for himself and his companions."[1]

Saldanha[2] says, in his essay on Quesada's writings, that Herrera, the historian of the Indies, was much indebted to the report Quesada had composed. According to a close analysis Saldanha makes of Herrera's writings, he deduces that Herrera took chapter viii. of the tenth book of Decada V. from the epitome Quesada wrote; also a good deal in Decada VI., Book I. In Decada VI., Book III., chapters xiii. and xiv., and in Book V., Decada VI., Saldanha says Herrera borrowed largely from Quesada.

This may be so; but it is certain that Captain Don Gonzalo Fernandez de Oviedo, the author of " La Historia Natural de las Indias " and several other curious books, met Quesada, as he declares in his own writings, in Madrid and Valladolid in 1547–8.

He calls Quesada " hombre honrado de gentil entendimiento y muy habil."

From Quesada, Oviedo got many details of the conquest of New Granada, " de viva voce," and also borrowed " un gran cuaderno "[3] from him. This he had in his possession for many days.[4]

He says himself that he composed his twenty-four chapters on the conquest of New Granada from Quesada's great unbound manuscript. It is in these twenty-four chapters, composed partly from conversations with Quesada, and partly from his manuscript, that the best and most authentic account of the conquest of New Granada is to be found.

Where, then, is this manuscript ? It may have disappeared or perished; but it does not seem improbable that it is identical with the " Epitome " Jimenez de la Espada found in the papers of the cosmographer Santa Cruz.

Quesada also wrote a book entitled " Apuntamientos y Noticias sobre la Historia de Paulo Giovio, por el Licenciado

---

[1] " En varios pasages dejó (Santa Cruz) que hablára en primera persona el descubridor y conquistador, ya en singular, solamente por sí, ya en plural por él y por sus compañeros ": Jimenez de la Espada, edicion de Castellanos.

[2] " El Licenciado Jimenez de Quesada ": E. de Saldanha, Cartagena de Indias, 1916, en Casa de Mogollon.

[3] A large memorandum book, unbound.

[4] Por muchos dias.

Gonzalo Jimenez de Quesada, Adelantado y Capitan del Nuevo Reino de Granada."

Paulo Giovio was Bishop of Nacera. He wrote in Latin, and his work was translated into Spanish by El Licenciado Gaspar de Baeza and printed in Granada in 1566.[1] It was very critical of the Spaniards and their policy in Italy. Quesada was indignant at its tone, and " could not endure such insult and discourtesy."[2]

So he determined to take up the defence of his countrymen and refute the charges of Giovio in detail and with circumstance. He began his book at the accession of the Emperor Charles V., touching on such subjects as the Rebellion of the Communities of Castile, the Conference of Calais, the Siege of Genoa, the Spanish Campaigns in Italy and Hungary, the Sack of Rome, the Attack on Tunis, and many other matters of the same kind.

At the end of the prologue Quesada says: " The faults of this book may perhaps be excused by the short time of five months in which I wrote it, and by the rudeness and barbarity of the people with whom I have conversed during so many years."[3]

The book appears to have been written in 1568–9, and was dedicated to Mendez de Quixada, who was Presidente del Consejo de las Indias at that date.

The historian Don Juan Bautista Muñoz[4] says he had the book in his hands, but he does not say at what time of his life. The book is lost; but it is quite possible that it may turn up in some old Spanish library.

Before writing this book Quesada had written another, " Anales del Emperador Carlos V." This work is also lost.

Lastly, he wrote a book entitled " Las Diferencias de la Guerra de los Dos Mundos." This, too, has perished, and is perhaps as much to be regretted as the loss of anything he wrote, except " El Gran Cuaderno " that he lent to Oviedo, for few men had greater opportunities of judging war than had Quesada in one of the Two Worlds.

Quesada also composed a Book of Sermons for his chapel. This, though it may seem strange to people nowadays, was quite in the vein of warriors of those times. Though they

---

[1] Prescott often quotes it in his " Ferdinand and Isabella."

[2] No pudo sufrir tanto agravio y descortesia.

[3] Restaba excusar las faltas de este libro por el poco tiempo en que lo escribi, que fueron poco mas de cinco meses y con la barbarie y rudeza de la gente con quien converso muchos años ha.

[4] Don Juan Bautista Muñoz was official historian to the Spanish court. He was born in 1745 and died in 1799.

did not write sermons, both Cortés and the Duke of Alba (he of the Low Countries) were deeply religious men. There is no reason for doubting that Quesada was equally religious. Indeed, the simple epitaph or text that he wrote for his own tomb, " Expecto resurrectionem mortuorum," shows him to have been a fervent Christian.

The most important of his works, after "El Gran Cuaderno," was undoubtedly that called "Los Ratos de Suesca." About this book a great deal of controversy has taken place. Suesca was a village near Bogotá at which Quesada had a country house. The book was written at this country house, at various periods, when he had gone there for retirement and rest. The name is curious, and is difficult to render quite exactly into English, but it may be roughly translated as "Times at Suesca," "Periods at Suesca," or "Leisure Hours at Suesca." Perhaps the last is best. The book is supposed to have been a history of the conquest, written in Quesada's declining years. It has disappeared so comparatively recently that there are hopes it may be found again. Jimenez de la Espada says it was known to have been preserved in the National Library of Bogotá up to the beginning of the nineteenth century. He gives us no authority for his statement, but seems to treat it as a thing well known.

Sir Clements Markham, in his "Notes for a History of New Granada,"[1] thinks it may still exist, as in a letter from Madrid, dated August 30th, 1878, the Argentine scholar Don Aurelio Rojas says he met in the north of Spain a Señor de Salamanca, who affirmed he possessed an MS. of Quesada's that he wished to publish, but had not the means to do so. Don Aurelio believed it to have been "Los Ratos de Suesca." One thing is certain, that Piedrahita[2] knew the MS., and availed himself largely of it in his chronicle; or, if not of it, either a companion book or a sketch for it. He says: " I found in one of the libraries of the Court (Madrid) the ' Compendio Historial ' of the conquests of New Granada,[3] that the Adelantado Don Gonzalo Jimenez de Quesada made, wrote, and transmitted to Spain."

It is known that "Los Ratos de Suesca" was sent to Spain to be published, and that on the 4th of November,

---

[1] Hakluyt Society, London.

[2] " Historia de la Conquista del Nuevo Reino de Granada," por Don Lucas Fernandez de Piedrahita, Obispo de Santa Marta.

[3] Encontré en una de las librerias de la Corte, con el Compendio Historial de las Conquistas del Nuevo Reino, que hizo, escribió y remitió á España el Adelantado Don Gonzalo Jimenez de Quesada.

1568, permission was obtained to publish it. In the Licence to Publish occurs the following passage: " Marshal Gonzalo Jimenez de Quesada, Adelantado of the Kingdom of New Granada: We have been informed that you have composed a book entitled ' Los Ratos de Suesca ' about affairs and matters touching the Indies. It appears to us that it will be useful and serviceable, and on it you have spent much time and labour."[1]

For all the Licence, the work was never published. The MS. has perished, been mislaid, or lost, and may perchance lie hidden upon the shelves of some forlorn, mouse-haunted library in Spain.

Therefore, as all his works are lost, it is not possible to judge Quesada as an author. He may have had the pen of a Cortés, an Alvarado, or of a Pedro Cieza de Leon. Certainly he could not have written in the vein of Bernal Diaz del Castillo, or in the manner of the author of the " Carnero Bogotano." Still, his books must have been of immense value on the early history of the conquest of the Indies. No writer so minute as was Oviedo could have thought so highly of them as to base twenty-four of his own chapters on the history of the conquest upon Quesada's works, had they not had some merit, or at least seemed to him that the matter treated of was of the first importance, to an historian such as he was himself.

Luckily for him, Quesada's fame is not impaired by the loss of his writings. It rests upon a sure foundation. If by the merest chance, in Popayán, in Pasto, in Bogotá itself, in an old convent in Tolima, or sun-stricken town in the Department of Bolivar, or perchance in a dusty archive in Castile, some of his writings one day come to light, all we can hope is that his pen was as well tempered as his sword.

There are said to be six portraits of Quesada[2] extant in Bogotá, and one in Mexico. Probably none of them were painted in his lifetime.

[1] El Mariscal Gonzalo Jimenez de Quesada, Adelantado del Nuevo Reino de Granada, nos ha sido hecho relacion que vos habeis compuesto un libro titulado " Los Ratos de Suesca," sobre materias y cosas tocantes á Indias, el cual será muy util y provechoso, y en él, habeis gastado mucho tiempo, y puesto mucho trabajo.

[2] The remains of Quesada now repose in " El Panteon del Templo Metropolitano," in a white marble tomb. The tomb stands in a little open space. Upon the south is his name, " Jimenez de Quesada "; to the west, " Al Fundador de Santa Fé de Bogotá "; to the north, " Expecto resurrectionem mortuorum "; to the east, " El Consejo Municipal de Bogotá 1891-1892." Quesada's helmet and mail shirt are hung up as monuments in the Museum in Bogotá.

APPENDIX III

LIST OF CONQUISTADORES OF NEW GRANADA, PRESERVED IN "EL CARNERO BOGOTANO" (RODRIGUEZ FRESLE).

CAPITANES.

Juan del Junco, soldado de Italia, persona de gran valor, nombrado por el Gobernador Don Pedro Fernandez de Lugo en segundo lugar, si faltase el general Quesada.

Gonzalo Suarez Rondon.

Juan de Cespedes, que fué de los de á caballo.

Antonio de Prado.

Antonio Diaz Cardoso de los capitanes de Santa Marta.

El Capitan Albarracin.

Juan de San Martin, persona valerosa.

Juan Tafur, de los nobles de Castilla, conquistador de Santa Marta, Nombre de Dios y Panama.

Martin Galiano, pobló la ciudad de Velez.

El Capitan Antonio de Lebrija, persona principal, trajó tres caballos; no hay memoria[1] de el.

Lazaro Fonte, vinó de España por capitan de un[2] navio con 200 hombres, murió en Quito.

Hernando Vanegas, de la nobleza de Cordova, vinó por soldado de á caballo.

Antonio de Olalla, vinó por Alferez.

Juan de Montalvo, soldado de estima.

Baltasar Maldonado, persona principal y caballero, fué alcalde mayor de este reino.

Juan de Madrid, discreto y valeroso capitan.

[1] This seems strange.

[2] Curious that a sailor should have been the best horseman in Quesada's army.

Juan de Ortega, el Bueno, á diferencia de otro Ortega, fué buen Cristiano.

Cristoval Arias de Moreno, descubridor de á pie.

FRAYLES.

Juan de Lascames, capellan del ejercito.

Fray Domingo, ó Alonso, de las Casas, del orden de Santo Domingo, descubridor.[1]

---

[1] The addition of " descubridor " to a friar's name is unusual.

LIST OF WORKS CONSULTED

ACOSTA (El Coronel Joaquin): " Compendio Historico del Descubrimiento de la Nueva Granada." Paris, 1848.

ACOSTA (El Padre José de): " Historia Natural y Moral de las Indias." Sevilla, 1596.

AGUADO (Fray Pedro de): " Historia de Venezuela."

BARCIA: " Historiadores Primitivos de Indias." Madrid, 1749.

CASTELLANOS (Juan de): "Elegias de Varones Ilustres de Indias." Madrid, 1589. Modern edition, 1886.

CIEZA DE LEON: " La Cronica del Peru." Amberes, 1554.

ERCILLA (Don Alonso): " La Araucana."

FRESLE (Juan Rodriguez): "El Carnero Bogotano." Bogotá, 1859 (edited by Don Felipe Perez).

GARCILASSO DE LA VEGA (Inca): " Comentarios Reales." Madrid, 1600.

GÓMARA (Fray Francisco Lopez): " Historia de las Indias y Cronica de la Nueva España." (In Barcia's Collection.) Madrid, 1749.

GUMILLA (El Padre Joseph de): " El Orinoco Ilustrado." Madrid, 1741.

HERRERA (Antonio de): " Historia General de los Hechos de los Castellanos en las Islas y Tierra Firme del Mar Oceano " (cinco tomos y ocho decadas). Madrid, 1729.

IBAÑEZ (Doctor Don Pedro M.): " Vida de Quesada." Bogotá, 1892.

JIMENEZ DE LA ESPADA: " Historia del Nuevo Mundo." Sevilla, 1890.

MARKHAM (Sir Clements): " Notes for a History of New Granada." London, 1912.

MARTIR (Petrus ab Angleria): " De Jnsulis, nuper inventis." Sevilla, 1511.

MILLIGAN: " Adventures of an Orchid-Hunter."   Cassell and Co., London, 1891.

MUÑOZ (Juan Bautista): "Historia del Nuevo Mundo." Madrid.

OCARIZ (Juan Flores de): " Genealogias del Nuevo Reino de Granada." Madrid, 1674.

OVIEDO (El Capitan Don Gonzalo Fernandez de): " Historia Natural de las Indias." Salamanca, 1547.

PIEDRAHITA (Doctor Don Lucas Fernandez, Chantre de la Iglesia metropolitano de Santa Fé de Bogotá, calificador del Santo Oficio, obispo electo de Santa Marta): " Historia General de las Conquistas del Nuevo Reino de Granada." Madrid, 1688.

RAMUSIO (M. Giovanni Battista): " Viaggi." Venezia, 1565.

SALDANHA (E. de): " El Licenciado Jimenez de Quesada." Cartagena de Indias, 1916.

SAN MARTIN Y LEBRIJA (Capitanes): " Relacion." In Ternaux Compans, " Recueil des Documents," etc.

SIMON (Fray Pedro): " Noticias Historiales de las Conquistas de Tierra Firme en las Indias Occidentales." Cuenca, 1627.

TERNAUX COMPANS: " L'Essai sur l'Ancien Cudinamarca " and " Recueil des Documents sur l'Histoire des Possessions Espagnoles dans l'Amérique." Paris, 1842.

TORRES (Simon Perez de Torres): " Viage del Mundo." (In Barcia's Collection.) Madrid, 1749.

VELASCO (Presbitero Don Juan de): " Historia del Reino de Quito." Quito, 1844.

XEREZ (Francisco de): " Conquista del Peru." Salamanca, 1547.

ZAMORA (Padre Fray Alonso de): " Historia de la Provincia de San Antonino del Nuevo Reino de Granada." Barcelona, 1701.

ZARATE (Agustin de): " Historia del Descubrimiento y Conquista del Peru." Sevilla, 1627.

INDEX